FIGURES OF THE REVOLUTION

FIGURES OF THE REVOLUTION

by LOUIS MADELIN

DE L'ACADÉMIE FRANÇAISE

Translated from the French by
RICHARD CURTIS

Illustrated from Linoleum Blocks by
KARL S. WOERNER

KENNIKAT PRESS, INC./PORT WASHINGTON, N. Y.

944.04
M 181f

FIGURES OF THE REVOLUTION

Copyright 1929 by The Macaulay Company
Reissued in 1968 by Kennikat Press
Library of Congress Catalog Card No: 68-16297
Manufactured in the United States of America

ESSAY AND GENERAL LITERATURE INDEX REPRINT SERIES

INTRODUCTION

A YEAR or two ago I paid a visit to one of our most famous statesmen. This distinguished veteran, still as vigorous as ever, had withdrawn somewhat disdainfully from public life. He was at last able to look back with satisfaction upon his life's work. At one period in his career he had fiercely championed the cause of the men of the Revolutionary era, who, he said, must either be praised or cursed *"en bloc,"* a remark that has remained famous. To him and many of his generation, these men of whom Michelet, Quinet, Lamartine and even Thiers, wrote in ecstatic terms, were divinely inspired; to others, on the contrary, they appeared as shadowy forms and then but as demons belched forth from hell and not worthy of the slightest consideration.

The old politician, who had clung stubbornly to his convictions on this subject, surprised me when he said: "You have upset my ideas on the men of the Revolution; they were people like ourselves and were often liable to grave errors of judgment." I was not sure whether he was a little annoyed with me nor was I certain whether I should consider myself responsible—the idea was certainly flattering—for this change of front. One must have experience in rousing men to action and of ruling them in order to obtain a sound judgment on past events, otherwise it is impossible to believe historians who must try to make an unprejudiced analysis of facts and so arrive at unbiased conclusions. In their view, gods and demons do not exist, not even demi-gods nor demi-demons. For them, men are always of flesh and blood and are endowed with minds which are very liable to become overexcited or rudely deceived, whether in the doing of good or evil; unfortunately flesh is weak, the mind is impressionable, and for that reason likely to be led astray.

Men have often been faced by critical problems which would upset the equilibrium of even the most balanced minds. I am not sure that even a Richelieu would have been able to remain unbiased in facing them. Nearly all those who have passed through times of political strife have lost their sense of perspective. Like the men of centuries long since past, they have had terrible experiences that will also be the lot of the men in centuries to come. Mirabeau, of whom we shall treat shortly, wrote at some time after October 10th, 1789: "When you take part in managing a revolution the difficulty is not to keep it going, but to hold it within bounds." Then forty years later, Casimir Perier, who was at first content with the July revolt of 1830, soon sighed: "The difficulty is not to get the people into the street but to get them out of it again." Both these men died very young, killed by the crushing anxiety caused by the very rebellions they had fomented. Some, less burdened by this anxiety, have managed to pass through years of horror, later to reap rewards of the revolution in which they had participated. According to the famous saying of one of them, Sieyès, "They have lived," and, like Talleyrand, have "lived" enough, ultimately to build a fortune upon the accumulated ruins while denying the doctrines to which they owed their rise. The majority have, on the contrary, perished tragically one after another. Of these,

Vergniaud was destined to cry, "Revolutions, like Saturn, devour their own children." Bailly, and Barnave, the Girondins, Manon Roland—their Egeria, Danton, Desmoulins, Hébert and Chaumette, Saint-Just, and Robespierre, were to experience the same bloody end. All of them, before succumbing to the knife, would have tried to arrest the revolt just when they saw it increasing in violence; they feared it would become a possible menace to themselves in their turn, and likely to sweep them away in the end. From 1789 to 1795 the same misconceptions, the same frauds, the same infamies followed one upon the other.

It is a psychological drama which we shall be able to follow in the ten scenes which comprise this book. While it is being played several of the actors, after but a moment on the stage, one after another, are roughly, even brutally, thrust out—never to return.

LOUIS MADELIN.

CONTENTS

LIST OF ILLUSTRATIONS

CHAPTER I

GILBERT DE LA FAYETTE

CHAPTER I

LA FAYETTE AND HIS DELUSIONS

THE first actor to make his entrance in the drama of the Revolution—and he really speaks the prologue—had this peculiarity: he outlived by more than forty-five years the events in which he was so eminently embroiled, and after experiencing the most dazzling triumphs and the bitterest humiliations and, further, having passed through crises which were caused by the first disturbance, he was never able to get a clear insight into his own attitude to the movement nor could he perceive the real meaning of the Revolution itself.

Gilbert de La Fayette was born, lived and died,—nearly an octogenarian—, in a mirage which I would describe as happy if it had not brought misfortune to the majority of those who supported him. People who knew him when he was very old, remarked very truly, that even then his brow was unwrinkled. Some would conclude from this that he had a faith that not only moves mountains but is great enough to ignore and to deny that there are precipices over which people may fall. Others would simply infer like Napoleon, that "the Marquis was a simpleton," which is certainly an exaggeration.

He came from an old Auvergne family and was born in the Château de Chavagniac between Brioude and Le Puy. In

3

an autobiography found after his death, he declared that, being an Auvergnat, he hoped to be a Gaul rather than a Frank because he always liked Vercingetorix better than Clovis. Possibly he was of pure Celtic stock. He was to prove himself a man of great physical courage, which often led him into foolhardy actions. He was, besides, a most persuasive speaker, vain of his ideas and his prestige, always absurdly liable to a change of front, and an impetuous seeker after adventures—all these characteristic traits were attributed by the Romans to the Gauls. One must conclude, therefore, that Gilbert de La Fayette was a Gaul and though I regret it keenly, I shall only have pleasant things to say of his memory.

At eighteen he was a big boy with light red hair, a smooth white complexion, and lustreless eyes. His face, impassive and usually expressionless, showed a touch of bucolic obstinacy. Although he had passed through the Military Academy of Versailles and had married early in life a charming girl, Adrienne de Noailles, he always seemed like a youth who had grown up too quickly and had still remained coltish. When he appeared at Court he provoked much laughter, and, because he was no dancer, became an object of derision to the young Queen Marie Antoinette. It is difficult to estimate the results of his impression upon this feather-headed princess, or to appreciate the still graver consequences of the embittered silence of this disgruntled young officer.

It was said of him that he was a "booby," but he was not. Without being particularly cultivated, he was an educated man and behind a rather unimpressive exterior, he appeared to be thinking. Gilbert de La Fayette was in the habit of thinking, but not widely or deeply; by which I mean that throughout his long life he followed only those ideas which had their roots in romanticism. There was something of the

Crusader about this Gaul from the Auvergne, but like nine-tenths of his contemporaries, this Crusader had as his creed the *"Contrat social."* It is difficult to realize how deeply philosophy had influenced all classes from 1760 onwards. The nobles, more than any other section of the community, were already steeped in it. The great ladies gave a warm welcome to Montesquieu, Voltaire, Diderot and d'Alembert, and more particularly to Rousseau. All those men born between 1749 and 1759 whom we shall study in these pages, imbibed philosophy along with their mothers' milk, but the squires more particularly, had, as mere children, played round the feet of the compilers of the *"Encyclopédie."* [1] La Fayette was a philosopher, but having a warlike strain in him he infused the obstinacy of his crusading ancestors into the thoughts of his generation. He did not expect to free the Holy Sepulchre, but went to find the Sleeping Beauty of Liberty in her tomb and to awaken her. He did not know where his ideal was leading him or whether this awakening of Liberty was going to prove a benefit to him, his people or his country. He was destined by nature to be her knight-errant, and love her without counting the cost or peering into the future.

La Fayette at eighteen had already discovered the ideal which he was to pursue until he was seventy-seven. He was one of those respectable and sometimes admirable men who are, however, extremely dangerous to the nation which gives them birth; they are suitable for export only.

He had just been sent to the garrison at Metz when he received the first news of the American Revolution. The Colonies were in revolt against England because she was thought to be levying taxes which were heavy out of all proportion.

[1] A monumental work by d'Alembert and Diderot. It was used to further the revolutionary movements in the 18th century.

Do not let us hide the fact that in this lay the chief grievance. In any insurrection however material its grievances—as for example unjust tea or cocoa duties—an appeal is always made to the highest ideals. It is one of the recognized rules of the game.

Tea-drinkers who were too heavily taxed became rebels and proclaimed themselves soldiers of liberty.

You will ask if this cause found adherents in the France of 1775, prepared as she was by philosophical works to acclaim any and every seditious idea. There was this further point. Was France to avenge herself upon England who for a century had beaten, robbed and humiliated her? Public opinion tended to drag the Government of Versailles into war. But the state had to be cautious. In order to help the rebels, it would be necessary to raise a loan. This would be inconvenient at a moment when the country, already faced with ruin, was uncertain—from Turgot to Necker—to which saint to pray.

Was it reasonable by a new war to hasten the hour—already dangerously imminent—when an impoverished monarch would, at his own risk, have to appeal to the Nation? In any case had Monsieur de Vergennes, the Minister for Foreign Affairs, the authority to wait, calculate, watch and then seize the opportune moment?

But when in the summer of 1776 it was learnt that the representatives of the rebellious colonies had met at Philadelphia and voted for the Declaration of Independence based upon *"Les droits de l'homme,"* among the broader-thinking nobility the urge to Revolution increased in strength. I once made a pilgrimage to Philadelphia; I saw the Independence Hall with its wooden tables, blackened with age, round which the founders of American liberty had sat in council, from John Hancock to Benjamin Franklin; there was also the Liberty Bell which to-day is cracked, but which on the 4th of July, 1776, at 11 o'clock, announced to the crowd that the decisive move had been made. I am probably a Celt myself because I was unable to hide my sympathy (evidently unshared by my Anglo-Saxon companions) before these austere witnesses of such a great event.

This emotion was aroused when I thought of the countries beyond the horizon towards which this Liberty bell had boomed out its throbbing notes. It cannot be disputed that its solemn toll crossed the ocean and came to France with its heartening message, to stir up men's thoughts and steel their wills. This word "Republic," which Rousseau had only used in the strictest practical sense of his conceived ideal, was to be writ in fiery characters across the sky of the new United States. Suddenly, minds which were least fitted to determine its substance, and to foresee its consequences, hailed this mystic word, to which the cold practical citizens of Philadelphia had not feared to give a very real meaning. It was scarcely taken into consideration that the idea which these men conceived might be totally different from the interpretation of French philosophers and their disciples' Liberty, Equality and the "rights of man." Suddenly the methods of Westminster, so beloved of philosophers, became unfashionable, and it was quite good form even at Versailles to proclaim the fact of one's republicanism *"à l'américaine."*

We can quite imagine that Gilbert de La Fayette would be very impatient in his garrison at Metz. Having proclaimed their independence at Philadelphia, the new United States soon would have to defend it—with their newly gained liberty. Therefore soldiers were wanted. Our young warrior did not look deeply into the matter, but after secretly negotiating with agents of the rebels working in France, he signed an agreement for a term of service and embarked for America

—all the more hurriedly because his father-in-law, the Duc d'Ayen, had obtained a *"lettre de cachet"* from the king which would certainly have prevented this hare-brained young man from going and disgracing his family and country in some unfortunate prank.

I am not going to give an account of this chapter in history or to describe the enthusiasm of the young marquis in the face of "this blessed equality" which resulted in there being "neither rich nor poor" as he wrote, a statement which might easily be disputed. I will not give details of his first meeting with that "grand old man" George Washington, who smiled paternally—perhaps rather ironically—when he interviewed this ingenuous young fellow. Nor will I describe the first few battles, in one of which this young Don Quixote received his wound. "We Republicans," this descendant of the barons of Auvergne wrote with gusto to his wife. The real American republican looked upon him with astonishment. They were sons of grave Puritan farmers of staid, cautious, practical habits, who carried on the struggle stubbornly but unimaginatively. This little officer wanted deeds of surpassing brilliance and astounding feats of arms. It was certainly the Gaul in him at work; already these Quaker merchants confronted with his restless valour evinced a rather bitter curiosity in him, concluding that "he was an outrageous young fellow, but oh, so French!"

The young man even ran off and made friends with the Redskins. They, of course, were held up by philosophers for a century as an example to corrupt civilisations. These savages—all the more virtuous on account of their savagery—did not disappoint him. He was given the name of one of their chiefs; Gilbert, received into their wigwams, was rechristened Kayerwla—let us hope this was complimentary!—and smoked the pipe of peace. What a joyous picture! He saw them as "the only real friends of France" and imbued with still greater virtues as they admired, after Voltaire and Rousseau, the writings of Raynal and Marmontel.

But firebrand though he was, his activities were viewed sympathetically. "My friend," Washington wrote to him, "The spirit of knight-errantry—lost to the rest of the world— has found a resting-place in the sensitiveness of your nation alone." It was with this saying—which did not cost the American a dollar—ringing in his ears, that he took ship back from Boston and continued to live with his ideals undimmed and his enthusiasm of the preceding year roused to a state of delirium.

This delirium France also shared, and it was inevitable— and justly so—that La Fayette should receive the greatest benefit from it. This journey of 1776 made despite a *"lettre de cachet,"* this crusade for Independence and Liberty—and against perfidious Albion to boot—stories of his American exploits, his friendship with that grand old man Washington, and his baptism amongst the Red Indians,—all these gave him immense prestige in a country already seething with the spirit of Liberty and Equality! The king smilingly punished him for his departure without leave with ten days' confinement at the house of his father-in-law who was now appeased. Then he was warmly received by his sovereign at Versailles where the authorities had decided upon intervention, and when at last an army was sent off to America under Rochambeau, La Fayette went also to act as pioneer and go-between.

These were two splendid years of his life; he fought magnificently and when he returned at the end of that period to France, he was, at thirty, celebrated, not only in his own country but also throughout the whole of Europe. There are no two opinions on this point. His demeanour of pretended modesty was but a poor cloak to his overweening vanity. He had indeed reason to be satisfied with himself, and adulation was poured upon him by court and town and countryside. But not even this triumphant welcome at Versailles nor the acclamations at the Opéra, nor his election to the "Masonic Lodge of St. John of Scotland" with all the distinctions reserved for heroes, was enough to content him. Why, even the favours of one of the most prominent ladies-in-waiting and the supreme triumph of being invited to dance—as clumsy as ever—with Marie Antoinette, were not enough; he sought the tribute of kings. How easy it is to be a Royalist-Republican!

Still in his glorious Republican uniform he went to Madrid where he came to the conclusion that the great men of Spain were but of little account, and from thence to Berlin where Frederick the Great, now an old man, received him; even Catherine II begged him to come and see her in the Crimea. He rather put these princes on a pedestal—this Republican—and Frederick II was much amused. There was no materialist like the King of Prussia. When this hero of Liberty was describing the American Republic to the famous Hohenzollern, the latter interrupted him: "I knew a young man, sir, who after visiting countries where Equality and Liberty reigned supreme, took it into his head to set up the same régime in his own country. Do you know what happened to him?" "No, sire." "Well, he was hanged."

I do not know if "our paladin," hearing the cries of the mob, freed at last, shouting "La Fayette *à la lanterne!*" would recall the sardonic expression on the face of the old king, but it is certain that in 1785 he was not the man to think of such matters. Besides he was off once more to immerse himself in American affairs, in a country now at peace, and where he experienced a triumphal procession: a Huron chief harangued him, Washington kissed him, and Liberty smiled upon him. In the midst of these heady successes what mattered the malicious insinuations of an old despot; and what of the moral?

These successes were food and drink to La Fayette. He wanted to free everybody from his hateful bonds; plantation negroes, French Protestants—black and white after the red. The State was also to be reformed. On no account should the old monarchy be destroyed, for La Fayette was above all a Republican only abroad. But, in the process of reformation, the State could be made, even at that time, into a model republic. As a matter of fact, in spite of everything, he still possessed an innate loyalism which, while struggling for an agreement with his philosophical ideals, led him into still greater misconceptions. Louis XVI, who, after all, was a good sovereign, would, if it had been the general will, have become president of the united states of France. All that was needed was to free him from an entourage which was insensible to progressive ideals, and which estranged him from the people. The latter he described as being good because they were simple—almost as simple, and therefore almost as good, as the Red Indians, who, after all, scalped only their enemies and then but in moments of mental aberration. Somebody once discovered an American Indian in full Huron dress by our hero's side. This savage called him *"mon père."* Paris went mad about Monsieur de La Fayette's Redskin.

All was being prepared for a drastic change in the Government. To prevent the meeting of the States-General, the Court demanded money from the Notables.[2] La Fayette was

[2] An assembly of the greatest in the land; the King would sometimes refer to it for advice in matters of great difficulty. Its most famous meeting was in 1787.

much too notable not to be a member of this experimental assembly but he openly opposed it, demanding representation by election.

"What," cried the Comte d'Artois, the future Charles X, "do you mean that you desire the convocation of the States-General?"

"Yes, your Highness, and even more than that!" And he was the first to pronounce the word "National Assembly," without having reflected for a moment as to what this high-sounding word might really mean. While waiting for his wish to materialize, he inveighed against the "oriental power of the king and extravagance at Court," in his letters to Washington. All that was to be done away with, but was a revolution necessary? Certainly not! Things must be allowed to take their course and a satisfactory conclusion would be reached "without any great upheaval."

Yes indeed!—"without any great upheaval." How easy it is to be wrong over these small matters!

This sudden unexpected meeting of the States-General which he desired, almost took him by surprise and perplexed him greatly. Each class of society was to elect its own representatives. But the Auvergne nobility had no sympathy at all with republican phantasies nor even with M. de La Fayette's liberal ideals: in fact it would have nothing to do with them. Such a state of affairs would scarcely have worried a Mirabeau, as we shall see. This mighty brain and indomitable spirit was to break away from his own Order and throw in his lot with the Tiers État. But in La Fayette a lack of decision was to show itself when he was confronted with signs of open rupture; for, though holding very advanced views, he firmly believed in rule by the aristocracy.

He did what some prospective deputies do in our own times. Because it was necessary for his election to the Assembly he accepted the reports of which he disapproved, and left that noble gathering, "elected but displeased" as he told a friend.

Hedged about by the duties he owed as a member, he felt paralysed for several weeks. Amongst the nobility, elected, as he was, by their peers, each faction displayed a willingness, from the very beginning, to join hands with the Tiers État in an endeavour to establish a common power. This was the first step towards the formation of a National Assembly —and, during the course of several stormy sittings, this party quickly gathered an increasing number of adherents among whom Latour-Maubourg, Virieu, Castellane, Liancourt and fifty others showed a disposition to set in motion the machinery of reform at once. But La Fayette whose inclinations were all for a "republic" (as he still declared to Gouverneur Morris, the United States ambassador at Paris) remained silent, not daring to declare himself. It may be perhaps that, though his mind was still constant, his spirit, which we know to have been irresolute, faltered. He knew that Morris profoundly distrusted the idea of so ill-defined a democracy, as he had expressed his views in the presence of the United States ambassador.

"I told him," wrote the latter, "that I am opposed to a democracy arising out of a love of liberty; that he and his friends were running blindly on to a destruction from which I wanted to save them. Their views, their ideals, and their projects are not acceptable to the various elements which make up the French Nation. It would be the most disastrous thing that could possibly happen if their plans and hopes were ultimately realized." Here we see the pitiless materialism of the Anglo-Saxon. La Fayette's reported answer is "that his party had gone mad and that he had told them so himself, but nevertheless he was determined to perish with them." I hesitate to believe the truth of this answer. It would presuppose a capacity for looking into the future on the part of La Fayette, hardly compatible with his character, or more particularly, with the delusions under which he laboured.

However the States became the National Assembly without the intervention of our democratic Marquis and proceeded to attack their immense problems. It was then that La Fayette once more appeared on the scene. On July 11, he produced his *"Declaration européenne des droits de l'homme et du citoyen,"* the code of laws brought back from Philadelphia and held in reserve by him for ten years. But the Assembly—fulfilling the expectations of Gouverneur Morris—already wanted something more extreme, this being to go a step further than America and to produce a constitution which was to be a model not only for Europe but for the whole world. I will come back to this. The scheme was put aside as being too anaemic but as a consolation prize for the author, La Fayette was elected vice-president of the Assembly on the 14th of July. This was the beginning of another turn of fortune's wheel.

It was on this 14th of July that the mob, bestirring themselves at the news of Necker's dismissal, seized the Bastille in the suburb of Saint Antoine, and, after massacring several officers, set up in the Hôtel de Ville a new municipal authority, a Commune with the astronomer Bailly as its president —the astronomer who, later, was to throw himself down a well. The *"bourgeois,"* terrified alike by the mob rising as by the threatened repressive measures of the court, had from the 14th maintained a force with a dual purpose—to protect them from the mob and from the Government. It was to keep intact the first victories of the Revolution while, at the same time, it was expected to keep order in the streets by a display of a middle-class spirit. This armed band of *"bourgeois"* eventually became the National Guard which was intended from its conception "to uphold our institutions, and if necessary, to fight against them," according to the forthright words of Joseph Prudhomme. But it had need of a prestige, which could only be provided by a popular leader who must also be a soldier and a patriot, if it was to have any influence with both the Government at Versailles and the mob in Paris. It so happened that on July 15th La Fayette, in his capacity of vice-president of the National Assembly, was appointed to escort to Paris the deputation entrusted with the task of complimenting the voters of Paris, assembled at the Hôtel de Ville, on the fall of the Bastille. No sooner had they caught sight of "the hero of two worlds" than with one voice they hailed him as chief of the city guard. La Fayette, as we know, could never resist the acclamations of the populace, but also—to be just to him—he saw in it a means of saving Liberty—still in its infancy—from the menace of mob rule and from the dangers of the counter-revolution. Drawing his sword he swore an oath to sacrifice his life "in the maintenance of Liberty."

The people were a very real anxiety to him. "This furious drunken mob will not always listen to me," he said, becoming anxious for the first time. But to calm them down he gave the order—in whose name is not known—to destroy the captured Bastille. Such a policy had more the effect of stirring up the mob than of calming it down; on the 16th, it had claimed two more victims in the unfortunate Bertier and Foulon whose heads were carried about on pikes. La Fayette, was, through his long career, to show astonishment at the fact that people, hailed as "generous" the day after they had torn good citizens to pieces, should show their generosity by a fresh massacre. On July 14th, de Launay and Flaisselles were cut to pieces by the people who were congratulated upon this act; they next murdered Bertier and Foulon. La Fayette, inconsistent as ever, grew alarmed and offered to send in his resignation. "I am in the terrible position," he wrote, "of seeing the evil without being able to remedy it." It was insisted that he should remain, which he did, and once more proclaimed the people as being "generous."

On July 31st, there was a touching scene at the Hôtel de Ville. The crowd in the square saw the Marquis appear on the balcony wearing a sentimental expression and as if inspired. He waved a new cockade in the red and blue of Paris combined with the white of the Bourbons and cried amidst the plaudits of the mob: "I give you a cockade which will be known the whole world over!" For once, at least, Gilbert de La Fayette was right—although he certainly did not realize under what conditions the three colours were to be paraded before the next twenty years, from the Rhine to the Nile and from Cadiz to Moscow.

La Fayette now "topped the bill." During those summer months of 1789, there was an outburst of patriotism in which the "General" played a part admirably suited to his character. There was in this man a strange mixture of divine faith, of vanity akin to frenzy, of heroic intentions, and a naïve desire to show off, which was abundantly satisfied in the Paris of August and September. He no longer appeared in the National Assembly, but, clad in the uniform of the National Guard and perched on his famous white horse, harangued the mob. Or standing on the tops of steps, balconies, and landings, he spoke as circumstances demanded, encouraging, calming or exciting the still "generous" people, who, delighted with being so generous, cheered every word of their tireless chief,—so much so that they could scarcely hear. He went to Notre Dame—religion still being in existence at this stage of the Revolution—to have the tricolour flags of the *"Garde"* blessed, then rushed off into the suburbs to kiss those citizens who had been kind enough to refrain from killing anybody for a week. He spoke with emotion of the God who protected Liberty, of the king who desired it, and of the people who had founded it. This lasted for two months. He was rudely awakened from this dream by the events of October.

On October 5th the Paris mob surged down upon Versailles to separate the King forcibly from his courtiers who had been accused (not without reason) of starting a counter-revolution: it invaded the Assembly and then tried to force an entrance into the Château. The rebels were hardly on their way when the National Guard showed a desire to support them at Versailles, and to return with the heads of those members of the bodyguard who had been guilty of anti-revolutionary actions. Perhaps they even wished to bring the King and Queen back to Paris.

Some days previously the General had conceived the unfortunate idea—with the view, as always, of gaining approval of the crowd—of announcing that some day or other, a march should be made on Versailles with the object of forcing the Assembly to come to a decision.

On October 5th, the National Guard re-assembled. La Fayette hurried off to dissuade them from such a determination which, in his opinion, was clearly harmful to Majesty, to the King and to the Assembly; he refused to lead them and made as if to depart. Cries came from all sides, "Good heavens, General, you must stop with us!" He gave in, as always, but made it appear that he was under orders from the City Commune. The Pontius Pilates of the Hôtel de Ville ordered him to go off with the rebels, "as it was impossible for him to refuse." This shows how Kerenskys of the future are made.

He was their leader; he followed them. Suddenly he appeared armed at the Assembly, and Mourier, a Royalist Liberal, questioned him sharply: "What was he going to do?" "I shall protect the King," he declared in all sincerity. If the Sovereign said a favourable word on behalf of the National colours which had been insulted by the bodyguard the day before, everybody would be satisfied. He started off for the Château and went in as far as the round-windowed room under the disapproving glances of the courtiers. They held him responsible for directing the affair when he was but a pawn himself; for being a leader when he was already a follower. "Look at Cromwell," someone cried. Shrugging his shoulders, he said, "Cromwell would not have come alone." He saw Louis XVI who received him with that smile, which was, alas, indicative of his usual state of lassitude. Since the General proposed to guard the Château with his men, he would withdraw his Swiss Guards and sleep under the protection of the "soldiers of the nation"; and so it was. The General posted his sentries; but he was tired, too, and went away to sleep, while the crowd, bivouacking in the avenues, howled in chorus, "We want the heads of the Guard!" Rivarol later wrote sarcastically of him, and called him from that time onwards, "General Morpheus": "When I was in bed, crime stalked abroad."

Then the sequel; the entrances were gradually forced by the surging mob, which penetrated the Château right up to the Queen's door, killing the Guards who barred their way. Marie Antoinette was forced to fly, half-dressed, to the King, who had to consent to leave Versailles, and the whole family —"the baker, the baker's wife, and the baker's brat"—was taken off by the crowd to the Tuileries. The Assembly followed the King to Paris, where, together with the Sovereign, it was fated to be controlled by the rebels.

We are told that the responsibility for this act did not lie with La Fayette. No matter; from this day onward, his enemies delighted to insinuate or to declare openly that perhaps he had deliberately—the phrase was to become famous—"slept while his king was stolen."

What he called the "love of the people" was adequate compensation for the disapproval of the Court.

And indeed this "love" was deep-rooted. Few men have reached such heights of popularity; even his famous white horse was embroidered on one side of the tricolour flag. "The General"—as he was called for short, for he seemed to have no other name—was the dominant figure in the Revolution, and Mirabeau, who hated him, accused him of being the man behind the throne. The latter, however, tried to further his ambitions by this man's marvellous popularity. I shall return to this matter when I speak of the great tribune, Mirabeau. He offered to ally himself to La Fayette, who was to be marshal while he was to be minister; and both of them would save the State by cutting short the Revolution which had already overshot its mark and would restore authority. La Fayette understood as little of Mirabeau as he did of Bonaparte ten years later and Louis Philippe 40 years later. His puritanism was disgusted at the self-seeking spirit of this "dissolute fellow." He could only see the intriguer in this clever politician, who would make use of him for his own ends and then cast him aside.

He met the hot-headed proposals made by the tribune with a display of frigid dignity. Mirabeau, when he came into contact with this mind, which he considered inept, became enraged with this "second-rate great man." He thought him a fool, a clumsy menial, a tub-thumping simpleton—"the

King of Clowns," he mocked. But as his popularity increased day by day, everybody wanted his co-operation; first there were the Jacobins as well as gentlemen of the Court, and, after Mirabeau, Talleyrand also sought his help. Indeed the Bishop of Autun even sounded him with a view to an alliance but he, in his turn, became quickly discouraged when faced by a man of such an expressionless countenance and finally came to the conclusion that "he was empty of ideas and decisions."

That was the truth: La Fayette had no idea of what was about to happen. On January 12th, 1790, he wrote to George Washington that he was pleased with what was being done; an excellent constitution was being built up "entirely adequate to ensure liberty." The future appeared to him to be a rosy one; in reality it was red. And carried away by a desire to appear in no whit a reactionary, he, the leader of the army of law and order, declared: "There must be disturbances in the Revolution; the old order of things was only a state of slavery and, in that case, rebellion becomes a most sacred duty." His vanity rose to further heights, however. "I have," he confided to Frochot, "overcome the King of England in all his might, the King of France in his authority, and the people in its rage."

Such pride was excusable, for his popularity reached its zenith on the famous festival of the Federation—when the sentimental side of the Revolution showed itself in a scene of impressive grandeur. It was La Fayette's supreme triumph. He appeared at the head of representatives from all the "National Guards" in the kingdom. When he went up to place his sword with a bombastic gesture on the Country's altar, raised in the centre of the Champ de Mars, the crowd became nearly frantic with enthusiasm. "They did not want him to descend from the altar," writes a witness. "They seemed to demand that he should remain there exposed to the public adoration. Scarcely had he come down when the Federates rushed upon him, some kissing his face, others his hands, and others, less fortunate, his clothes. He was barely allowed to mount his horse. Hardly was he in the saddle when they kissed whatever part of him was available: his thighs, his boots, the horse's harness, even the horse itself." And when, riding out of the Champ-de-Mars, he seemed to be borne along on a wave of cheers, someone cried, "Look at M. de La Fayette riding into the unborn centuries!"

Then, suddenly, this bubble of unprecedented popularity burst. The Revolution increased in intensity, and already a whole gang of leaders pushed it in a new direction. Had not the rebellion been proclaimed "a most sacred duty" by the leader of the National Guard himself? Later, men of Danton's type took the same view when it became imperative to put aside those who, after guiding the first childish steps of Liberty, then wished to stop it, as it were, in its course, and thus became "traitors." La Fayette was still a loyalist, and in spite of some rash words about democracy, wished to re-establish order; this they guessed, and so he began to be a nuisance. On the day after the festival of the Federation Marat had denounced him as a false friend of the people whom he had hatefully deceived. Amidst all this, La Fayette was stirred by the revolt of the troops at Nancy. He was a soldier; suddenly he saw for a moment the danger which threatened, if the dissolution of the army, following—logically—on that of the nation, was not prevented by rigorous disciplinary measures. He advised the Assembly to adopt such measures and then took an active part in the suppression of the rising.

This gave grounds for offence to the factions of disorder, and it led the people—already alienated by the political writers of the extreme Left—to hesitate—if not to change front completely. How is pure gold changed into mere dross? Marat attacked the man with ever-increasing harshness. La Fayette—they used his patronymic Motier de la Fayette— was no more than "the infamous Motier, the vile supporter of the Court." Desmoulins denounced "this artful thief of popularity" as a traitor. It rained pamphlets. When the Queen, who hated the General, dissuaded the King from confiding in him, a libel was published, called the "Amorous evenings of General Motier and the beautiful Antoinette." He had one very brief moment of doubt which is betrayed by a letter to Washington. It was time to retaliate: he would retaliate. But he repelled the intermittent advances of the Loyalists. On whom was he to rely for support? The flight of the King forced the General to assume a kind of dictatorship, and when, later, the unfortunate sovereigns were imprisoned in the Tuileries after their recapture and return to Paris, he had almost to assume the rôle of gaoler. When, in the evening of the day of their return, he sought an audience of the King with an air of frigid deference—which the Court considered the height of impertinence—in order to receive the orders of the "suspended" sovereign, the latter smilingly replied, "It appears that I am more at your command than you are at mine." Marie Antoinette, however, pale with suppressed fury, received the man who was supposed to be guarding them.

La Fayette was faced by a situation which, to him, was becoming hopeless. The strain of it was exhausting him and he firmly resolved to oppose any excesses in the Revolution. It was his opinion that, once the Constitution was in being, the King, now suspended, should be re-established on the throne, and supported this time by the National Guards against the extreme Revolutionaries; he was firmly resolved to suppress any protests which this scheme might arouse. When on July 17th, 1791, Desmoulins and Danton, the leaders of the second gang, had assembled the mob on the Champ-de-Mars to make a demonstration against the re-establishment of the King, the General marched there at the head of the National Guard to disperse the rabble. With him was the Mayor, the unfortunate Bailly, who was also involved in this disturbance. After the Riot Act had been read to the rebels, La Fayette, as impassive as ever, an erect figure on his white horse, drew his sword and suddenly gave the signal to fire. Several hundreds of the rioters were mown down and the rest thrown into howling, headlong, flight. It was the end! What was left of his popularity crumbled away in that sea of blood, towards which, alas, the events of the last three years had been fated to lead. This climax was certainly unforeseen by Gilbert de La Fayette, who, but a year before, on this selfsame spot, had been kissed by the crowd, even down to his horse's crupper. La Fayette ceased to reign even before Louis XVI.

However, he had no regrets, and blinded by his faith, was incapable of learning any lesson from these events. He was cold-shouldered by the Court and disowned by the Revolution; he considered himself a greater man than ever, but his position in Paris was impossible. A new Assembly was elected in which, indeed, his friends appeared to be in the majority, a circumstance which would have ensured his retention of the command of the National Guard, but he was disturbed by signs of his intense unpopularity in Paris. He resigned and obtained command of an army on the already threatened frontier. He was a brave soldier but no general, and when war was declared, he seemed at a loss and did nothing. Besides, the Girondin gang had managed to get the power into their own hands, as we shall see. They hated the man, but at the same time were a little afraid of him. Hack-writers demanded his recall, arrest and punishment. He went on to meet his fate. When the mob had been urged to attack the Tuileries by the Jacobin Clubs in June, 1792, and had insulted the King without daring to go further, the General's innate loyalism burst forth once more. I have said that he did not lack courage. Suddenly, abandoning his army at Metz, he appeared at the Bar of the Assembly, where he denounced the crime of *"lèse-majesté"* which had been committed, and although the Left demanded that he should be tried for having deserted his post, the Legislature paid no heed and went on with the business of the day. The latter thought that he was followed by his army, and being, as a matter of fact, greatly disturbed by the revolt of the evening before, trembled in anticipation of the outburst due the next day. They had already planned a display of force which should unite the leaders of the Second Revolution, which was to effect the subjugation of the Assembly, and to overthrow the throne.

But La Fayette had not brought a single soldier with him. He was still the paladin with unspotted sword, and being, besides, proudly convinced of a popularity which was in reality non-existent, he thought that his name alone was sufficient to destroy those who were inimical to himself and the Constitution.

To the Court, whose attitude of mistrust was maintained towards him, he proposed certain repressive measures. His overtures were coldly received by the King. "I am aware," the Queen said, "that M. de La Fayette wants to save us, but who will save us from M. de La Fayette?" The latter assembled his old soldiers of the National Guard in order to review them. The new mayor of Paris, Pétion, who was hand in glove with the Jacobin leaders, and who had received an absurd warning from the Court, countermanded the review, so bringing to naught the General's ill-planned scheme.

Profoundly disappointed and annoyed, he went off; the storm burst behind him. The Assembly was asked to pass a vote of censure on him but this was gently refused. His dismissal and arrest were demanded; even in his own army signs of discontent were evinced when he wanted to review it and he felt that his control over the army was insecure. He was, in fact, no longer their real leader. When he received the news of the Revolution of August 10th, which had overthrown the monarchy, he felt dreadfully alone. His enemy, Danton, was the real leader of the new Government, and the General might be arrested at any moment in the midst of his own soldiers, who would undoubtedly have surrendered him. On August 19th the Assembly, which was now under the control of the Jacobin Clubs, issued a warrant against "Motier de La Fayette, formerly general in command of the Northern Army." On that very day at Sedan, when he had been warned of what lay in store for him, he wrote to the municipal authorities of the town which he was now leaving: "It was his great desire that the sacred cause of Liberty and Equality, which had been profaned by the crimes of one party, might not be allowed to remain for very long in the bonds of slavery." With his following of liberal nobles, as disappointed as himself, he crossed the frontier. Everyone was amazed at the unruffled serenity of his countenance.

He could not hope, however, for a warm reception from the Austrians. The whole of Europe, which had been aroused by the emigrés, considered him as one of the worst abettors of the Revolution; he was treated as a prisoner and placed in a fortress where he remained five years.

Sometimes it is of inestimable advantage for a public man who has just passed through a terrible crisis to have a period of quiet retirement, even though it is in a prison. There he can meditate and reflect upon past events, and learn a lesson from them. But under no circumstances was Gilbert de La Fayette a thinker. Even though he had had a hand in everything, the happenings of the last four years had really very little meaning for him, or rather, he put his own interpretation upon them. He had wanted to dig deep the foundations of Liberty and had worked to that end. One party, however, had seized Liberty and, having suppressed it, proscribed it; but this, far from shaking him in his convictions, merely served to confirm them. That was all. Though he was one of its victims, he would not have agreed for one moment that this great Revolution was necessarily the offspring of the First which he himself had helped to let loose. The downfall of his hopes—incredible as it was—did not dispel his illusions. This bright mirage followed him into his dark cell at Olmütz and helped to lighten it.

Seven years later, he came back to France. Bonaparte's advent meant nothing to him; he refused to "identify himself with the Emperor's government," although, in 1815, he helped to overthrow it without having any idea of what form of government should follow it. Under the Restoration, his policy was one of opposition, though he had no settled plans. Towards the end of his life, he witnessed the July Revolution of 1830, and played an active though ill-defined part in it. Under Louis-Philippe, so long an object of dread to him, he brought about the proclamation of "the best of Republics," and at the age of 72 he reassumed command of the National Guard, imagining himself still in 1789. Then he declared himself in sympathy with a general crusade to secure liberty for the peoples of Europe, but, becoming an embarrassment to the régime which he had himself fashioned, was again thrust aside.

Although it was nearly time for him to join those of his family, guillotined in his stead, who lay in the cemetery at Picpus, he still continued to speak of the Revolution with deep affection. On January 23rd, 1833, at the Bar of the House, he once more apologized for the 14th of July, 1789, describing it as "the signal for the emancipation of Europe" just as July 14th, 1776, had been "in the American era the signal for the liberty of the world." In 1834, he declared himself a Universal Republican. If he had been spared for a few years longer, he would have taken part in the Revolution of 1848 and would have found in it complete satisfaction, for a moment at least,—as well as the fruition of his ideals. But no one can live forever, even though immersed in the distorted visions of an unending immaturity. On May 10th, 1834, he died at the age of 77; and so he was saved another self-deception.

He had learnt nothing. Upright, honest, generous and brave —these he certainly was—and if not a "simpleton" as the Emperor unkindly described him at St. Helena, he was certainly entirely unfitted for the rôle which a mischievous fate had offered him: and this had proved most unfortunate for his country. He never suspected this, and that is why this septuagenarian had an unwrinkled brow. It is rather distressing to think of this unlined countenance since he had experienced so much public and private sorrow. One prefers to dwell upon the furrowed forehead and the despairing expression of Alphonse de Lamartine after the shattering of his illusions in 1848.

La Fayette died without learning that, to quote Mirabeau,

"it is easier to start a revolution than to end it." Had he known that he would have thought twice or even ten times before drawing his sword on behalf of untrammelled ideals.

Revolutions! If this noble old man had lived, he would, with the very best intentions, have set another ten in motion. Let us beware of such generous people.

CHAPTER II

COMTE DE MIRABEAU

CHAPTER II

MIRABEAU, OR THE REVOLUTIONARY DESPITE HIMSELF

On May 5th, 1789, when the States-General met, deputations from each bailiwick proceeded to the "Salle des Menus Plaisirs." This procession excited no interest, composed as it was of obscure provincials who were, for several weeks, to remain unknown.

Suddenly a noisy tumult of cries, murmurs, and malevolent curiosity arose. The deputation from the Seneschal's district of Aix-en-Provence had just entered the room. Dressed in the drab uniform of the Tiers État a deputy stood out from amongst the group of Provençal bourgeois, in whose midst he was advancing,—already wearing a defiant smile upon his lips. As this broad-shouldered man thrust his way through the crowd, his eyes glowing like coals in his careworn face, a name passed from lip to lip, a well-known name, indeed too well known: the Comte de Mirabeau.

How was it that he was so well known? How was it that, bearing one of the great names of his province, he was here in the black dress of the Tiers État and what were the reasons for the odiously distrustful reception given him by that body? That is what can only be explained by examining the life led before the Revolution by this dreaded, redoubtable man, Gabriel Honoré de Riquetti, Comte de Mirabeau.

"I was too prodigal of life in my earlier years and this fact somewhat weakened me in those that were to follow and drained me of a part of my vitality," he wrote. As a matter of fact, he had used up more than a part of his energy; in those years he had pledged his credit in advance. As he was a born statesman, this powerful brain and courageous spirit could perhaps have seized unaided the Revolution in a strangle-hold, not so as to stifle it but to prevent it from deviating from its course; he might have mastered it and led it, with France in confusion, to a port of safety. That was his wish; to this end he laboured but failed because, owing to unfortunate circumstances, the only man capable of envisaging such an enterprise was, in 1789, somewhat hampered by his dreadful reputation. "How the public welfare has been damaged by the excesses of my youth!" he cried.

"Shall we never hear about anything else except this profligate Mirabeau family!" For a century this had been an uncontradicted saying in Provence: the last to bear the name has told us herself quite recently, under the popular signature of Gyp, and in simpler terms, that, down to the last generations, "All the Mirabeaus had a weak strain." This strain was hereditary, long before Gabriel Honoré was born as the last of the Mirabeaus has observed "after a close study of her family's mode of life."

The fief of Mirabeau which stood on the banks of the Durance—itself a mad river—had been elevated to a marquisate in 1686 in favour of the Riquetti, who had come from Florence a long time before. Historians—Monsieur Louis Barthou was the most successful—who have tried to apply to Mirabeau Taine's theory of hereditary influences, have given us the results of their study based on the early inhibitions of the family. These are really astonishing. It was, indeed, a family lavish in its courage and its vices, in its thoughts and actions.

The terrible Gabriel Honoré was born slightly crippled, with a twisted foot, two huge molars in his mouth and was tongue-tied. This was the Tribune of the future. What a responsibility was his who, without a qualm, freed that tongue by cutting the thread. When he was three years old—to make things worse,—smallpox pitted his face, which would have been hideous if his powerful forehead, piercing eyes and eloquent lips had not been the saving grace. Even so, his father wrote to his brother, the bailiff, "Your nephew is as ugly as Satan."

He was almost uncontrollable in his turbulent moods, but had a quick, intelligent mind and an astonishing memory; his tutors, however, were struck by a particular quality of precocious magnanimity. "He is sharp, but good-hearted," as the Abbé de Castagny said in his report. "He wants to crush the life out of everything and then is ready with his pardon at the earliest opportunity." That was Mirabeau already to the life. But he was too much for his father; the family traits which appeared so early in this redoubtable son rather frightened the Marquis. "My real cross," he wrote, "is my son who is growing up," and according to the custom of the time his impatient father sent the boy off to join the Berri Cavalry regiment.

Like all his stock, he was courageous—a soldier who only lacked a battlefield. Soon, however, as a result of several escapades, he suffered his first imprisonment on the Ile de Ré. Here began his extraordinary journey round France—a regular prison tour; first the Ile de Ré, then the Château d'If, the Fort de Joux, the Castle at Dijon and finally the dungeons of Vincennes. He was, indeed, well qualified to write *"Mes Prisons."*

As a lieutenant, he had been sent to Corsica and when he returned home from that island full of ideas and theories he astonished his uncle, the bailiff, who said of him: "His head is full of thoughts whirling round like the sails of a windmill and full of ideas, some of which are decidedly original." To his father, who was unimpressed by these attractions, he remained a scourge,—"the Squall" as he called him.

However, he appeared to reform; he was married and had a son but he treated even these events in his life as opportunity for fresh outbursts and caused his father and father-in-law, both terrified out of their lives, to join forces against him, a spendthrift young husband who was already considerably in debt. That was not all; he quarrelled with everybody and soon his household was divided against itself and separated by their mutual grievances. From this resulted his incarceration in the Château d'If, then in the Fort de Joux. The old idea of imprisonment was a broad one and there are many examples of it in history; in this case the results were unfortunate, for the young man was often able to visit the neighbouring town of Pontarlier (visits which did it no good)—and made the acquaintance there of Sophie, the young wife of the old President Monnier. He ran away with this charming lady and fled to Holland. There he wrote his first essays in literature, which already showed his bitter hostility to despotism in general. But behind these two lovers, the scandal of the elopement assumed enormous proportions. The Tribunal of Pontarlier condemned the seducer to suffer the extreme penalty, and before he could find refuge, he was handed over to the constables of France on an extradition warrant. He was arrested at Amsterdam and imprisoned at Vincennes, where he remained three years.

These were the most useful years of his life. It is a splendid thing for people of such a temperament to be separated forcibly from the attractions of life and made to undergo long periods of restraint. What is there to do in a cell if one does not read? He read and wrote. His famous monograph on the *"Lettres de Cachet"* was smuggled out from this accommodating gaol where, fortunately, some latitude was allowed in the locking of doors.

One curious feature was that he remained under a sentence of death. To be condemned to death and still live was, to say the least of it, an absurd situation. One memoir, in which he drew attention to this fact, was published, thus reviving the old scandal; the injured husband was more embarrassed than annoyed and offered to come to terms. They compromised. Sophie de Monnier's seducer, far from being executed, was set at liberty, while she was placed in a convent. It would seem that it is sometimes dangerous to be loved by great men!

However, once his mistress had taken the veil, it was his intention to make his wife live with him again. He summoned her to join him and on her refusal he instituted troublesome legal proceedings which he lost. Then came a duel with the Marquis de Galifet, the devoted adherent of the Comtesse de Mirabeau—one scandal after another. To avoid the consequences he fled the country, going to Geneva and then to Prussia.

The intelligentzia in the Europe of that time greatly desired to make the acquaintance of Frederick II. We have seen how La Fayette fared under his gentle gibes, but Mirabeau, who was no La Fayette, heaped ridicule and sarcasm on the Prussian king and his country. Soon an anonymous work entitled "The Secret History of the Prussian Court" appeared in the middle of a succession of scandals; it threw the diplomatic corps into confusion, even to the extent of forcing the Minister of Foreign Affairs to take some legal action.

In 1781, this terrible man came back to France. The Notables were summoned and though he was anxious for a place in the Assembly he was not successful. The direct result of this incident was to arouse his resentment against the Government, so that at the approach of the Revolution he was far more worked up than any of his contemporaries.

He made a violent attack upon Necker, the idol of the moment. The suppression by the Council of State of a pamphlet written by him did not damp his spirits: the Bastille was still missing from his collection of prisons! He made good his escape and from the Austrian Netherlands launched his "Second Letter on M. Necker's Administration."

Ten works of minor importance followed in pamphlet form dealing with the events of the time but these were soon forgotten. In quite a different category was his study in three volumes on "The Prussian Monarchy" in which he showed himself to be a deep thinker as well as a great stylist. It is a mistake to quote only one of his sayings, many of which will remain true forever: "War is the national industry of Prussia." For the work abounds in truisms of that kind and there are other remarks which would have opened the eyes of many ministers of that century.

Nevertheless, the States-General were summoned: the die was cast. But Mirabeau was still perplexed; he was not in accord with an emotionalism, which, like others of its kind, yearned for the advent of a liberty, endowed beforehand with every virtue. Emotionalism usually fails to foresee any probable consequences. He was a thorough monarchist; it was on account of his monarchism that he called for a revolution.

Here we touch upon the least studied problem of the Revolution and, at the same time, on the secret of that strange career. It is time to speak of it. Alone, perhaps, in the whole of France among partisans and adversaries of the Revolution, voters, and deputies, ministers with and without portfolio, nobles and bourgeois—yes, alone, or almost alone, Mirabeau had a clear perception of the Revolution, which was in the making.

As a Royalist, I would add that he followed the example displayed from century to century by the great ministers of our kings. For hundreds of years the French Crown had tried to free itself from the yoke of feudal privileges which had weighed heavily upon it and still more so upon the people. These privileges had long been allowed by the feudal system which for centuries had threatened the very existence of the throne and had finally hemmed it in on every side and become a serious embarrassment.

For many decades, the country had been in agreement with its statesmen. In 1789—I will come back to this date —it did not in the least want a Revolution directed against its King: nothing was further from the thoughts of its people. Undoubtedly, despotism was mentioned, but to show that St. Louis' descendants were not held responsible, the excuse was always made of "a ministerial despotism" and the blame for all the irritating measures of the government was laid on the Ministry—that impersonal scapegoat. As a matter of fact, the dynasty was very popular with the masses and Louis XVI more so than any of his predecessors.

The nation only wanted the abolition of an out-of-date feudal system and, by the suppression of "privileges," the establishment of a social and political state of which the king would be a beneficiary and not a victim.

It was most important that, at Versailles, the new spirit

should not be misunderstood; that it should not be regarded as a rising against the throne, but, rather, as a movement tending to free the Crown and even to strengthen it.

These were Mirabeau's ideas. He was convinced that none of the leaders were possessed of clear vision. On December 28th, as he did not wish to approach Necker, his enemy, he addressed himself to Montmorin, Minister of Foreign Affairs, and explained his ideas; at the same time he presented a plan in outline for a constitution and, to his intense disappointment, obtained no reply. But by this time, he had entered the political arena where he caused a great sensation.

He was the Comte de Mirabeau, of the nobility of Provence. Boldly and almost insolently he demanded his nomination by them. But, alas, his reputation preceded him; he was known as a rebellious son, a faithless husband, a troublesome friend, a fickle lover—in short, a most unpleasant person. People recalled his cynical misdeeds, his broken promises, his almost fraudulent practices and his debts which, owing to his excesses had increased from year to year. Many hardly dared to read what he had written, it was like burning-hot lava, sweeping over a cultured century—in a word, he was a hateful candidate for "honest people." Even his face, with its dreadful bloodshot eyes, and foaming mouth, together with his air of terrifying insolence, was enough to put anybody off. His ideas which were well known by this time were particularly repugnant to the Provençal nobility who were still far from seeing the necessity for personal sacrifice, particularly at a time when he of all people was going to sacrifice them in the common interests of the nation and the throne. He was repulsed and excluded from the patrician assembly.

His fury is seen in the grandiloquent message which even time has not destroyed. "In every age, the aristocracy has mercilessly pursued the people's friends, and if by some happy circumstance, such a friend is raised up in their midst, then it is he whom they have struck down. So perished the last of the Gracchi, at the hands of the Patricians. But mortally wounded, he cried to the avenging gods to witness his extremity: then in this hour of bitterness, a Marius was born—a Marius, known as the exterminator of the Cimbri but famous as the destroyer of the Roman aristocracy." These beautiful words are almost unintelligible to most French people to-day and have rather a hollow sound. But in the Rhone Valley, with its memories of the Legions and chock-ablock with souvenirs of antiquity, what a clarion call was such a challenge! People felt as if the mistral had burst upon them; Aix and Marseilles already strove for the honour of making this turncoat the representative of the common people of Provence.

Mirabeau's electoral campaign began and we can follow every move in it, thanks to the diary kept by his valet, Legrain. Oh, how useful these valets often are to historians!

On March 6th, 1789, Mirabeau entered Aix; the town was illuminated and he was presented with bouquets. He made a speech and the crowd answered to his roaring with delirious applause. "I'm a mad dog, am I? Right! Then elect me! Despotism and privilege shall die of my bite!" As he was leaving the meeting of the nobility, he remarked of them, "They will make me a tribune of the people *in spite of myself*, if I do not take care." As you know, he took very little or no care and became a tribune "in spite of himself," just as when carried away out of his depth towards high-sounding formulæ, he became, "in spite of himself" one of the leaders of that Revolution of which he almost entirely disapproved.

In the meantime, the people became drunk with his oratory. "He has been fêted like a king," wrote Legrain. He had an enormous influence upon the mass but though he could rouse enthusiasm, he was able to quell a rising in Marseilles, for instance, with his little finger. The crowd decked his coach with flowers and kissed the very wheel-tracks, while he, intoxicated with, but a little frightened at his success, cried: "I see now how men become slaves; gratitude begets tyranny." On April 4th, he was elected at Marseilles, on the 6th at Aix, and after selecting this town started for Paris. He was carried in triumph as far as Avignon, which goes to prove that the real Midi—the Midi of Roumestan, ends at the Château of the Popes.

Filled with resentment against the nobility who had disowned him and against the Ministers who had refused to listen to him, he still remained an ardent Royalist. "I feel deeply," he wrote, "how great is our need *to kill ministerial tyranny and to raise up the authority of the throne once more.*" The whole political creed of the great tribune is contained in this one sentence. As he understood it, the throne was to fight its supreme battle against a moribund feudalism with the help of the country's representatives. It did not take him long to see that, as the Ministry had no definite plan, the Court, crowded as it was with the privileged classes would, on the contrary, persuade the King to protect these threatened privileges. Although this situation was not, as yet, clearly outlined, he trembled with anxiety. Was this Revolution so dear to his heart, to fail him from the very beginning owing to the stupidity of the King; was it fated finally to turn against himself?

It was that incapable fellow Necker's fault. On May 2nd, he founded the "Journal of the States-General" which was suppressed on the 7th by a decree of the Council of State because in it he made several virulent attacks upon the Ministry. If the nobility, fearing his bitter tongue, kept him at a distance, neither was the Tiers État as enamoured of their weird colleague as had been the Provençal people. They did not understand his attacks on Necker who was idolized by the *"bourgeois,"* some of whom, being puritanically minded, viewed Mirabeau with suspicion on account of his depravity and thought that he was already purchased by some political party. Malouet wrote: "It was he, indeed, whom I looked upon as the arch-plotter, for, at that time I believed, as everyone did, that there was a conspiracy afoot." And Mounier, the most typical of the Moderates in the Tiers, left this troublesome compeer well alone.

This explains the reason for the clamour and unkindly curiosity that was aroused when Gabriel Riquetti de Mirabeau made his way through the ranks of his fellow-deputies with the light of battle in his eyes.

In the first debates in the Tiers, on the question of bringing about the union of the Estates, he adopted a violently hostile attitude towards the privileged class. It was with the gravest anxiety that he saw the Crown falling more and more under the influence of the privileged section of the community. It alarmed him to see the King enter into a quarrel which was certain to harm him. It had been his dream to see his monarch boldly taking the side of the people against "Privilege."

He thought of dragging the Crown out of the grasp of the Court by giving his King a thunderous message of warning. The question was whether the King would order or simply authorize the joint assembly of the Estates; in that case he would be taking the nation's part. If, on the other hand, the King forbade it absolutely, he would be throwing in his lot with the privileged class.

For six weeks nothing happened of a definite nature, but, on June 23rd, the government decided to summon a joint meeting of the Estates which was to be called "Royal" and in which the King would, at last, make known his wishes. At the joint assembly, Louis ordered the three Estates—Clergy, Nobility and Commons—to separate and vote, each in its own House. Then he withdrew, followed by a satisfied nobility and a hesitant clergy; but the Tiers, silent and brooding, remained in council. They had the courage to disobey but not enough to brazen it out. Then the Marquis de Brezé, one of the masters of ceremonies, appeared on the scene and in the King's name summoned the deputies to leave their Chamber. The black-coated throng of the Commoners wavered; not a word, not a cry passed their lips; their grief only showed on their drawn faces, and judging from the despairing gestures of some of them, they were, even now, ready to submit.

Then from out of this hesitant mass, a man stood forward—the redoubtable personage that we know. He advanced towards Brezé; his eyes flamed like coals, his dress was disordered and he rolled his shoulders from side to side in a kind of fury. Witnesses of this event all describe it differently; some grandiloquently, others coarsely; but the traditional version is as follows:—"Go and tell *your master* that we are here by the wish of the people and that we shall not go out from here except at the point of the bayonet." These were the words inscribed on his bust.

History tells us how the King yielded, how the Estates met jointly, and, becoming the National Assembly, started on its task of reforming the State. But Mirabeau was not satisfied. He had wanted the King to lead the Revolution and not be dragged along in its wake, as was the case, allowing it to take its course until he should have an opportunity of turning against it. By his attitude to the movement, the King showed himself to be scornful in his humiliation, pathetic in his dishonesty. This attitude grievously wounded Mirabeau's loyalist instincts and alarmed him beyond measure.

From June 23rd onwards, he was in a difficult position. The famous remark which he had hurled at the Marquis de Brezé became legendary and made him appear as an adversary of the Crown. From that moment onwards, the Court, the Ministers and the King looked upon him as a foe; the Assembly hailed him as their defender against a possible recurrence of despotic rule; the people welcomed him as their tribune. He became at once a declared leader of the Revolution which, because of the temporary checks which it had suffered early in its career, was no longer moving forward with the King; rather, it was advancing without his co-operation, awaiting an opportunity of attacking him when some fresh misdeeds of the Court offered pretext. The prestige which his attitude of June 23rd had given him in the party of the Left, flattered him; his sudden popularity with the mob sometimes stirred him; but he was desperately alarmed by the reverse that he had suffered, by the bitterness of the Royal House, and by the mistrust of the party of the Right. In spite of the convictions and ideas which he cherished, he was acting contrary to them. If the Court tried to oppose the Assembly then he would be forced, as a newly-crowned hero of the people, to bring himself to follow a distasteful course of action and to become, despite his own feelings in the matter, the leader of a movement from which he seemed to be already alienated.

Besides that, he was possessed by a devil; his great powers of oratory were torture to him and caused him to go much further than he would have desired had he been able to indulge in reflection. But he was always to suffer from this drawback. So it was that the Comte de Mirabeau, Royalist, was forced by circumstances to become, apparently, an adversary of the King and not only a revolutionary but the most virulent one ever known. It is the psychological aspect of the case which is particularly interesting during these few months; for while the great drama of public life was being played, another drama of a singular type was taking its feverish course. A thousand thoughts strove against each other behind that darkened brow.

On July 14th, the King's dismissal of all those ministers who were supposed to be in sympathy with the new ideals made everyone fear a sudden attack on the Assembly. Mirabeau was silent. He was delighted at the dismissal of his enemy, Necker, but fears of counter-revolutionary measures began to assail him. For three days he was silent and, in order to be doubly safe, did not appear in the Assembly on July 14th. But when, on the 15th, thrown into confusion by the events in Paris, it met again, he could hold back no longer. He entered the Chamber and made his fateful speech. The Assembly had decided to send a deputation to the King begging him to withdraw the troops that appeared to threaten it, and to recall the patriot statesman who had been dismissed. But, as the deputation was making ready to leave, suddenly Mirabeau arose. His speech was like a volcanic eruption, a dreadful philippic, directed not so much against the Court as against this King of theirs who had been so feeble as to yield to the request of the Assembly;

he also boldly denounced the Queen. Some of the Tiers État received this bitterly indignant outburst with mad enthusiasm; others heard it with the gravest consternation.

And he repeated it; when the King's approach was announced he cried: "The blood of our brothers is now flowing at Paris. Let the first welcome made to the King by the representatives of an unhappy people be one of mournful respect. The silence of nations is a lesson for kings."

As you know, the King yielded once more to the Assembly; he went to Paris where he ostentatiously submitted, and so blundered still deeper into a policy which consisted of humiliating surrender followed by half-hearted resistance: he could not have chosen a worse. Even Mirabeau himself, who was becoming maddened by the dreadful uncertainty of the situation, also had a hand in making this tragic misunderstanding more complete. He seemed to be following a policy which every day became more alien to his first convictions. The Queen's party now hated him but, on the other hand, the Jacobins acclaimed him; he was made almost as desperate by the hatred of the Court as by the plaudits of the multitude.

Mirabeau was a materialist. The Assembly and its incredible idealism offended his common sense. When, in the night of August 4th, in a kind of legislative frenzy, it abolished the whole feudal system in a few hours and without any sort of preliminary work, Mirabeau could not be displeased, as the Revolution had been undertaken for this purpose. But it was this delirium which offended him. This was not the way to bring about a reform in the State. It was not fitting to cast aside a system, ten centuries old, after an emotional debate lasting only eight hours interspersed with crying and embracing. He involuntarily shrugged his shoulders at this mad act, though it both pleased and alarmed him.

Confronted by an Assembly composed of metaphysicians, he returned to his first ideas of State; stirred by the sight of his country, a prey to anarchy, he could not suppress his desire for the restoration of order.

The Assembly had decided to make a "Declaration of the Rights of Man" and I shall return later to this declaration which is so characteristic of the idealism which Mirabeau detested. He was never tired of repeating that, when a country becomes a prey to anarchy, it is not a declaration of rights that is wanted but a *declaration of duties*. How was it possible to vote for a sensible constitution after establishing positive ideals which would, later, have to be changed or partly destroyed? "We are not savages landing on the banks of the Orinoco to form a society; we have ancient prejudices, a government and a king which have already been in existence for a long time. As far as possible, all these things must be grafted on to the Revolution and *the suddenness of the change avoided.*"

In short, he considered that the Assembly was already astray. It had abolished the feudal system. That was quite enough. The revolt of 1789 had attained its end. Now they were sailing along aimlessly, and, having destroyed an out of date social system, wanted to destroy everything in France, without producing any reasonable plan of reconstruction. And, in the meantime, the whole country, influenced by the happenings at Paris, was breaking up; the State was foundering, and with it, all ideas of law and order. The time had come when Mirabeau must definitely range himself on one side or the other.

Mirabeau had many sides to his character; and this was his weakness.

The tribune had given full rein to his fancies; he had learnt how powerful a weapon was his oratory. His terrifying appearance helped to enhance his prestige. "They do not know," he said, "the power in my ugliness." When this strange figure appeared, the first feelings of his audience were those of repulsion. His head was enormous and covered with extravagantly kinked hair which made it seem even larger; his face, congested, worn and pitted. His brow was haughty, some said "seditious"; his eyes glowed like fire and became bloodshot when he was rudely contradicted. His mouth—an outstanding feature—was bitter, jesting, imperious—each in turn; his thick-set body, in spite of his crippled walk, seemed to bear resolutely down upon an obstacle and shatter it. That offensive gesture of his which nailed his adversary to the pillory and doomed him to the gibbet! Such was Mirabeau. At first sight people were impressed adversely—although deeply—by these characteristics.

He was therefore generally given a distrustful reception. The Right looked upon him as the most formidable of demagogues, but to the Left he was always the aristocrat who had gone astray, and whose disquieting ambitions smouldered under a mask of idealism. "This man," wrote a member of the old Tiers État, "is a wild beast, a mad man. He has a tiger's face. He can never speak without convulsions."

In everyday life he was a good fellow, cordial, gay and full of racy remarks on a variety of topics. At times his shattering irony was a delight. His love of flattery, when fame was his object, was clearly one of his weaknesses; another, still graver fault, was that, as everybody knew, he continued to throw his money about. It was said that he accepted financial assistance from anyone who would give it without any scruples whatever. He was reputed to be mercenary and made but a poor defence to this charge, simply giving as his excuse that if he had received money from all those who were said to have purchased him, "he could have been king of the whole world."

But after he had been speaking for five minutes all these moral and physical imperfections were forgotten for an hour.

Though endowed with a wide intelligence and with a moderately cultured knowledge of many subjects, he was too lazy to prepare his own speeches. It has long been known that, not only the necessary notes but even the text of the speeches were provided by a regular troop of assistants: "Mirabeau's portfolio," wrote Rivarol, "was like the courtiers;—filled with other people's belongings!" Ten of the names of these jobbers are known. Any doubt on this point was dispelled when the papers of one of them, the Genevan Raybaz, were published in 1874. In them, the tribune appears to have asked this jobber to write whole passages in his speeches and seems even to have gone as far as to beg him to follow the debates closely so that he might provide him with suitable matter for his answers. "I beseech you, try and find some noble answer to the reproach that I have been unfaithful to my principles." But his genius enabled him to adapt the ideas of others and to fit them into his plans, giving them a strong, personal touch. For though he coloured the subject matter of others with incisive utterance and burning phrases, his voice alone was enough to give his speech a range and striking force of its own. "His voice was full, virile, and sonorous," said a contemporary. "It was always sustained but at the same time flexible; it satisfied and charmed the ear."

At the beginning of his speech, he was nervous and often hesitated but in such a way that interest was aroused. He seemed as if to seek the strongest expression, to discard unsuitable expressions, and to choose and weigh carefully the words he used, "until," an eye-witness wrote, "he became an animated being and until the *forge-bellows began to work*." Then he carried even the most hostile of his listeners with him. There was only one opinion about his powers of rhetoric. "In a countenance which seemed so repulsive at first sight, what grace, what expression was to be seen!" cried somebody. Madame Roland, who hated him, could not but admire him, and on the Right, an opponent was heard to cry, "Oh, what a brute! but what a talent!" Desmoulins, later on, called him "Mirabeau the Thunderer," and this name stuck to him.

He was called versatile and impressionable but, though he appeared to vacillate, his main ideas really remained the same. That was what he meant when he said that he had never received payment to sully his ideas but to further them. And La Fayette admitted "that he (Mirabeau) had never been paid except in accordance with his convictions."

We know what his convictions were and I shall not refer to them again; they remained the same. The Revolution had been necessary to free the authority of the King, not to destroy it. He was not the type of a Cardinal de Retz, whose only instinct was to harass the State in order to procure an office for himself; his tendency was rather to make himself the Richelieu of a liberated monarchy. A Richelieu—how often this great statesman's name occurs in his writings and speeches!

The Revolution seemed to him to have achieved its end when privilege was abolished. As he understood it, its consequences were to be defended from attempts to restore the old order of things from a wholesale destruction of the State by people who hoped to take an unfair advantage of the inevitable disturbances.

As early as the autumn of 1789, it was clear to him that he was the only statesman who could with the approval of an enlightened monarch and the support of an Assembly, which had been won over to the government, take firm hold of the Revolution and place it on a sound basis. He alone could build up a new state, and, as a second Richelieu under a second Louis XIII could calm the country and restore it, in triumph, to its monarch's rule.

But, as time went by, the Court's hatred of him grew in intensity, and the Assembly which had so often been sub-dued by him, also learned to dread him. So he meant to regain the Royal support as well as to win the Assembly round to his point of view. He had a great friend in a Bel-gian nobleman, the Comte de Lamarck, who had the ear of the Queen, Marie Antoinette. He took him aside, one day, and said, "Make it known at the Château that I am more on their side than against them." In fact, as early as September, 1789, he made every effort not to appear in the House except to defend the King's prerogative in the new Constitution which was then being debated. So it was that be upheld the necessity for the Royal *veto*, for, he declared, "I cannot imagine anything more terrible than the aristo-cratic rule of six hundred people." Certainly there must be some control of the nation, but an unconstitutional parlia-mentarianism without restraining influence was unthinkable. He spoke now with an authority which gained in strength every succeeding day. At times, he carried his audience with him; his famous speech on "hideous bankruptcy" is still famous; he made the terror-stricken deputies rise to their feet as if a monster had in the flesh reared itself up under their very noses. But when he had come down from the Bench, his colleagues, having regained their self-possession, were blind to everything but his intriguing nature, made even more dangerous by his great oratorical powers. What would become of the Assembly if this man was called upon to govern the State?

Then, opposed by these "red jack-asses," he made despairing efforts to force himself upon the restive Assembly and tried to obtain an audience with his sovereign in the hope that they might help him to attain this end. But the Queen had an absolute horror of him and she made the King dismiss any idea of an interview. Mirabeau now had every reason to be discouraged. Quickly the Revolution was moving forward and there was not a day to lose. He was mad with rage: "The King and Queen will perish," was his prophetic cry, "and the people will batter their dead bodies."

However, he did not despair of forcing his way to the front. The Constitution was voted and the State reorganised on a most indifferent basis. Then as soon as the Constitution was in being, the King was obliged to choose a Minister from amongst those who having played a part in the Revolution, yet would declare for the re-establishment of law and order. It was useless for Mirabeau to act alone; so he tried to form a coalition in which portfolios would be shared, with certain influential members of the Constituent Assembly. As we know, he came up against the mediocrity of La Fayette as well as the scepticism of Talleyrand, who was afraid of being tricked and who therefore met these advances with stinging jests. One day when Mirabeau had made complimentary remarks about the future President of the Assembly, the Bishop of Autun, smiling mischievously, said: "Monsieur de Mirabeau missed only one point in his speech of a moment ago; this was that the President must be pitted with smallpox."

Compelled to do without these politicians who distrusted him so much, he sent the King and Queen an endless succession of notes, as he was unable to meet and convince them personally. These letters are really admirable, vigorous, witty, eloquent, and extraordinarily clear-sighted. Above all, Mirabeau tried to win back the support of Marie Antoinette to whom Lamarck showed the letters. "The King has only one man on his side, and that's his wife." He was always harping on the old strain: "I always thought, like you, that the monarchy was the State's only sheet-anchor."

"The monarchs dread the advent to power of the Jacobin ministers," Lamarck told him.

"Is it not generally known," he replied, "that once a man is made a minister he becomes a totally different being. . . . *Jacobin Ministers would never be Jacobin in office.*"

As there still seemed no possibility of obtaining a hearing at the Tuileries, he turned to the Assembly. It was beginning to be unpopular and there was a growing desire for its dismissal; the deputies, in a great state of anxiety, seemed to favour dissolution. Mirabeau's intention was to gain popularity by adopting a reassuring attitude. He and his colleagues could prolong the session without any scruples. "I swear," he cried, "that you have saved the State." Parliamentary representatives of any age are prepared to listen complacently to remarks of that kind and do not find it difficult to applaud them. But the applause in this case did not last more than a minute.

In spite of everything, he was isolated by the incurable distrust of the Constituent Assembly and he realized it. If one is to believe the statement of the deputy, made on February 18th, 1790, Mirabeau said: "No party likes me, not even the one to which I have had the happiness of doing some service." In reality, the Assembly submitted to his action but with the intention of holding him as a hostage, and of keeping him forever in their grip, thus preventing his rise to power. While he observed a gleam of hope—at last! —from the Tuileries, all his other hopes were suddenly shattered.

He had meant to precipitate the solution of the problem. In order to obtain a summons to the Tuileries, he had made a request that the Ministers should be sent for by the Assembly. There he counted on annihilating them verbally, and forcing them to resign. That was a false step; the Assembly understood his hidden motive and rejected the proposal. "His suggestion was simply the sum total of his ambitions," and to cut them short, his enemies took the offensive with the result that Mirabeau who had more power over the King than any Minister, became an out-and-out despot; the Assembly which he had so often extolled up to that time, came into conflict with him. On November 7th, the young Breton deputy Lanjuinais brought forward his famous proposal which later became a basic clause of the future Constitution. It declared the holding of ministerial office by a nominated representative of the people as incongruous and made an even more far-reaching change by forbidding a deputy, on his resignation, to become minister during the three succeeding years. The deputy for Nantes made no attempt to hide the personal character of his proposal. "An eloquent genius is carrying you with him and subjugating you to his will; what would he not make a minister out of?"

In principle, the proposal was ill-omened, absurd. By preventing the King from taking his ministers from the Assembly itself, it made much too clear-cut a distinction between the new executive and legislative bodies and this was later to estrange them forever. Also it condemned deputies who were most fitted to hold office to a sterile and curbed existence. Further the measure disarmed the King by taking away from him the liberty to disarm his opponents. The Right had really no particular interest in the proposal but, on the Right as well as on the Left, there was only one thought and that was to ruin the hopes of the tribune, hated by one party and feared by the other. The Right, therefore, supported the Left in voting for this measure. Mirabeau had made a despairing effort to thwart the hostile actions of "his stupid enemies." He became ironical, as he always did in his bitterest moments. He declared the measure a fatal one in itself. "This is the amendment that I would propose; it is to except M. Mirabeau, the deputy for the communities of the Seneschal's district at Aix, from the suggested exclusion." People smiled but Lanjuinais' measure was voted by a very big majority.

This date is an important one in Mirabeau's life and also, perhaps, in the history of the Revolution.

The Right had made sure of Mirabeau's exclusion from the government by their blind hatred of the tribune. On his part, he hated the Right even more bitterly than the Left from whom the proposal had come. He was disgusted with the weakness of a party which had not *understood* the only chance that he had offered it to bring the Revolution to an end. Full of fury against the members of the "gambling-hell," embittered by his rebuff and worried by his own position, he rained anew his bludgeon-like blows on the King's friends. The Left, delighted at having brought off the double coup of closing the doors of the ministry to a future despot and of getting their tribune once more into their power, now paid the ransom of its deception in applause.

However, he did not allow himself to become more than somewhat intoxicated for he hoped more than ever to become powerful, and so he redoubled his efforts to make himself agreeable to the Tuileries. For, reconciled to his sovereigns, he could demand that they bring their influence to bear upon their friends in the Assembly in order that "the stupid decree" might be repealed.

On the other hand, he continued to explain to the King how monarchy had been freed from its shackles by the overthrow of the feudal system, because "Liberty had in one year crushed more people inimical to the Crown than Royal authority had in the course of several centuries." Then, as a proof of his desire to support the Throne, he entered bravely into the debate on the right of a prince, alone, to declare war or to make peace. He was then attacked by the Left who were frightened to find the Tarpeian [1] Rock so near the Capitol. His convictions carried the day and it was to Barnave, his opponent in the debate, who—as we shall see later on—began to realize the intoxicating effect of popularity, that he said these famous words: "I have also seen the days when they wished to carry me in triumph! And now in the streets the people cry aloud the Comte de Mirabeau's duplicity."

There was no definite evidence of any treason. He had always defended the Royal authority except when it seemed

---

[1] Tarpeia was a Roman maiden who gave the Capitol into the hands of the Sabines. Later, they threw her down from the rock that bears her name. This phrase means that disaster often follows close upon success and shameful defeat is not far removed from glory.

to him to protect, in a troublesome and unorthodox manner, the privileges of the two higher classes to its own detriment. So now he defended it against possible encroachments by the Legislature.

At last it was realized that he was favourably disposed towards the Château and it was on the 3rd of July, 1790, that the memorable interview with the King and Queen took place. He had desired and waited a whole year for it. He was extremely competent, unaffectingly modest, deferent without cringing; he could flatter delicately, with an insinuating, persuasive air. The King and Queen, who, according to Lamarck, had "made a monster of him," were agreeably surprised and appeared to be satisfied. Mirabeau, on his part, left the Court very well pleased and sincerely devoted to them. "Nothing shall stop me," he wrote, "I would rather die than break my promises."

But once more he was deceived. They listened to him now in the Tuileries but there was no wish to place him in power. His prestige was damaged in the eyes of the King and Queen by the very conditions in which he became their counsellor. In exchange for his promise of help the King had offered to pay the tribune's debts, but the latter declared that he did not know how much they amounted to and said that he would be content with a monthly salary of a hundred louis. Louis XVI generously gave him three hundred and spontaneously added to this promise another of a million which should be paid to Mirabeau at the end of the session of the Legislature. It may seem strange to us that Mirabeau did not think that he had sold himself. But this kind of pension was very common at that time. What does seem rather distasteful are the outbursts of joy with which he received the news of these financial arrangements.

The fact is that he had not felt so free for years from the continual distracting worries mainly created by his unpaid debts, which he imagined were unredeemable and from which he now hoped soon to be freed. The idea that he was his sovereigns' tool did not seem to enter his head. "He took their money in order to rule them and not to be ruled by them," as one of his trusted friends wrote of him. This exactly expresses his feelings.

To rule them! He never managed, however, to be in a position to do this. Having urged the King on every possible occasion boldly to take the lead in the Revolution, he thought that he had made his meaning clear. But neither Louis XVI nor Marie Antoinette had resigned themselves to that necessity. Neither the Court nor the entire Right in the Assembly could understand Mirabeau's idea. In the Tuileries, the main hope was to paralyse the Revolution by a strong display of force; and each time the tribune gave his support to the Left there were murmurs of "treason" from the Right. He explained this very frankly. "I am in favour of the re-establishment of law and order but not of the establishment of the old order." Sometimes at the Assembly he allowed himself to get carried away in the heart of the debate and rather far from his original proposal when confronted with the Right's unconquerable hostility. There was an increase in the number of these incidents which resulted in Mirabeau being in opposition to and exasperating the Court—whose secret counsellor he was! And, in order to have an excuse for his seeming breach of faith, he became more estranged. One day as he confessed to Malouet, after a bad reception from the Right when he went up formally to the dais to give it his support, he abruptly changed front and unmasked his batteries. "What could I do? I could not fight happily on the side of those who wanted to see me hanged." In rather a vague way he had arrived at an idea which, for once, was completely wrong: this was that by dint of going one better than the Left's schemes and thus definitely gaining the popular approval he would be pushed by it into power. Then he would ruin the whole of the revolutionary work and would build up Royal authority on a new basis.

He was quite sincere in this gigantic misconception, but pulled in every direction by the contrary exigencies of this foolish undertaking, he became exhausted. Side by side with his public life, he continued to lead a feverish private existence poisoned by every form of indulgence. When the candle is burnt at both ends to that extent it is soon all burnt away.

Although he railed at "his riotous life" he did not realize its effect on him. He thought now that he was nearing his goal. The daily increasing graciousness accorded by his sovereigns to the reception of his views deluded him, and, towards the end of 1790, his popularity, far from bringing him to the Tarpeian Rock, seemed to be carrying him towards the Capitol. His speeches, which were passionately read, excited the people to frenzy and he became as much loved in the capital as in the provinces. Whereas at this time, the other leaders of the Revolution, especially La Fayette, seemed to be losing in prestige, everybody flocked to hear him. At a performance of "Brutus" he was carried onto the stage, where he was proclaimed as the people's protector and crowned with laurels. He was elected to the Executive Council of that part of Paris, then placed in command of his district's battalion of the National Guard, and finally became President of the Jacobin Clubs. And, as a supreme act of homage, after having desired the Presidency

of the Assembly so much—although declaring after each
reverse that "he didn't care a fig for it"—he was installed
in the Chair on the 29th of November, 1790. From this elevated position he showed qualities that were still more extraordinary in that they were contrary to his fiery temperament.

He was enthroning himself in every heart. Could he succeed in getting the fatal decree repealed at last by the King
and by the Assembly—that decree which rivetted him to
his bench? He believed so. Already he was arranging meetings between some recanting republican and some of the
King's friends in which they were to discuss the famous
restoration scheme which was going a long way to bring
about his triumph in the Assembly itself. Could he have
done this? And when once in power would he really have
been the second Richelieu which he aspired to become?

The Revolution had borne him along with it, but it had
ended by wearing him out. He had too many different anxieties, too many conflicting, partially realized ambitions in
which he was disappointed; too many of his hopes originated
in fits of madness and were abandoned in moods of despair.
He was brimming over with jealous passions and righteous
anger. Millions of ideas jostled and clashed together in his
teeming brain and his restless heart was filled with feverish
emotions. Then there was, besides, his life of folly with its
constant entertaining, and endless feasting—a life uncon-
trolled, a mere whirl of pleasure.

When at one of the conferences with the leaders of the
Right, Malouet left much impressed by the appearance of
his ravaged face. "His flaming bloodshot eyes were starting
out of his head; he was horrible but never have I seen
such energy, such eloquence."

In January, 1791, he became afflicted with disease. A purulent ophthalmia forced him to go to the Assembly one day with a bandage over his terrible eyes. On March 26th, he was seized with violent nephritic pains; but he had to speak in the Assembly, though he wore a tortured expression. For three days, he fought against his sufferings but on the third he saw Death staring him in the face. "Misfortune has served to steel me, to stimulate and set me on fire," he wrote to a friend, "and I still burn though I am only a cinder now."

Talleyrand visited him. I shall speak later on of this unfrocked priest,—given to refined debauchery. This was the prelate whom that heathen, Mirabeau, desired to have at his death-bed; he also asked for flowers. The tribune gave him a speech which he had prepared on the question of succession. Suddenly turning his despairing eyes on him, he said: "My friend, I am taking the last shreds of monarchism with me!" This was reported at the Tuileries—but too late. The sovereigns sent anxiously to learn how he was. "This would be a great misfortune" was the statement made at the Court. The King's messenger passed the Jacobin envoy on the doorstep. The tragic misunderstanding, which was the cause of his death, still remained.

On the 2nd of April, he realized the end was at hand: "My friend," he said to Cabanis, "I shall die to-day. And at such a moment there is only one thing to do—to be sprinkled with perfume and decked with flowers; there must be sweet strains of music so that one may sink peacefully into that eternal sleep."

Strictly between ourselves, it would seem that "at such a moment" something else remains to be done. There is no real courage in these words pirated from the ancients. At such a time, the really great man has other consolations than the vain bombast of an actor who listens for popular applause right up to the fall of the curtain.

But we must not be unjust. This man, who was the morbid product of his age, did not believe the soul immortal, but he was not without nobility and his care of the citizen had always been disinterested. He died, partly, of despair caused by a revolution which he had helped so largely to unloose: now he saw clearer than anyone else that the Revolution would ruin the country which he seems to have loved so well. "I see very clearly that we are in the clutches of anarchy; that, every day, we are sinking further in." This he wrote to the king a year before: *"I am furious at the idea that I have only helped to bring about a huge destruction."*

He had, indeed, done nothing but share in "this huge destruction"; but he had at least the merit of realizing his mistakes and of admitting them; he even hoped to repair them.

I will leave my moral there since history does not preach. It judges.

This man was very nearly a genius. But was this genius sufficiently strong—even had he lived long enough—to master this revolution that he had so desired? Even the most powerful personalities can only very rarely stop at will such movements as these before they exhaust all their venom. Whatever one's opinion on mankind may be, it would be superhuman, if it could turn back a raging torrent in the full force of its first flood and at a point some distance from its source.

On the evening of Mirabeau's death, Louis XVI's minister, Montmorin, said to Malouet: "I am in despair. We shall all be massacred." And they were.

I am convinced that Mirabeau, had he lived, would have been massacred with them. But I will agree with one who knew him very well, that: "He is the only man to whom one can pay the compliment of believing that, had he lived, France's destiny would have been changed."

And this honour is really the only one that can be paid to Gabriel Honoré de Riquetti, Comte de Mirabeau.

CHAPTER III

CHARLES MAURICE DE TALLEYRAND-PERIGORD

CHAPTER III

TALLEYRAND—REVOLUTIONARY

For fifty long years, Charles Maurice de Talleyrand-Périgord was the foremost figure in the public life of his country. His career started when, as the little Abbé de Périgord, Agent-General of the Clergy, he was entrusted in 1788 with the interests of his Order; the year 1840 marked its conclusion. All Europe grieved at the passing of this old Prince de Talleyrand (as he had become); five times Minister and formerly Ambassador Extraordinary of the July Monarchy in London. Starting as Abbé de Périgord, he later became in turn, Monseigneur the Bishop of Autun, Citizen Maurice Talleyrand-Périgord, His Highness the Prince of Benevento, and then last of all, Prince de Talleyrand, whose prestige was past belief. He appeared in approximately ten different rôles and sometimes he played the lead. He was a deputy in the States-General, the Constituent Assembly, and was the true founder of the constitutional Church— since to him alone it owed its inception; then he was a member of the Paris Executive Council in the last year of Louis XVI'S reign, a propagandist envoy for the new Republic in London, and, after an amazing visit to America, he held office as a (supposed) Jacobin minister in the Directorate, and the Consulate. This was not all; he was a minister and great dignitary of the Empire, President of the provisional government in 1814, again Minister in the First Restoration, President of the Council of the Second and, in the interval, Plenipotentiary of the most Christian King at the Congress of Vienna. Finally, after remaining in sullen opposition for some time, it was he who was entrusted by the French King, Louis-Philippe, with obtaining the recognition of the Tricolour Monarchy by the Court of St. James. What a career! Almost without a breathing space in it. And he was lame in one leg!

Of that great career, the three most important years are those which this marvellous actor spent in the First Assembly and which are so vital in history. In confining myself to this chapter in the life of this great statesman, it will be possible, without going too deeply into the matter, to touch upon the question as to what part was played by the Clergy in the early stages of the Revolution. The name of the Bishop of Autun is in fact intimately connected with two of the most outstanding events, the nationalization of church property and its separation from the state. When he had accomplished this he hurriedly disappeared from the scene of action, for several years.

But in order to obtain a clear understanding of the part which he was going to play, we must first see what manner of man he was and under what circumstances he came to set in motion the anti-clerical movement which was to be mainly responsible for altering the course of the Revolution, and, consequently, the whole course of history.

Nearly all those who played a part in the Revolution may be said to have had their fate rudely altered by it. They were often snatched from a hopeless existence and cast on to the tribune, into political combat, into war; it made them

famous and powerful; it showered honours upon them; sometimes even it brought them to their death.

I would not go as far as to say all that of Charles Maurice
de Talleyrand-Périgord. It is by no means certain that he
would not have been ambassador, minister, twenty times mil-
lionaire, or prince without the oath of the *"Jeu de Paume"* [1]
and the taking of the Bastille. In his very interesting book,
M. Bernard de Lacombe has given us a very full account
of Talleyrand as he was prior to 1789, or the "prehistoric
Talleyrand" as I described him in an article. It certainly
seems as if, whatever lay before him, he was intended for
intrigue and glorious successes.

He was certainly born at an advantageous time; under the
old Régime the pickings fell to the best of the nobility. He
came of ancient and almost formidable stock, for did not a
Périgord in the tenth century deliver his challenge to the
first Capet: "Who made thee King?"

Almost directly descended from this rough baron, the
breed had continued to show great restlessness; sedition and
intrigue were in the blood. To mention only one Périgord,
Henri de Talleyrand, Comte de Chalais—a closer relation
of our hero than the above-mentioned Talleyrand, he it was
who was executed by the orders of the great Cardinal on
a charge of conspiracy. And this, if it sometimes leads to
the headsman's block, can also be a way to highest honour.
Of this, Cardinal Hélie de Périgord is an example; a great
intriguer and a friend of Petrarch, he had both at Rome and
Avignon, been dubbed the "Pope maker,"—and this leaves
the impression that he "overthrew" perhaps as well. Mon-

---

[1] The famous oath, which the Tiers État swore on June 20th, 1789, that
they would not disperse until they had given their country a constitution.
Louis XVI had refused to allow them to meet in their Chamber.

seigneur Dupanloup,[2] who had been the Bishop of the famous unfrocked priest's diocese, had taken an interest in the Talleyrands and discovered Cardinal Hélie's tomb at Rome. The epitaph, couched in singularly candid terms, declared that he was *"religione tenuis terrena sequendo,"* or "apathetic towards religion for he sought this world's goods." This made a precedent; our Talleyrand, if he had been born thirty years earlier, would probably have become à Cardinal in a very short space of time; but we may well suppose that "while seeking this world's goods," he would have been "apathetic towards religion," no matter what might really be the cause.

In the Talleyrand family, there were certainly other very virtuous divines. They, for some unknown reason, seem, as a general rule, to have afforded less interest than other prelates to historians and their students and pious people have very little to say about them. The family also gave good officers to the service of the King, and Talleyrand would perhaps have been of their number if he had not been lamed by a fall when quite a child. Following the excellent notion, common at the time, our injured hero was considered unsuited to serve the King, but fit to serve his God. Ungrateful, he sometimes used to curse his twisted foot which had made him a cleric. But he was wrong. His infirmity, while it caused him to become a priest, then Bishop, and afterwards deputy for the Clergy, also contributed to making him a prince.

He was born on February 2nd, 1754, in a mansion in the Rue Garancière. His father, Lieutenant-General Comte Charles Daniel de Talleyrand was in the service of Louis

---

[2] 1802-1878. Famous for his theories on education and his increasing efforts in defence of the temporal power of the popes.

XV and came of a great military family. These Talleyrands were a good type; they not only had an indomitable
spirit but also they never suffered from infirmities in the
legs! This, unhappily, was not the case with Maurice; being
lame, I repeat, he was immediately appointed to take Orders
without anyone thinking it necessary to consult his conscience
or his personal wishes in the matter. And this was his excuse
for what followed. These are the circumstances which we
must recall if we are to understand rightly this unfortunate
man, so blessed by fortune in the eyes of men but who,
doubtless, in the eyes of God, was never anything but a
mean creature.

He became acquainted with the gloomy seminary of Saint-
Sulpice just as Chevalier des Grieux [3] had done. But he also
learnt that Saint-Sulpice abutted on the Rue Férou, where
a young actress was living. Since she inhabited his street,
she must have been fonder of darkness and obscurity than
actresses generally are. Saint-Sulpice seemed to him an agreeable place, when situated so close to this street which had
been "illuminated" as if by a miracle by one so charming. I fear that this fascinating Manon did not have to go
and rout her noble Des Grieux out of the school-parlour!
Certainly, Maurice had a limp, but he was destined to
prove that he knew how to travel greater distances than
that which separated the Place Saint-Sulpice from the Rue
Férou.

Man is a complex being, more particularly so is the type
which comes of restless stock, is endowed with a mind
devoid of simple emotions, and is capable early in life of
many different feelings. To judge from M. Bernard de Lacombe's account of him, Talleyrand was not, taking it all
round, a bad boy while in the seminary. Far from it. And

[3] Manon's lover in the opera of that name.

what seems to go to prove this fact is, that, all his life, he was loud in his praises of Saint-Sulpice and it must therefore have seemed to him a most attractive place—when he had left it.

The little Abbé de Périgord (he was always known as that) was next seen at the Sorbonne, where he prepared his theses which were accepted. But the best thesis of all seemed to him to be his meditations before Richelieu's tomb. In spite of the fact that the latter would have most certainly beheaded any and every Talleyrand, yet to Maurice he always remained the ideal statesman. I suppose that the little Abbé went to the Church of the Sorbonne; there, perhaps, he stood before the imposing mausoleum in the same spirit as that in which the heroes of Maurice Barrès [4] leant on their elbows in front of the marble vault at the Invalides where the "professor of energy" slept his last long sleep. As his thoughts were more particularly fixed (like those of his great-uncle the Cardinal) on "the things of this earth," his meditations there must have been more upon life than on death.

If he felt that he had the makings of a statesman, he did not boast about it, for he was prudent; though, perhaps, his plan was to govern the State, for the moment, he only aspired to govern a diocese. But he began, regardless of consequences, to injure his reputation and in certain sections of society where, in spite of the loose morals of the time, —even Church dignitaries were not free from blemish—his behaviour was scandalous. He was ordained priest on December 18th, 1779, elected Secretary of the Assembly of the Clergy in 1785 and, thanks to his great talents which were then already evident, succeeded to the very important post

[4] A reference to the principal characters in Maurice Barrès' book "Les Deracinés."

of Agent-General to his Order. But, by 1788, the Abbé Périgord was more famous as *"homme du monde"* than as an ecclesiastic. A candidate for a bishop's throne, and (even at this time) for a Cardinal's Hat, this young cleric spent his days in riotous living, got into debt and found it all very pleasant. He frequented all the well-known salons where, to judge by far too many precedents, he was right in hoping to find the royal road to even the highest ecclesiastical honours.

However, he did not expect preferment during the present reign, for Louis XVI, a most devout prince, hated the idea of appointing bishops in whom, he said, the Holy Spirit was noticeable by the spirit alone.

On being urged to nominate as Archbishop of Paris, the scandalous Loménie de Brienne, who, later, as Cardinal unfrocked his priests and presided over the Jacobin Clubs, wearing the while his Hat surmounted by a tricolour bonnet, the King, with much foresight, cried: "I want at any rate the Archbishop of Paris to believe in God."

This God-fearing King had, indeed, no more confidence in the Abbé de Périgord's faith or even in his morals than in those of other churchmen. For five years, he was proof against insistent requests to bestow on him a bishop's mitre. However, late in 1788, he reluctantly yielded and appointed him to the See of Autun. The Abbé de Périgord was thus one of the last bishops to be enthroned under the "Concordat" [5] which, more than anyone else, he was to be instrumental in destroying. Twelve years later, by an amazing

---

[5] A treaty between the French King and the Holy See, relating to religious matters.

In 1801, another "Concordat" was signed between Bonaparte and Pius VII, re-establishing the Roman Catholic Church in France. This agreement lasted till 1905.

coincidence, this unfrocked Bishop of Autun became one of those who negotiated the New "Concordat."

The See of Autun conferred on its bishop high-sounding titles but very little wealth. According to the practice of the time, a rich abbey was made an adjunct and an additional source of income. Therefore we must admit that, in these circumstances, the whole system was unsound and that, on closer inspection, the Church was not the most wronged of those institutions overthrown by the Revolution. People said that the revenues from this prebend would merely encourage the bishop-designate to indulge in pleasure on a larger scale than ever, for many people thought this new apostle of the Gauls to be a very weak vessel indeed.

And they were right. Paris had too many attractions and held too many possibilities to be easily renounced by the Bishop of Autun; he could not bear to leave the salons of virtuous ladies—and of others—to withdraw from ministers' audience chambers and from the ante-rooms in the neighbouring palace of Versailles. This ungrateful fellow did not appear at all in a hurry to go and administer the diocese which Syagrius of happy memory had, in the dim past, made illustrious by his singular virtues.

Maurice, indeed, lingered in Paris and it is to be supposed, that it was not to the things which made Syagrius happy that he gave his time. Certainly he wrote admirable pastoral letters for, as everyone knows, he was neither a fool nor an ignoramus. He wrote to his Curés that, in future, he would take Bossuet and Fénélon as his models. With the former, he had nothing in common; with the latter only his strong desire to become a Minister. The fact of the matter is that he was more absorbed in politics than in mere pleasure. If sometimes his thoughts turned to Autun between visits to that charming Comtesse de Flahaut, it seems to me that it could not have been on the blessed Syagrius that he paused to reflect but rather on that former Bishop of Autun, Léger, who had been *"Maire du Palais"* in the time of the Merovingians and who, in the seventh century, had made and unmade kings. Talleyrand, ex-bishop of Autun, was, likewise, to make and unmake kings.

Suddenly, he appeared at Autun on March 12th, 1789. How could it be said, therefore, that he did not bother about his diocese? So great was his love for his clergy that he had come thither to embrace them. Let us say quite openly that he was the candidate for their election. The States-General were about to meet; when they assembled Maurice de Talleyrand wanted to be there as their deputy. In 1614, in similar circumstances, Armand du Plessis de Richelieu had started his career as deputy for his diocese of Luçon, that "squalid see" which he was so anxious to leave.

Autun was quite taken in by their young bishop, who wrote such edifying letters to his Curés and whose political programme is still extant. He was a "Conservative," which shows that already he was an opportunist, for, unlike many Curés, those in the diocese of Autun were conversant with neither Rousseau nor Voltaire.

He was elected on April 2nd by a large majority. The Autun clergy could never understand how, after one year, his promises, once golden, should have assumed a leaden hue. The fact is that the gold, to begin with, was hardly pure, and also in the crucible of the Revolution, metals of a purer alloy were bound to be fused together in its fiery furnace and consequently debased. We should hasten to point out that, a deputy, at this stage in the proceedings, never makes a false move in the eyes of his electors. But Heaven knows if this is a solitary case.

Since the duty of a conscientious deputy is to live in Paris, the Bishop of Autun did not stay more than a fortnight longer in his diocese. On April 12th, he left the town where Syagrius had found happiness, already casting off the mask which he had assumed as long as it was necessary. He was destined never again to return to that town.

It must not be imagined that he had settled upon the line which he would take in the Assembly and in the House of his Order. His position as deputy did not weigh at all heavily upon him, for the Clergy were divided among themselves and nobody, at that juncture, could have predicted with any degree of certainty which of the two parties would gain the day.

The clergy were indeed divided. The truth is that many prelates who were less fortunate or less talented than the Bishop of Autun had been compelled to give up any idea of standing for election: in their stead, a whole mob of Curés, pushing aside their spiritual superiors, had come forward, warrant in hand, to represent the French clergy. And this section of the Clerical Order seemed inclined to unite with the Third Estate and, with its co-operation, to bring about the abolition of "Privilege."

It is impossible to conceive the enthusiasm with which the clergy (more particularly the Curés and certain religious orders under the spur of their orators) had welcomed the Revolution.

After a close scrutiny of clerical records and of the events in the electoral campaign of 1789, I have been astounded by the almost complete unanimity with which the new ideas had been hailed in clerical circles,—ideas one day destined to bring about their ruin. Of this, I have given an explanation elsewhere.

It is quite enough to recall the fact that in the whole course of the election, the clerical assemblies had been the most disorderly and that in many places the Curés had forced their Bishop into so humiliating a position that he had been obliged to leave the meeting followed by their abuse. The representatives of the Clergy became so insulting that the Comte d'Antraigues was heard to exclaim, "These damned Curés will be our ruin," and his judgment was of value.

But that was nothing out of the ordinary. I have shown in greater detail than is possible here how the incredible inequality in riches between the majority of the upper clergy and even their most favoured Curés had, more in this section of the community than in any other, established a class possessing enormous privileges over the wretched masses of the people. And to show the accuracy of my statement, I do not merely rely on figures alone but I can call upon the testimony of Cardinal Mathieu who in his first work, "The Old Régime in Lorraine," has, better than anyone, described and stigmatized in no uncertain fashion, a grievous situation which was even fraught with danger.

A typical case of inequality was that of a Cardinal de Rohan, who threw millions out of the window at the Château de Saverne while one of his Curés could hardly make ends meet. From out of this disparity a feeling of discontent arose. This feeling was intensified by a rather too frequent display of riches under the very noses of their clergy by certain of the bishops, for the most part gallant, honest souls but with characters more often worldly than spiritual.

The Curés, therefore, were ready to welcome these claims to equality. And, for thirty years, they had been reasoning on philosophical lines. In common with the admirable and impartial author of "The Religious History of the Revolution" (M. Père de la Gorce) I have quoted this very significant fact: I refer to the discovery in the district of Périgord of two lists of signatories to the *"Encyclopédie"* which, out of forty names, give twenty-four as being priests. In view of this, no figure is more likely to have appeared among this number as that of the good Curé Barbotin whose letters have been published and who declared that his favourite authors were Mably and other philosophers. But Rousseau himself made them weep as he did everybody. I am prepared to wager that certain Curés of 1789 would have accepted as a "pocket-curate" the *Savoyard* which Jean-Jacques had given them.

After May 5th, when the question arose of individual or Order-voting, and brought the State-Reform party and its antagonists to grips, it is not surprising that the Tiers were unanimous for the individual vote. On the other hand, the nobility rejected it by a large majority and the clerical party was more or less split in two. It is a fact that out of the 247 clerical deputies, 114 approved of the proposal and only 133 rejected it, including nearly all the bishops. But, on the succeeding days, violent episodes in the Clerical House brought Curés and prelates to grips. When an eminent Abbé had severely reprimanded the Tiers État, lo and behold! a Curé cried: "Hold thy tongue," and another, Jallet by name, roughly chided the bishops, exclaiming: "My lords, here we are all equal!" On June 13th, after a month of uproarious meetings, three Curés went over to the Commons amid scenes of wild enthusiasm; they were later to be followed by nine others. Finally, on the 19th, by a majority of 149 votes, the House of Clergy decided to follow *"en bloc"* these daring pioneers and, led by five bishops, it joined the Commons

while the remainder of the bishops went off to beseech the
King to prevent this union.

Autun was not one of these five bishops. I have said that
he was always careful to see which way the wind was blowing,
but, up to June 24th, his guesses had been wide of the mark.
The truth is that it appeared to him quite impossible that the
government could allow the reunion of the Three Estates once
it had vetoed it. In case a reaction set in (which at that time
he thought was inevitable), he was not at all anxious to find
himself compromised as being one of this clerical vanguard.
He boasts in his memoirs of having advised the King, on the
evening of the *"Jeu de Paume,"* to call out the troops. But
when he saw the King's gesture of hopelessness, like a flash
his whole outlook was changed. The system from which he
had reaped such unmerited advantages and of which he was,
frankly speaking, one of its "living abuses," seemed to him
henceforth to be doomed to destruction; and he was not the
man to cling to wreckage. On June 26th, he took his seat on
the side of the Tiers without any kind of noisy welcome, for
any applause which would mark so belated an adherence
might have done him more harm than good. No one noticed
this thin bishop with his expressionless countenance, sitting
in the midst of the *bourgeois*. Aristocratic in his notions
which no warmth of feeling could broaden, he hated them,
disdained them, and almost despised them.

Now that he had taken the step, he meant to profit by it.
With cold assurance, he weighed the chances of the future.
From the moment when the Revolution went unchecked from
its outset, it was inevitable that it must go very far, so far
that any conclusions were admissible and any conjectures
plausible. Doubtless, for the first time, Talleyrand saw in
that Revolution an entirely different career from that of his

dreams. A Cardinal's Hat, even with a career of a Retz or a Richelieu to match,—what did that matter now? Since he had been rigged out in a hateful cassock for ten years by a most curious turn of Fate, he intended to make the best possible use of it. Now he feared that it would trip him up. While awaiting the moment when he might be able to throw off this cloak of Nessus,[6] he certainly did not want to be compromised by it. That is why this prelate, who a short time before, was opposed to the Revolution,—this refined nobleman to whom democratic ideals were later to be entirely obnoxious—suddenly took the lead in this movement towards union which the Curés had but planned in outline. Further still, he conceived the idea of freeing himself absolutely from his Autun constituents who expected him to adopt an entirely different attitude. In a clever speech, he did more than anyone to ensure the rejection of the motion that deputies should be bound by the wishes of their electors. In the words of Malouet, "It was the Bishop of Autun who had, henceforth, the greatest influence in all the activities of the Assembly." That, I think, is perfectly true; he had released the deputies from their constituents' control and in the face of public opinion which, I still insist, was only slightly inclined to reform, the Assembly was going to effect a complete revolution.

In the future, the Bishop of Autun will appear not merely among those, but more often at the head of those, who were shortly to despoil the clergy and then attempt to pervert

*A centaur who wished to abduct Deianira, the wife of Hercules; he was mortally wounded by the latter with an arrow dipped in the blood of the Lernæan hydra. The young Nessus gave her his cloak as a talisman which would bring back her husband to her if he proved faithless. Being deceived she acted on this advice and so caused the death of Hercules.

them. No one will ever have a better right than the French clergy to say that "Treachery begins at home."

On August 11th, 1789, the Assembly struck its first blow, —the suppression of the tithe payable by clerics to the nobility. This was what the deputy Chasset had demanded so vehemently.

At this time, the French clergy were still far from moderating the ardour which they had evinced on their entrance into the revolutionary movement. When after the memorable night of August 4th, in the course of which La Fare, Bishop of Nancy, besides making other sacrifices, came in the name of his late Order to renounce his privileges, the dawn broke over Versailles, and even the bishops, overcome by a new tenderness and feelings of good-will, sang the *"Te Deum."*

Under the influence of this "new tenderness," Monseigneur de Juigné, Archbishop of Paris, perceiving that the Assembly was prepared to suppress the tithe, made a complete renunciation in the name of all the Clergy at the beginning of the session of August 11th.

What henceforth would be the part played in the House by the pale, thin Bishop of Autun? Having taken his seat, he made a very careful distinction between himself and his colleagues. The latter "gave up" the tithe-payments, but paying a delicate compliment to the Left, he nevertheless wished the Nation to "receive them back" instead of "accepting" them. He found fault with Chasset's amendment and put it to the vote. Thus the Left realized that the Bishop of Autun was a super-patriot; thenceforth we see him regarded with approval by that party.

That was Talleyrand's first step on the road to treason.

But how insignificant is this in comparison to that *"coup de Jarnac"* [7] which he later dealt his own party.

It appears that he intended to win the good graces of the Assembly by bringing a rapid solution to the most harassing problem which had ever faced it. This was the financial situation.

It is a popular supposition that financial worries are never the cause of death, but many differ on this point. And in any case, if it does not kill men, it certainly inflicts great suffering on nations,—as we know to be the case at this time.

But after all, the States-General had been convened only because the Monarchy was threatened with bankruptcy and intended to appeal to the Nation for financial assistance. Then, for five months, the representatives of the nation continued to discourse in touching language upon "The Rights of Man" and the need for a Constitution; but they had not found a penny for the empty Treasury. Quite the contrary, for the country was now in confusion, and had therefore ceased to pay the customary taxes, the first thing the taxpayer always does when the country is faced by a crisis. What was the good of levying additional taxes when even the old ones could not be collected? Attempts had been made to borrow; but money is not readily lent to sick folk and France undoubtedly seemed to be ailing. Then there had been appeals for patriotic subscriptions; the deputies, to set a good example, had come to the House one fine day, bringing their silver shoe-buckles; worthy souls during these sharp attacks of "tenderness" on the part of the Assembly, had sent—some, their silver-plate, others, a modest five crowns each, but the

---

[7] A French captain who killed La Chatagneraie in a duel in 1547, by a most unexpected stroke. He cut open his adversary's calf by a back-stroke; from this has arisen this phrase which expresses a decisive, but also most unexpected blow.

total failed to reach seven millions. Necker, still Minister of Finance for a few days longer, struggled amid these difficulties. He had considered organizing a national bank but it is easier to do that in times of restoration, (as we shall see under the Consulate), than during a revolution. Each day brought an idea—and a disappointment. The deputies came with cheerful faces and made the most ingenious suggestions. "Give me twenty minutes of your time, gentlemen," cried one of them, Wimfen by name, "and I'll find you 600 millions!" The twenty minutes became sixty,—not a pound was forthcoming and Necker declared that hardly a sou remained in the Treasury. Since he showed no skill in alchemy, he lost favour; in the same way, during the past hundred years and even quite recently, we have seen more than one Necker cast down from the Tarpeian Rock in less than a month,—merely because they had failed to discover the Philosopher's Stone.

Under these circumstances, a number of candidates were keeping an eye on this office, one so difficult to fill. Mirabeau had denounced the "hideous bankruptcy" only to advance his own claims; and Talleyrand, with less ostentation, was working for his own ends.

Throughout his life, he was to show his love for money matters. In reality, the Bourse was our prelate's real vocation,—at least, for several weeks, he talked of nothing but money. If he happened to solve the financial problem at one stroke it would give him supreme control of everything. Also, it would be his lot to succeed Necker. Talleyrand, a Catholic, a priest, a bishop, had a definite proposition to make,—the recovery by the Nation of the Church's wealth. This, Necker, a Genevan, a Protestant, handicapped by his origin and hidebound by scruples, dared not do.

In the eyes of many people who would not admit it, this was the solution of the financial difficulty and the idea was not a new one. "Kings," as Louis XIV wrote in ms Memoirs, "are lords with as complete control of secular as ecclesiastical property; this is in order that they may make prudent and economical use thereof, which means use in accordance with the needs of the State."

The wealth of the Church was considerable, being close upon three milliards; for a century, it had been a sore temptation to many a Minister with an empty Treasury. There had been plenty of accommodating theorists ready to remove any scruples there might be in seizing this wealth. Built up by legacies from private individuals, this wealth had been nothing more than a vast reserve under the control of the Church. To quote the words of an orator: "The Church is the body corporate of the faithful, not consisting of priests alone." But who are the faithful but ourselves? That was clearly a clever bit of reasoning. Actually, there was need of money. A deputy wrote thus in his private diary when the proposal raised such a storm of protest: "How do they want their debts paid?"—a very simple but forcible argument. I will add that there was one small but definitely anti-clerical party in which the Protestants were conspicuous; in times past, they had had real cause for grievance, like the Pasteur Rabaut-Saint-Étienne. This group thought this an excellent opportunity of robbing the Catholic clergy, and at the same time, in a minor degree, of provoking it to break away from the Revolution. In spite of this, no money-grubbing *bourgeois*, no noble of the Voltairian persuasion, no Protestant deputy,— in fact nobody at all, would, as yet, dare formulate their desire. Who then would be the bold fellow?

It was at this juncture that, on October 10th, 1789, the Bishop of Autun slipped on to the tribune. He had recently given up the idea of a Cardinal's Hat in favour of a port-folio.

As far as one could see, however, he had come forward with the most innocent proposal. His bearing was frigidly calm but, at times, he became almost genial. He spoke of the national distress; like all those who are going to attack the right of property, he declared it to be sacred,—that's a trick of the trade; but, in this instance, the property in question was not a sacred property. In a word, he proposed that ecclesiastical estates and revenues should be declared the property of the Nation, on condition that, under the new régime, a proper yearly grant of money should be guaranteed the Church and reasonable stipends be paid to even the humblest of its clergy.

Amid the bewilderment of some and the obvious enthusiasm of others, Talleyrand limped down the steps of the tribune and though for many long days his motion was eagerly discussed in the Assembly, he sat in his seat like a graven image. Even when the terrible Abbé Maury, in one of the crushing speeches of which he was a master, bitterly opposed the proposal, quoting Talleyrand himself, (for the Abbé de Périgord had in 1784, as Agent-General of the Clergy, maintained that Church property was inviolate,) the ex-Abbé de Périgord never turned a hair. It was ages since "M. le deputé Maurice de Talleyrand" had been acquainted with the insignificant Abbé de Périgord, a candidate for a bishop's mitre and a Cardinal's Hat. Perhaps he murmured to his neighbours as he was one day to repeat, "I haven't changed, but time and circumstances have!" Whatever the case might be, he was never again seen on the tribune. He loathed violent discussions; his prim, elegant speech caused outbursts in the House. His famous saying "Moderate your zeal" was often heard, ten years later, by those connected with him in office.

Already, he disliked becoming over-zealous to no purpose. He made little or no impression and supported no party. That aristocratic bishop with his delicate finger had touched the spring, and lo! the war of words had started. He was satisfied; in silence he voted for the nationalization which he had proposed and which was fast becoming a reality.

On the evening when the division was taken, he once more made his appearance with that off-hand manner which he would always assume after bringing off a successful coup. He did not seem to notice either the backs turned on him or the scornful expressions of those round him. He had already become that very Talleyrand whom a rude Marshal of the Empire described later to a brother-officer as "a damned fellow." "I would kick his back-side while he talked with you, you can bet your life!" Perhaps he swallowed these insults with the fixed impression that he who laughs last, laughs longest. And, actually, after 1814 when Monseigneur le Prince de Talleyrand, as Minister of the Most Christian Monarch, was destined to see so many people bowing to his will who, since the session of October 10th, 1789, had treated him as a "rascal" and as a "lame devil," it would certainly appear to him then that he was laughing—up his sleeve,—but that he was laughing last.

At that time, the Marquis de Travenet, famous both as a wit and player of backgammon, never played a game without calling the devil's point, Autun's. Besides, libels against him, the lame devil, became common. He was not merely a traitor; people were indignant at his double-faced behaviour. Their thoughts were in the same vein as those of Marie-Joseph Chénier when, later, he wrote this poem:

> "All those who zealously for knowledge seek,
> May take their lessons from a clever man,

Our Maurice, with heart of ice and brazen cheek,
He deftly lays his doubly trait'rous plan.
One foot, with furtive step, shuffles along
With those whose creed is power without restraint.
The other, to the enemy doth belong,
This is the one that limps. Oh worldly saint!"

He certainly was two-faced,—at least. The same hand that
wrote his speech on nationalization drew up his order of
October 12th. In it he ordered prayers for a period of forty
hours, in all the churches of his diocese "for peace in this
time of national unrest."

"Thine anger, O my God," he cried, "is kindled against
Thy flock. Will Thy hand reject us? O Lord, call to remem-
brance this people, which has ever been in Thy service. Be
not forgetful of the covenant which Thou hast made with it.
Rise up to defend its cause. It is our cause that Thou wilt
defend." There were three pages in this mystic style; and
who knows if this passage was not written on the evening
when that great American, Gouverneur Morris, interrupted
the Bishop of Autun, who, with the episcopal ring still sparkling on his finger, was fondly embracing the Comtesse de Flahaut? He was a jack-of-all-trades, was Talleyrand.

However, he suffered a grave disappointment. The Assembly, in its distrust of its leaders, more particularly of
Mirabeau and Talleyrand, had just dealt them and several
others a treacherous blow. By the famous decision of November 12th, with which I have dealt at length à propos of
Mirabeau, the Assembly decreed that the King could not
select his Ministers from among the deputies. We have seen
how the fiery tribune took no pains to disguise his fury and
how, in consequence, he weakened his influence for some time
to follow. Maurice de Talleyrand did not hide from his

friends the bitterness that he felt but, in the Lobbies, he held
his peace. He acted wisely, for while Mirabeau was not to
sit in the Presidential Chair till much later, the Bishop of
Autun was installed by the Left as early as February 16th,
1790, as one way of compensating him.

His advances had been repulsed by many who formerly
had been his friends and he despaired of becoming a Minister of the King at once, so he went still further in this new
direction. He hoped, in this manner, to achieve some still
greater success, at no far distant date.

Then came the great day of the Federation—July 14th,
1790. As a fitting celebration for the first anniversary of the
taking of the Bastille, preparations were made for a stupen-
dous festival, the like of which had never been seen before,
to extol Fraternity and Liberty. An altar was erected in the
middle of the Champ-de-Mars, where grassy terraces could
hold 300,000 spectators. There Mass was to be celebrated and
the colours, presented by La Fayette to contingents of the
National Guard from 83 Departments, were going to be
blessed. A procession started from the École Militaire flanked
by a long line of priests, with tricolour scarves over their
albs. Behind them, one could see one solitary golden mitre;
leaning on his pastoral staff came the Bishop of Autun, limp-
ing less than usual. Many people, however, thought that he
was making a *faux pas* of the first order,—frankly, it was,
indeed, a blunder. Picture him mounting the altar steps,
chalice in hand, amid the blare of a thousand trumpets. On
one side the Abbé de Renaudes, his coadjutor and tool,
served as deacon; on the other, the Abbé Louis as sub-deacon.
Twenty-five years later, when Baron Louis, Louis XVIII's
Finance Minister, came to consult with the Prince de Talleyrand, President of the Council, would they manage better
than the augurs themselves, and keep a straight face?

When the Bishop of Autun approached the altar and passed in front of La Fayette, who saluted him with his sword, some maintain that he said, *sotto voce,* "Don't make me laugh." This story seems hardly probable. Talleyrand would not have let slip words of this sort as he certainly never considered sacrilege as a joke of which to be proud. And as for that heavy fellow, La Fayette, he was absolutely incapable of ever making anybody laugh.

The Bishop of Autun said Mass with dignity. After all, I am not sure that he did not find this ceremony in atrocious taste and the rabble that attended it extremely stupid, for he was always thoroughly opposed to any undue ostentation. He thought, however, that the Government certainly deserved a public Mass.

But, one day, this famous Mass would appear very insignificant beside that other to be celebrated at the Église de l'Oratoire. This ceremony of February 24th, 1791, out of which arose, canonically established, the Constitutional Church, was the last chapter in the lamentable history of a downfall which, for selfish ends, was unchecked.

The new Constitution of the State was not, on the face of it, the work of Talleyrand. His part was merely to labour towards its fulfilment. I do not believe that he wanted it at first. He took no part in any of the noteworthy discussions which resulted in the passing of the law relating to schism and, later, to oaths. Nevertheless, his name has been quite rightly coupled with that memorable event with which I am briefly going to deal.

Talleyrand certainly had a hand in the formation of the Constitution because this fatal measure is actually the consequence of the law which nationalized Church property, and this is how it came about.

The Act which put Church property at the disposal of the State was not, as I quite recently explained, entirely the outcome of considerations involving money alone.

A considerable section of the community saw in this measure a means of forcing the Church to break away from the new régime. That section consisted of Protestants and Jansenists.[8]

When, in 1789, a violent movement developed against the old régime, all those who had suffered under it, had hoped, now it was being attacked, to find some opportunity of taking their revenge. The Protestants, outrageously persecuted since the revocation of the Edict of Nantes, and the Jansenists exasperated beyond all measure after Louis XIV had made the Bull *Unigenitus* a law of the land, had counted upon getting their revenge and upon witnessing the discomfiture of the Pope and Louis' grandson, at one and the same time. It was obvious that these hopes, the result of these bitter feelings, were being entertained and I am surprised that, so far, historians have hardly ever noticed them. A deputy wrote in his diary that the Revolution had been accomplished with three Latin words: *Deficit, Veto* and *Unigenitus*, and this shows the great importance he attached to the attitude of the Jansenists, who had the Abbé Grégoire as their leading representative. On the other hand it is quite enough to read the letters of the Pasteur Rabaut-Saint-Étienne to see how without a shadow of doubt, the sons of victims of the persecutions, as well as the posthumous friends of the ruined Port-

---

[8] Followers of Jansenius, a Dutch theologian. His doctrines tended to limit free-will and to defend predestination. Jansenism was fiercely attacked by the Jesuits, and Pascal from his retreat at Port-Royal wrote his famous *"Lettres provinciales"* in defence of it. In 1713, this doctrine was condemned by the Pope in the Bull *"Unigenitus."*

Royal,[9] were determined to avenge their dead. When the Act nationalizing Church property had been passed, Rabaut had given a cry of joy,—a proceeding which was particularly astonishing in a man generally so very circumspect. "No longer is the Clergy an Order," he wrote. "The priests will be able now to march in time with the State. *It only remains to get them married.*" And when that artlessly candid Carthusian monk, Dom Gerle, who had voted for the spoliatory measure, came forward on April 16th, 1790, with a request that, as a measure of compensation, the Assembly should declare Catholicism to be the religion of the State, he was astonished to hear the cries of indignation which arose from the Benches of the Left. Also, when Mirabeau in opposing the motion in the Assembly elaborated upon the legend of Charles IX firing on the Huguenots from a balcony at the Louvre on St. Bartholomew's Day, he knew quite well—the clever tactician that he was—that he would be triumphantly successful in obtaining the support of the entire anti-Catholic party.

This group had been disappointed to see, during the past year, the Church of France offer her left cheek as soon as the right had been smitten, and to witness the Holy See allowing, with a most surprising resignation, those anti-clerical measures to become law.

Nevertheless, this party was beginning to show signs of unrest. If the majority of bishops showed an extreme condescension, there were at any rate some who, at least in word

[9] An abbey near Chevreuse, Seine-et-Oise; it was originally a Bernardine convent. Under d'Angelique Arnaud, it became a house of retreat. Pascal, among other men of letters, lived there. Later the recluses of Port-Royal threw in their lot with the Jansenist party and, after quarrelling bitterly with the ecclesiastical authorities, caused their Abbey to be closed by order of Louis XIV in 1705; it was destroyed in 1710.

if not in deed, revolted against the policy followed by the Assembly. The Bishop of Tréguier, in an order to his diocese, denounced "those perverse men," who had fastened on to a movement which was primarily a spiritual one, in order to distort it. The diocesan order was immediately denounced and a definitely anti-clerical campaign was set in motion. Strictly speaking, it was something more,—a campaign against Rome. Not only did the philosophers, the Protestants and the Jansenists take part in this attack but also the extreme Catholics who thought of Rome as something more than an adversary—as an age-long enemy.

Some argued that it was necessary to adapt the Church of France to the new organization of the State—for the Jacobins were already immoderately attracted by geometrical uniformity; others, provincial priests who formed the party in opposition to the policy of the Assembly, advocated the reorganization of the Church in conformity with the newly reorganized State.

I need not enter into the mechanism of the Civil Constitution as it was when passed by the Assembly on July 12th, 1790. Whole Sees were swept away by a stroke of the pen; dioceses were cut up to fit in with the Departments; chapters were abolished wholesale, parish-boundaries were altered; vicars, Bishop-Coadjutors were submitted to the popular vote and appointed, no longer by Rome but by the Metropolitan—and there was only one. These are the main points. Some of these changes were probably acceptable to the Holy See which, at the King's request, would doubtless have fallen in with some modification of the Concordat of 1516. But actually,—and this was unjust—there was not the slightest pretence made of paying attention to whatever the opinions in Rome might be—a fact that is not astonishing since the leaders of the movement meant, before everything, to force the Holy See into a complete and lasting rupture with the Church of France.

We know the reception given by the Clergy to this Constitution. The Order affected to know nothing of it until Rome had pronounced her opinion, and, prejudging this opinion, the nature of which was known beforehand, declared "the new law to be null and void."

Then it was that the leaders, anxious to make the situation even more difficult, asked for a new measure which would force ecclesiastics of every rank to swear allegiance to the Constitution or hand in their resignations. Those priests who refused to take the oath would be then replaced according to the procedure laid down in the law,—that is, by popular election. The measure which was passed on November 27th, 1790, was sanctioned by Louis XVI (who was, as a matter of fact, stricken with remorse) and the Clergy were thus driven into taking the oath. We know how the majority of them refused their allegiance to it and how the religious war was an immediate consequence.

If the members of the Constituent Assembly had been logical, they would have simply separated the Church from the State. Since there was no desire to have anything further to do with Rome, some consistency should have been shown and the law carried out to the letter. Anything was certainly preferable to these exaggerated pretensions of reforming and overthrowing the Church, without any reference, and in opposition, to the Holy See,—this, the Catholic Church which even its enemies in recent speeches had repeatedly called the *Roman* Church. But the Constituents, some of whom, as early as this, would dearly have liked to separate the Church from the State, found themselves unable to do so. Everyone had held that to the nationalization of Church property there was an inevitable corollary; the establishment of budgets: for the religious bodies. One hundred and sixteen years later, in 1906, French deputies let themselves be quite unmoved by such a consideration, but the law was too recent and this solemn undertaking too fresh in men's minds for it to be possible, so soon, to do away with these "budgets of the religious bodies." The Church might have had the right to say "Give back the money" and if there had been a desire to do so, it would have been impossible as the property of the Church was already transferred and part of its wealth expended. It was directly in consequence of this nationalization of Church property that the deputies were forced to pass this scandalous and artificial reform which cut the clergy off from Rome and doomed them to persecution. So it was that Talleyrand, though, I repeat, having no actual share in the reform, was one of those directly responsible for it. That is indeed a heavy responsibility, for, in the opinion of all historians, it was the civil Constitution which changed the course of the Revolution and brought above the divorce of Church from State. The consequences of this, far from diminishing, increased in importance, and, having thoroughly exasperated Louis XVI, who, up to that moment had been placid enough, thrust him into the conflict in which he was to lose his head.

But further, if Talleyrand's only share in the passing of this schismatic constitution and the law of oaths was by the slipping of his voting-paper into the urn on two separate occasions, he was one of the first ecclesiastics to show his adherence to the régime which was, at this juncture, condemned by Rome.

He certainly made no display of the fact that he was supporting this party. Whereas bishops and priests when called upon to take this oath in the House, set an example by refusing to do so, Talleyrand sneaked up on to the tribune early in the session of December 28th, 1790, and, in the presence of a very few deputies, took the oath in a whisper as if carrying out an unimportant formality.

In reality, all this suited him down to the ground, for there can be no doubt that, being resolved to cut adrift from the Church, he found this kind of transitional stage most convenient as it would give his first steps towards apostasy the appearance of being nothing but a civic act.

Besides, he wanted to win the gratitude of the party of the Left. It was he who offered to consecrate the new bishops who were elected a little later to replace the "refractory" ones. The three other bishops, who, with Talleyrand out of a possible 120, had taken the oath, refused to proceed with this frankly schismatical ceremony.

A saying was attributed to them (which goes to prove that at no time in France's history, even in the most tragic circumstances, was there a sense of humour lacking), "We swear, but we do not consecrate (*"nous ne sacrons pas"*).

Talleyrand swore and consecrated. On February 24th, 1791, assisted, *in partibus,* by two bishops, Dubourg-Miroudot, Bishop of Babylon, and Gobel, Bishop of Lydda, he presided at the ceremony in the Église de l'Oratoire which Rome considered such an odious act of sacrilege.

He performed this office without enthusiasm and though apparently untroubled, he was really extremely apprehensive. That same morning, assailed by the fear that some fanatic might, by an attempt on his life, avenge the religion which had thus been ridiculed, he passed the night in a house adjoining the church in the Rue Saint-Honoré; besides, for several days, he had been carrying two pistols on his person and seemed most anxious to show them. As Maury would have said, they were the two chalices for this extraordinary Mass.

On March 24th, he appointed the unfortunate Gobel to the

See of Paris, though he had refused it himself. Nearly four years later, watched by all the members of the Convention, Gobel would trample on his priestly habit. This was the last time that the Bishop of Autun bestowed the mitre or, wearing his golden chasuble, officiated in his holy office. For, much less ostentatiously than Gobel, Talleyrand anticipated him in making his apostasy complete; he not only divested himself of his episcopal dignity of which Rome was always threatening to deprive him but he also laid aside his priestly distinction. Then, having by his act of consecration on February 24th, 1791, laid the foundations of the new Constitutional Church, he had abandoned it to its wretched fate,—which is what it really was—and, still noiselessly, he slipped away into civil life.

And so, early in the summer of 1792, Citizen Maurice Talleyrand, formerly Bishop of Autun, felt the soil of France scorching his very feet. After serving (very much in the background) as Councillor of the Department of Paris, he managed to be appointed to London on a diplomatic mission, from which he did not return straight to his own country. This was a kind of alibi,—the desertion of his country without its really seeming so. The Revolution was becoming frankly brutal; every day it grew more violent, more clamorous, more bloody and this refined personage no longer found a place in it. Then, leaving London for America, ex-bishop-deputy of Autun deliberately and calculatingly plunged for the time, at any rate, into oblivion.

Even those who thought of him as being a tireless, dangerous and inquisitive framer of intrigues thought that the former Abbé de Périgord's career was at an end; it was said that the cripple had definitely stumbled.

Anyone who said that he would appear again as Minister

of a decadent Republic, of a great warlike Empire, then of the *fleur de lis* Monarchy once more restored to power, would have amazed everyone—except, perhaps, Talleyrand himself. He was entirely unscrupulous and was incapable of astonishment. So many of his contemporaries had thought of the Revolution as an arena but, if we may make use of M. Bernard de Lacombe's very apt expression, it struck him at once as being a chess-board. Because it was convenient to do so, he called "check"; but he still went on watching the board where everything seemed in confusion, never losing sight for a moment of the game in progress and viewing it all at a distance from his lofty seat. Smiling faintly—to show extreme mirth—he had foreseen that those who employed force would destroy themselves so that, once the board was again clear, the politicians might continue their game.

He had betrayed his family, his class, his friends, his Order, his King, and his God. But he did not despair at all of finding himself once more in the good graces of his family, his class, his friends, his Order, his Church, and finally his God. This was the *tour de force* of a career which, immoral through and through, was to prove more conclusively than any other career that in politics the player is not impeded by his past acts.

Charles Maurice de Talleyrand-Périgord, Bishop of Autun, is surely a good example of the higher politician. The ruins which his delicate hands wrought so unconcernedly, show what a great factor is the destruction of the soul in the downfall of a nation.

Talleyrand had indeed left in ruins the sanctuary where, on December 18th, 1779, Monseigneur de Grimaldi, Bishop of Noyon, had solemnly ordained him. Passing through these ruins which were the results of his personal ambition, Maurice de Talleyrand disappeared, temporarily, in the summer of 1792, from history.

CHAPTER IV

CHAPTER IV

THE CONSTITUENT ASSEMBLY

In 1789, the Manège (or riding-school) of the Tuileries stood between the Château and the Place Louis XV—to-day Place de la Concorde—and on the terrace which in our time forms one side of the Rue de Rivoli. After the Court had moved definitely to Versailles, no use was found for this great, rectangular building; it was almost abandoned to its empty silence.

Then, on November 9th, 1789, much to the excitement of people in the Quarter, a regular crowd was seen to pour into this hall which had been fitted out to suit quite another purpose; more than 1,400 men were there, all talking and gesticulating excitedly while another stream of people packed themselves into the public seats.

This was the National Assembly, which, up to that time, had sat at Versailles and then temporarily in the Archbishop's palace; it had now come to take up its quarters here—in an out-building of the Château.

Benches in tiers had been constructed and a very roomy dais installed opposite the narrow, lofty, presidential desk; in front of the tribune a kind of balustrade was fixed known as the Bar of the Assembly, before which the delegates passed after they had made known the wishes and, soon afterwards, the orders of the people.

This Manège des Tuileries, destroyed at a later date, was to be the home of the Constituent and Legislative Assemblies and, finally, of the Convention till May, 1793, when it moved into the Château itself. It was one of the principal scenes in the great revolutionary drama.

The Assembly had already been in existence for six months —and very stormy they had been. But not until its removal to the Manège did it really assume a definite character; and this, if it is to be understood, will necessitate a review of the circumstances in which it came into being and was so rapidly transformed.

On December 27th of the preceding year, the King had convened the States-General. Following the age-long practice, each of the three Orders elected their representatives separately but, on this occasion, the Tiers État which, up to that time, had elected the same number of deputies as each of the privileged Orders, was doubly represented. It was the business of the electoral assemblies to provide deputies with memoranda or "reports" containing the wishes of the country. April and May had been spent in drawing up these memoranda and electing deputies but, on May 5th, those elected by the nation,—and they reached the enormous figure of 1,700—had met together at Versailles. It will scarcely be necessary to recall the circumstances in which the States-General had become the National Assembly, contrary to the wishes of the King and then, with his assent,—when it was forced from him; nor how the National Assembly arrived at its decision to give the country a constitution and, in fact, to destroy the old system in its entirety.

The feverish, almost insurrectionary spirit which had prevailed during the formation of the Assembly, had considerably changed the outlook of many of the deputies. That is why it is best to stop for a moment at this point.

Nine-tenths of the members elected in the spring of 1789 would have been amazed to hear it prophesied that they were to legislate *against the throne*. They considered themselves to be good royalists and, indeed, their electors were even more fervent.

A careful examination of these parish-reports, the results of the deliberations of local authorities, leaves one with a very definite impression that our ideas of what the people's wishes were in 1789 are entirely erroneous. *Equality in matters of taxation and justice* were demanded much more than a *"Liberty"* which no average Frenchman, and much less the peasants and workmen, either understood or desired; and if the question of giving the country a constitution was mentioned in the "reports," that did not mean at all the subordination of the monarchic system of government to the control of the Elected Houses, but the more regular organization of the kingdom ruled by a King freed from any hindrances that yet remained. Recast in the form of "a bailiwick-report," these modest "parochial memoranda" were already changing in character. By the side of claims made by a rural people against feudalism, there began to slip in recriminations against the abuses of the Ecclesiastical Order, appeals for "liberty" against "despotism," ideas of "national representation," all tempered however with expressions of deepest love for the King.

The notaries of little towns and bailiwicks had put pen to paper and this was the result. The more humble *bourgeois* for more than a quarter of a century intoxicated by philosophical theories, lived at this time in a curiously ideological state. In the minds of this generation of *bourgeois* (they were men of from thirty to fifty years old in 1789) there had arisen rather artificial ideas only very distantly connected with the views of the peasants and work-people.

The lawyers, who were more than any other class brought up on philosophy, proceeded to tack on to the original wishes of the people all the ideological theories of the time; in addition, it was this legal type which was most ready to stand for election and, in consequence, the Tiers État was composed to a great extent of these lawyers. There is something very significant in the complaint of a certain villager, Du Barrois, who stated that the lawyers of Bar-Le-Duc had "made away with everything."

True to their type, however, these idealists had gone off to Versailles without reckoning at all what would be the result of their theories, crying, *"Vive le roi"*—and in this they were sincere enough. Only the more advanced *bourgeois* were made restless by their hatred of despotism which was to appear later in so virulent a form at the first blunder made by the government of the King,—as we have already seen in Mirabeau's extraordinary case. The opposition of the King to the fusion of the Orders, interpreted as being evidence of the alliance between the Court and the privileged classes, suddenly brought about the revolt of the Tiers État which, despite itself and as a consequence of the contagious fever of mob-impulses, was thus forced into making resolutions of incalculable importance. So it was that the Tiers proclaimed itself the *National Assembly* at the suggestion of the Abbé Sieyès, and overcame, first, all opposition from the two upper Orders and then from the King himself. On June 20th, when the oath of the famous *"Salle du jeu de Paume"* had been taken not to disperse "until the Constitution was established," this Assembly which had been convened solely to find money-supplies, found itself converted into that political academy which was going to sit in judgment upon all political, social, economic, religious, administrative and international ideals; which was to uproot and destroy the oldest State in Europe, and going even further in its unexpected activities, was to undertake the regeneration of the human race. As for the humble "parish-reports" expressing far more modest wishes, which were still those of all reasonable people in France, after six months they were no longer of any importance whatsoever. A deputy who was much behind the times, practically stupefied most of the members and caused much mirth when, at the beginning of 1790, he referred to these "parish reports." A member of the Assembly wrote later that "the reports have no more significance now than old wives' tales." That is exactly what had also befallen many of the electoral programmes.

On the other hand, from Montesquieu, who was more particularly the inspiration of the Constitutional Right, to Jean-Jacques, whose doctrines sustained the entire party of the Left, and then on to Voltaire who armed the enemies of the "Infamous" [1] with their weapons,—all the philosophers who had by their ideas given life to great movements were there—in spirit: Diderot and d'Alembert, d'Holbach and Helvétius, even the minor prophets, Duclos, Mably, Raynal and Condorcet.

The Assembly had besides the *Contrat Social*, the whole *Encyclopédie* as its gospel. By the autumn of 1789, the "reports" made by those worthy villagers were ridiculously behind the times, so far had public opinion progressed; and of that everyone was very proud.

Having thus abolished feudalism and, on the night of Au-

[1] The Church as symbolizing superstition. Voltaire's motto was: "Écrasez l'Infâme."

gust 7th, destroyed a system one thousand years old in a few hours, the Assembly had decided to establish a *"Declaration of the rights of man and of the citizen"* which might apply to the whole world; it was also making attempts to build up an ideal Constitution. At this point, in October, the people whose deputies had approved, not without some embarrassment, the rash act of July 14th, came to Versailles; they invaded the dismayed Assembly and then the Château and did not depart without taking with them, besides the Royal family, the Assembly itself to which it gave the disrespectful name of "the blooming shop."

It was in these circumstances that the Constituent Assembly, after a brief sojourn in the Archbishop's palace, became installed in the Manège des Tuileries. Here raised to fever-heat by close contact with the capital itself in a ferment, the debates became more chaotic than ever. These discussions were endless, interrupted by innumerable incidents and touching upon every subject under the sun. Nevertheless, little by little, the parties began to take definite shape and men of ability to show their powers, whilst the general character of the Assembly became more distinct. Therefore it is only at this stage in its development that it is possible to examine it properly and to describe it, wholesale and retail.

Anyone who studies its general composition cannot help being struck by the extraordinary manner in which its members were recruited. There were great nobles from the First Chamber mixed higgledy-piggledy with poor country-squires, but these peers had not served their King in diplomacy or with the sword. Not one ex-ambassador, not a single Marshal (and, at that time, there were many more than six), only a few generals and hardly thirty senior officers had seats. The peers in the Assembly were more often wits, the majority of

them being enervated by their life at Court as well as estranged by the philosophical vogue; in any case, they were
entirely unfamiliar with the practice of politics.

Among the 266 clerical members, there were 48 bishops,
representatives of the episcopate as it was at the end of the
18th Century; if not entirely lacking in virtue and moral
worth it very rarely possessed both these qualities. Beside
them were a vast number of priests and monks who, elected
to oppose the bishops, owed their seats for the most part to
the support given them by the lower clergy who had revolted
against the abuses to which they were subjected. Among
them, there were approximately forty curés who viewed
things from a philosophical standpoint.

The most striking fact of all is that there was an enormous majority of lawyers among the 700 deputies in the Assembly. As we have seen, they were primarily responsible for
altering the people's wishes, of which they claimed to be the
interpreters and, in all sincerity, believed themselves to be.
More than four hundred of the *bourgeois* were in fact bar-
risters, solicitors, notaries, sheriffs, or magistrates. To these
must be added fifteen doctors, fifty traders and thirty-eight
farmers. "Father" Gérard is the only real example of the
villein; he played the part of the country bumpkin in this
Assembly where wits abounded and belonged to this last
class. He refused to change his coarse wool clothing for the
black habit of the Tiers, a departure which brought him an
ovation, so an eye-witness said, during the procession on the
first day. But he was thought a most annoying creature on
that June day, in 1790, when, in supporting the motion that
deprived absent deputies of their allowance, he made the
extraordinarily blunt pronouncement that "the Provinces
have certainly not sent us here *for us to mess about.*"

Another striking feature is the absence in this Assembly of

high officials representative of the bourgeois. It is very characteristic that Malouet was the only Intendant and alone represented the class with administrative experience; neither was there, of course, a single ex-minister who had managed men or had had close contact with State affairs. Men with ideas there were, however, in plenty. The American, Morris, wrote in January, 1790, that the "madmen" were recruited from amongst those who were called *"pettifogging lawyers"* in his country. They had a great influence on the mass of deputies who were, strange to say, dumb. Madame Roland, always a great admirer of eloquence, called them scornfully, *"the pile of logs at 18 francs a day."* Most of them were "logs," but not quite all, unfortunately, I am tempted to add, if Malouet's testimony on this point is to be accepted. The latter declared that a great number of his colleagues did not shine on the tribune nor even put in an appearance there; however, in the committees, the equivalent of our *commissions*—they showed a certain "sound education," but he added, "this abundance of shining-lights has made this Assembly uncontrollable." The fact is that each of at least three hundred of its members thought that he was better versed in this, the greatest of inspired doctrines, than anyone else, and this resulted in unending attacks on everything, in struggles to outbid each other in making proposals on any and every subject; in a riot of thought that made them arrogant, and, as in Mirabeau's case, caused them to fear and hate alike any influences, whether coming from the Right or the Left, which seemed at all superior.

Cardinal de Retz has written that "the greatest embarrassments of a party-leader are his party." Members of the Constituent Assembly who were somewhat superior in ability to the rest, soon despaired of ever becoming leaders of these parties so lacking in cohesion. One has only to remember the cry of poor exasperated Mirabeau, "Red jack-asses!"

Soon it was just possible to distinguish a Right and a Left; in between came a shapeless mass bearing for some time the name of the *"Impartials."*

As it was pointed out earlier, the Right was composed of a great majority of gentlemen; this, with fifty curés, and three-quarters of the bishop-peers, made a large total of aristocratic deputies. The two outstanding figures were, however, the Abbé Maury, a priest of plebeian descent and the Comte de Cazalès, a soldier of fortune.

The Abbé Maury's influence was increasing; the qualities which made him popular were in strange contrast with his violently reactionary attitude. He was a shoemaker's son from the Comtat-Venaissin, one of the few men in the Assembly to become well-known, if not celebrated, before 1789. For four years a member of the Académie Française, thanks to his success in the pulpit, he had acquired the reputation of being as great an intriguer as he was an orator. Although unprincipled, he had, while coming to the fore in the early days of the Assembly, assumed the rôle of an indomitable defender of the two basic principles—throne and altar. His eloquence was of a very high order and, in the Assembly, he was soon considered the only man who could stand up to Mirabeau; the latter sometimes acknowledged himself defeated by his masterly methods. He was a jovial southerner, witty and even extremely caustic, trivial and always aggressive. The people hated him. "To the lamppost with Abbé Maury!" cried a mob who attacked him. And his answer, "Will that help you to see clearer!" That made them laugh. On another occasion, some more assailants shouted out, "Abbé, you'll be made to celebrate mass in the air!" "Excellent," he retorted and, taking two pistols out of his pockets, he cried, "And here are the chalices!"

People were, at times, disarmed by his demoniacal wit. He was, in reality, suspected of insincerity and even the Right denounced him; in any case, his extravagant counter-revolutionary proposals, which provoked and exasperated, were of service to the hotheads on the Left; but they offended the Centre.

In strange contrast to Maury, Cazalès owed his persuasive powers not only to a rare elegance of speech but much more to the moving sincerity of his loyal nature. "He talks like a god," one of his colleagues cried. Two violent opponents of his ideas, Lindet, a fellow deputy and Madame Roland, despite their feelings towards him paid him their homage as an old soldier and a stout-hearted champion of the Royal cause and the honour of France. "Above all others, deserving mention," they both described him in 1791, "abounding in ideas, full of fire and vehemence, he was the foremost orator in the Assembly since Mirabeau's death." Madame Roland expressed astonishment that a soldier should have such a wonderful mastery of language. But as a soldier he had kept his touchy sense of honour; his hand was always on his sword-hilt. He weakened his cause by these ever-changing moods and was quite likely to give up everything if discouraged for even ten minutes.

Besides these two orators, mention must be made of Malouet, a cultivated bourgeois and once an important official. Besides being quiet-mannered and of moderate opinions, he was a man of experience. But the Assembly which had no use for men who were not tribunes thought him rather *gauche* and according to a witness, "he never grasped its tone."

These were the striking figures on the Right, the rest were a strangely mediocre collection. They were a mixture of great lords who were soon quite at sea, then exasperated country squires, and bishops, courtesy itself, but quite incapable of doing anything but preach a rather flowery sermon; a few reasonable or timid bourgeois made up the number. On the whole, it contained little of any value; it was a large party but owing to continual absenteeism and later to the discouragement of its members, it fell into the habit of taking no part in debates or divisions.

The Impartials who were soon known as Constitutionals sat in the centre. They were faithful Royalists estranged from the Right's Extremists by their philosophical principles and conciliatory character. Determined supporters of the new political theories, they were naturally held by the Right "to have done all the more harm because they had appeared as moderate at first," and this is the traditional attitude. Liberal nobles, episcopal politicians and *bourgeois* visionaries belonged to the Centre. All these men had in reality definite leanings towards the Right (much more than it thought) but they were continually being driven over to join the Left owing to the former's scornful, bitter attitude rather than its principles.

The noble liberal party had some leaders with resounding names. There was Noailles who on the night of August 4th, had given the signal for the great sacrifices; Tally-Tollendal who was called by Rivarol "the fattest of sensitive men"; Clermont-Tonnerre, according to a lady, "inflamed with philosophical notions and who undertook to procure the Jews enfranchisement"; La Rochefoucauld-Liancourt, a Castellane, always a pig-headed philanthropist, who, having come right through the Revolution, always declared that man is good, which had been his master, Rousseau's, saying and he stuck to it through thick and thin. One day, he cried, "Kings are made for the peoples and not peoples for the Kings," and this was much applauded on the Left. Finally, there was the Comte de Virieu, both an ardent Catholic and fiery democrat; as a soldier, he was a vehement speaker but, at the same time, was a man of deeply religious beliefs. A supporter of *"The Rights of Man,"* he would have liked to have seen this work —the new democratic gospel—prefaced by a prayer to the Almighty and marked with the "stamp of God"—as the phrase ran. He was a forerunner of our Christian Democrats, perhaps even of Albert de Mun.

The *bourgeois* Mounier, a lawyer from Grenoble, was, however, quite the most outstanding of all the Constitutionals. He had been the great leader of the provincial Estates when they met at Vizille and initiated the proposals for doubling the representatives of the Tiers and for great reforms in the State. Therefore, when he arrived at Versailles, he enjoyed a popularity which was then unique. He was a distinguished orator, "precise as a professor of mathematics and energetic as a critic who weighs every word," wrote the deputy, Biauzat; a generous, noble, upright character of great refinement, he was liable, however, to be easily discouraged. In the opening struggle, he took an eager part, but after the first few months, he saw that the Assembly had overreached itself and was on the wrong track. The more he championed the new theories the more he despaired when he saw them distorted. Being a sensible, methodical man, he protested against the street disturbances which his colleagues thought so glorious and against the preposterous suggestions which arose in course of their discussions. He was violently attacked by the Clubs and, less than six months after the outbreak, his popularity dwindled to nothing. Thus the Revolution, even at its outset, was beginning quickly to "devour its own children."

A famous astronomer, the venerable Bailly, a Member of

three Academies with a great and glorious reputation, was, like La Fayette, the first representative in the first Assembly and belonged to the Party of the Centre. He was not, however, a real force in its deliberations. He was a mathematician and of a dreamy disposition—for mathematicians are poets— and he was consequently quite the opposite of a statesman. His overweening vanity and exaggerated ideas of self-importance were his undoing and made him an object of ridicule to even his best friends. Everyone was disappointed in him as Mayor of Paris, an appointment he owed to his almost unbelievable popularity—as well as in the Assembly where he proceeded to come crashing down from his high pedestal. Even as early as the end of 1789, it was declared that "He has not come up at all to our expectations of him." But an annual review coupled his name with La Fontaine's fable, *The Astronomer who fell into a well*, at the outset of his career. By his tragic end on the scaffold, this virtuous respectable old man made up for all his shortcomings, which were not so much his fault as of those who thrust him so enthusiastically into the political arena. Here was another victim, rapidly devoured by the Revolution.

His friend, La Fayette, shared his illusions and his popularity. Like many others, he wavered between the Centre and the Left. After all, the Centre was composed of sincere liberals and well-intentioned men who took from six months to two years, according to the circumstances, to recover from their enthusiastic outbursts; it soon found itself tossed about between the two extreme parties. Morris wrote that "the Central party is very willing but has, unfortunately, taken its theories of government from books; we can only admire their ideas on paper." Malouet relates how he saw these poor people "cursed by the aristocrats" and then "stoned by the people." That is what has always happened.

On the Left, the most striking, outstanding figure was Mirabeau. We have already seen how extraordinary was his influence and how his crushing eloquence was so much admired by this Assembly, distinguished for its oratory and how his singular qualities made him dreaded by it. We have shown how he could carry it with him, thanks to his imaginative powers and by his vigorous speech, but was powerless to direct its course because he lay under its censure. So when he aspired to be the foremost in everything, he was reduced to playing the rôle of a tribune who enjoyed but fleeting triumphs. We have also studied his neighbour, the Bishop of Autun, Talleyrand-Périgord, who was so unlike him. He was a man with an ingratiating, persuasive manner, a mischievous wit, who brought treason to a fine art; moreover, he had the ear of the Left while his support was of service to it but he also, being denounced because of his immorality, was totally incapable of uniting a party.

Beside these two men sat another priest, the Abbé Sieyès. He was called upon to play the strangest part in the Revolutionary drama and as he will have later on a chapter to himself, it will not be necessary to deal at length with him now. He was a philosophical politician, enveloped in the prestige which his pamphlet "What is the Tiers?" gave him in the year 1789. He was received with an almost superstitious veneration and immediately posed as an oracle. But, in this rôle, he shrouded his ideas in solemn, obscure formulæ— "hermetically sealed" we should say to-day. And though we may persist in looking upon him as a man of great depth (because we do not understand him), it is not surprising that the Assembly, more inclined to follow the hotheads, broke away from this pontifical person who was left soured and exasperated on his pedestal.

The Left was a large party and became the refuge of all

impassioned speakers because their violent utterances expressed the turbulent emotions of this group and were vigorously applauded. A tribune is always prompted by boldly original, extremist ideas which will quicken the pulses of his hearers and the Left swarmed with these bombastic tribunes.

One hundred names could be mentioned but they would all be orators. Of the 400 members of the Left, one hundred were orators—at any rate in their own opinion.

This Party of the Left, so impetuous in its proposals or, in any case, always prepared to accept the wildest proposals, lived a feverish existence, determined from the beginning to upset and overthrow the established order of things. Though they were encompassed about by illusions and turbulent emotions, members of this party were firmly convinced that the task of reconstruction would be accomplished by them.

Violent as was this party, there were others more violent. One section soon broke away—if not purposely at any rate actually to form a kind of Extreme Left.

It was quite a small group, but everyone in it thought himself, for once, quite a superior fellow; these were the future Jacobin leaders. Three deputies from Brittany founded it as the Breton Club after the great events at Versailles, and it was the cradle of the famous Jacobin Clubs. The first three Jacobins were deputies from Nantes; Le Chapelier, fated to die by the guillotine, Defermon, later Comte Defermon, a minister under Napoleon Bonaparte and Lanjuinais or Comte Lanjuinais as he became, who was made a peer by Louis XVIII. It is a characteristic trio, and sums up an epoch. But, by 1790, these Bretons, so hated by the Right, were quite outshone by another Triumvirate—"*The* Triumvirate" as it was called: Adrien du Port, Alexandre de Lameth, and Pierre

Barnave who, alone, is worthy of our attention because the other two, after all, were only his assistants.

Barnave! How long would this name, from the Benches of the Right to the Assemblies at the Tuileries, make men shudder with hate and shake with fear? And even by 1791, the mere mention of his name would evoke roars of indignation from the revolutionary Clubs in their turn. Barnave! one of the most poignant examples of a man's soul tortured by the tragic events of the Revolution.

When in 1788, he fought along with Mounier at Vizille, in the struggle for Liberty, he was only twenty-six. Of humble *bourgeois* stock, he suffered in his early youth the bitterest humiliation at the hand of a certain nobleman who wounded his feelings as a devoted son. So his pride rose within him at this affront and, having read avidly the theories of the philosophers, he sought to heal his wounded pride by preaching their doctrines of equality. A gambler, an ardent lover, he was scorched by all the flames of passion; above all ambition maddened him and spurred him on. Riches, power, the highest honours—all these he aspired to win; and, imagining that he was being thwarted in his object, he attacked with particular violence the régime which his countryman and erstwhile friend Mounier only went as far as to criticize in judicious terms. He was a deputy at twenty-eight but he soon left the Assembly. "You have made your reputation, I want to make mine also," was his candid admission.

He was handsome in a quiet kind of way and hid under a cold exterior a heart of fire. "A fire glowed within him," one of his colleagues remarked. Madame Roland described him as a "gilder of phrases," but he was something better than that. His reasoning was trenchant and implacable in its severity. Ambition, always predominant, led him to join the Extreme Left. One of his adversaries described him as a "young tiger" after his share in a certain ghastly incident. When, on July 17th, 1789, it was announced to the Assembly that Foulon and Bertier had been brutally murdered and their heads carried about Paris by the people who shouted like cannibals, the deputies from Right and Left alike shared in the general consternation. Then a young man rose from his seat and his dreadful remark has never lost anything of its tragic significance. *"What! gentlemen, was this blood then so pure!"* The victims became criminals: That is a rule in the horrible game of Revolution. Recovering from their panic, the Extremists gave the wretched fellow a great ovation. According to the statement of Abbé Jollet, written that evening, it was "a speech worthy of any Roman." Having justified this bloody act, it seemed that he was to bear its stains forever. Moreover, right up to 1791, he always took a foremost part in all the most outrageous motions—still with that cold expression upon his face.

Then, suddenly, his whole attitude changed when an unhappy queen smiled upon him; he began to incline to moderate methods and, losing his popularity in consequence, became (how history repeats itself) an object of loathing to those who once idolized him. Thus was he hated even to the hour when he in his turn was dragged off to the scaffold. As he waited for the knife to fall, he would hear the people cry that they wanted the death of this traitor, this Judas: they wanted to see his blood flow, blood which was no longer "pure."

And while he manoeuvred before the astonished gaze of the Assembly, another Triumvirate, already formed, was preparing to take the place made vacant on the Left by the desertion of this trio.

The members of this new Triumvirate did not become famous till much later. From 1789 to 1791, they *waited;* but so extreme an attitude did they adopt that even the Left, for once, seldom supported them. Their names were Buzot, Pétion, Robespierre.

We shall shortly come across them again but it is necessary to say something about the last mentioned of this trio at this juncture. Picture him in the Extreme Left on the Extremists' bench; a mean face under his carefully powdered hair, a small figure in his well-cut, tightly-fitting clothes; his eyes were hidden behind blue-tinted spectacles, and there was always a bitter expression upon his lips. If a spectator had asked, "Who is this mournful-looking young deputy?" people would have answered, "A deputy from the Artois, M. de Robespierre,"—and this name would doubtless have been more than once on the lips of those in the public galleries. The sad, soured deputy for Arras was already there, in the Assembly. One day, he would be seen in all his splendour as leader, pontiff, almost a dictator; but not yet. Now he was mocked at, his speeches which were said to savour both of the oil of his lamp and the vinegar of his mind, provoked much laughter. "M. de Mirabeau is the 'Torch of Provence,' M. de Robespierre the 'Candle of the Artois.'" Humiliated, bitter and frowning, he stored up his hatred; all these fine gentlemen who now made a mock of him, he would have them all right one fine day. Then, certain that the Revolution would go still further, he made himself the protagonist of a complete Revolution; it would carry him with it little by little on its advancing wave from the bench where for three years he had sat exasperated, to the altar of the Supreme Being. There this little man with his plumed hat would be seen one day standing above the Convention which bowed low before him.

There they were, the leading orators and speakers of the Constituent Assembly, from Maury the outstanding figure of the Extreme Right to Robespierre, the most remarkable of the Extreme Left.

Orators, speakers, certainly, but not one leader. Nobody, either from the Right, Centre or Left could boast of being able to lead the Assembly or even to guide a party or a group. Whoever managed at one session to obtain the half-hearted support of the Chamber to a measure by an eloquent speech, found it impossible the next day to get even one-tenth of the votes.

This shows the general characteristics of this panic-stricken assembly.

Idealism continued its mad career, for everyone, or nearly everyone, considered himself as the possessor of the very latest and best theory, and alone able to obtain its acceptance. The irritated deputies adopted a strongly egotistical attitude which estranged them from each other and, in the same party, made the friends of one day the enemies of the next. Also it prevented the formation of those *groups* which are really the cohesive elements of a parliamentary body.

One of my Lorraine compatriots, Duquesny, with the great discernment typical of his province, made a criticism of his extravagant colleagues: *"A detestable metaphysical Assembly,"* he wrote in his diary. Condorcet who was himself an idealist but not yet a deputy, felt that he had been left far behind. *"An Assembly of twelve hundred metaphysicians!"* was his opinion. A member of the Left declared in March, 1790: "We are feeling our way!"

If they had to grope their way, it was because they were most of the time in the clouds, a thousand miles away from hard, cold facts. As we have seen, they were nearly all the spiritual sons of philosophers. As the materialistic Czarina Catherine said to one of these most distinguished theorists,

"You are using suffering humanity as your paper." Certainly, they had just crammed their heads full of the outpourings of fifty philosophers' books. Then when the humble masses of France sent them to bring about the reform of an out-of-date social system, they were soon content with nothing less than the reform of humanity. This was because as humanitarians, internationalists and pacifists "of a cosmopolitan spirit" they meant, still "using suffering humanity as their paper," to force their ideas on the government of a great State which had stood for fifteen centuries and had at all times followed the policy imposed upon it by the necessities of its economic life, the traditions of its race and the dangers of its geographical position. Economics! History! Geography! Not a soul thought for one moment of counterbalancing with practical considerations the axiomatic theories of Philosophy.

I shall only mention two famous examples of this extraordinary idealism though two and a half years of discussion on this point have provided me with twenty. These are the debates on *"The Declaration of Rights"* and *"The War."*

There had been a strong desire to draw up a *"Declaration of Rights"* which was, so it was stated, a necessary preface to the formation of a Constitution. This *"Declaration"* ought, logically, to have been based on the "parish reports" since the proposed legislation was to take place in France and on behalf of France. Clermont-Tonnerre had drawn up eleven very straightforward articles from these "parish reports" but his ideas did not originate in Philadelphia or Geneva. Were they going to labour for one nation alone? "We want to make a Declaration for all men, for all countries, to serve as an example to the whole world!" was the cry of one deputy. Foreigners smiled at this pretension; so did Morris (who in fact, did come from Philadelphia) and Dumont who was a citizen of Geneva. "What a puerile invention" was what the latter wrote of it. But had not Condorcet said: "A good law is good for all men just as a proposition is true for everyone." For the Assembly, this was quite enough justification.

Now, as no proposal had really been outlined in committee, the Assembly, therefore, at a sitting to which the public was admitted, set about its task, and amendments followed one after the other as everyone tried to outvie his neighbour in advancing fresh designs for this fantastic humanitarianism. This *Declaration* was, on paper, a philosophical achievement magnificent in its liberality; as a political achievement it was absurd, being formulated at a time when a rebellious and lawless nation required to be shown (to quote Mirabeau), *not its rights but its duties.*

But was it certain that even these rights would receive satisfaction in the ensuing Constitution? No, that was impossible, for it would be ultra-democratic and almost anarchical in character. Therefore, if there was no intention to vote for a constitution of that kind, why frame a preamble which would be immediately contradicted by it? "Why go and take men up to the top of a mountain," Malouet wisely said, "and show them the whole domain of their rights since we are forced to bring them down again, to impose restrictions upon them and then cast them back into this workaday world where they will feel fettered at every step." What did that matter; it was imperative that this chaotic state should be justified by grand idealistic theories. But the people considered that in the Constitution which followed they had been betrayed. "All men, being born equal, must have equal rights" was, in short, the promise of the *Declaration.* Then came the answer of the Constitution: "But they will not have them." Then again the Declaration: "Rebellion is the most holy of duties." But members of the Constituent Assembly probably added that "if they rebel against us, they must be shot down at once," and the same assembly had to struggle along for two years in this dangerous situation, created by its own idealists in order to give an "example to the world." Anarchy, justified in the Assembly, resulted from it, and the pacifist discussion of May 22nd, 1790, was directly responsible for the detested war which shortly burst upon them.

At this time, Europe which had been closely watching the increasing disorders in France, was preparing to invade the country so as to profit from the confusion that was rife everywhere. The question was what measures were to be taken in order to save France from invasion; were fortresses to be built or was the army which was melting away, to be reformed? Those were the methods of tyrants, of despots (they were not yet called imperialists), and the relics of a system that had long been destroyed. Instead of building up a strong army, perhaps France should strengthen her alliances? But when Montmorin, the Minister for Foreign Affairs, spoke on April 20th, 1790, of utilizing the pact with the Bourbons in Italy and in Spain, he was met with a blunt refusal to support a treaty concluded under the despotic régime—and with despots.

Robespierre rose to protest in the name of the pacifists. In his harsh voice he said, "It must be proclaimed that *France gives up her conquests* and looks upon her boundaries as imposed by age-long destiny." This proposal appeared so exactly in accordance with the internationalistic spirit of the Assembly that, for once, Robespierre, bursting with pride, was warmly applauded. It must be noticed, however, that his motion was directly contrary to the national

policy followed for a thousand years by all the great statesmen of France.

In vain did Mirabeau, much more of a materialist, point
out that it was impossible to be without a foreign policy,
and that the country's position must be maintained and
preparations made for war as long as Europe remained under
arms. His cry that "Until then, it will be dangerous to dream
of perpetual peace if it causes France to disarm when all
Europe is armed" was unavailing. This time the "Torch
from Provence" was not bright enough to lighten their darkness, being outshone by the "Candle from the Artois."

Cazalès also tried to protest; but he was a soldier and
as a soldier was naturally anxious for war. Although he
made a magnificent patriotic speech it was received with
hoots, for his expressions were those of one thirsting for
blood, or so it seemed to the Assembly. The President even
went as far as to ask him to apologize for having dared to
say that France would defend herself. He was provoking
war!

Then on May 22nd the famous measure which became
Article IV of the Constitution was passed, though never to
be kept. "The French nation abandons all idea of waging
wars with the object of making conquests."

Albert Sorel has shown clearly that Europe, taking the
measure as an avowal of France's decrepitude, decided to
make every preparation to tear this deliquescent country to
pieces. Great territorial gains were the result of the conflict which followed and lasted for so many years. This
period of France's history is, for once, a valuable lesson
for all countries and all times.

But these two examples show how reasoning on idealistic
lines was liable to lead these men into making the most
terrible mistakes and how the wisest spirits failed dismally

when lashed by the tribunes' fiery tongues and harassed by the attacks of those whom Condorcet described as "the 1,200 metaphysicians." The Civil Constitution of the Clergy, the history of the Assembly and twenty other instances, all go to prove this.

This idealism which destroyed all reason and defied good sense would, alone, have been enough to upset the working of the Assembly. But, like most deliberative bodies, it was permeated with passions of a baser sort, all the more dangerous because owing to the general inexperience of parliamentary procedure, they were not easily discernible. Intrigue, personal ambitions and sometimes even viler influences did their work and on January 26th, 1790, a date to remember, matters were brought to a climax on the occasion of the first case of bribery, the very first in parliamentary history. Consequently, the Assembly immediately reacted by a return to more upright behaviour which caused them to adopt the most extraordinary proposals.

It was fear rather than rancour that turned hearts to stone and clouded men's perception. One deputy wrote, "If the Assembly does raise altars to the gods, *it must be to Fear and Vengeance.*"

Fear indeed had it in its grip and there are proofs of this on every hand; fear of the Court, of the troops, of the streets, of the Clubs, of riots and even of itself. And fear became an instrument of blackmail. Latterly, six hundred châteaux had been burnt and fifty of the King's officers murdered in the provinces and when the deputies of the Right tried to oppose a revolutionary decree, those shameless members from the Left cried, "We shall refer you to your departments,"—and everyone knew what that meant. Indeed speakers from what was called the Black Group were continually interrupted by threatening murmurs from the public benches which were packed with members of the Clubs. A deputy from the Left cried, "We are deliberating in the presence of our masters," and that explains why certain improbable demagogic motions arose; "they were deliberating with their masters' eyes upon them."

Assailed by these thoughts, the Assembly was finally thrown into a confused, feverish state even at periods when idealism failed to carry them to delirious heights. The disorders which now prevailed in the Chamber ended by being their undoing.

No Assembly has ever shown such inability to control its unruly factions. After being carefully prepared in committee, legislative measures were wrecked at one fell swoop in the debates which sometimes, as on August 4th, descended to the lowest depths of folly; on other occasions, they became one tangled mass of improvised amendments. More often, the point at issue was entirely lost in countless interminable speeches. At this time, eloquence was generally synonymous with grandiloquence or perhaps more particularly with loquacity. The most nebulous notions were hidden in an unending stream of emphatic statements which seemed to convey no definite meaning even after an hour. There were speeches so long that a deputy who, ironically enough, was called Bouche, proposed, (if I may say so) to shut the mouths of others by placing an hour-glass on the tribune to prevent a speaker from remaining there after the sand had run through. So rambling were these harangues that when the Assembly voted that the speech of one of their number, a certain Toulouse-Lautrec, who was also a wit, should be printed, he added with a chuckle tnat he would also move that it should be bound.

But, for the greater part of the time, these dissertations were hardly heard at all. In the Chamber the dreadful din never ceased; there were from 1,200 to 1,400 deputies who could never be prevailed upon to sit down. They were moreover intolerant and excitable, brooking no contradiction nor allowing anyone to combat their opinions. Suddenly they would hurl themselves at each other, sometimes going as far as to exchange blows or even cross swords over the matter,—outside. Therefore the hubbub was so great, for much of the time, that it was difficult to know what was being said. One day, a worthy deputy who must have been, I think, a very artless fellow, made the following inimitably touching announcement: "I approve heartily of everything without knowing what it's all about."

The democrat and Curé Thomas Lindet gleefully described the Assembly "a field of battle with the two opposing armies drawn up upon it"; he added, "they are evenly matched," and this certainly gives food for reflection.

How can it be said that this equality had been achieved when we know that between May, 1789, and April, 1791, revolutionary measures always found a majority. It is true however that after January, 1790, this majority became much smaller.

Indeed, only one-third of the Assembly was composed of members of the Right. But after the period of disillusionment and regret had begun for so many of its members, the part of the Centre showed its penitence for past conduct by suddenly showing signs of resistance. It is highly probable that if the Right had remained firm in the battle-line it would have won the support of one hundred to a hundred and fifty members from the Centre and so have revenged their early defeats. Another very noticeable fea-

ture was the relatively very small number of those register-
ing their votes after the end of 1789. Thus when the Nationalization of Church property was passed (a measure which
indeed opened Pandora's box), there were 368 votes for
and 348 against or 716 out of a possible 1,500. It was the
same in almost all the important motions and what can
that mean except that one-half of the deputies did not
vote at all and probably no longer put in an appearance in
the Chamber.

In fact, following the example of the depressed Mounier,
the majority of deputies from the Right and, later, from
the Left, gave up the struggle in a most precipitate fashion.
As a woman of wit wrote forty years before, "Bad schemes
are sometimes successful, but abandoned ones never." They
were demoralized after continuous defeat in these abusive
and almost dangerous debates. Educated men disliked their
surroundings and were violently displeased with the jeering reception accorded them by the rag-tag-and-bobtail of
that party; this drove away many peers and prelates from
the Right. Others were assailed by that fear of which I
have already spoken and for that one cannot blame them
seeing how, as "pure-blooded" deputies, they were liable to
be attacked by roaring mobs on leaving the Assembly. The
deputies of the Centre felt entirely differently. These idealist
Liberals had suffered disillusionment, disappointment, almost
despair when they saw the hopes which they had cherished
at the beginning of their career, dashed to the ground, one
by one. Whatever the reason was, 120 members nearly all
from the Right and Centre, having officially resigned almost
"*en bloc*" during the winter 1789-1790, at least a hundred
others as well refrained from making an appearance.

Finally, those who came did not stay. Mounier said in
the summer of 1789 that it was impossible "to get them

to come to the Chamber at the beginning of the session or postpone their meal times so that they might stay till the end." Vaublanc said the same thing adding, "The revolutionaries profit by it." These worthy people were men about town and it was quite natural that they should go at five o'clock to talk to ladies in their salons or at six o'clock to eat their dinners. Thomas Lindet in explaining to his brothers, on the day after the closure of the Constituent Assembly, what his policy should be in the Legislative Assembly in which he was going to take his seat, showed how he gloried in the Right's indolence, which had been their undoing. According to him, the most extreme measures were passed thanks to the absence of the "Blacks" between the hours of six and seven, "and so," he added, "the Revolution was shaped by candlelight." It was a lesson that perhaps ought to be taught many members of parliament in our time.

The Right and the Centre, completely sundered by their ancient jealousies, were unable to act together. These parties had no leader to enforce discipline and, if the Left were not willing to submit to the control of a chief, they had at least the advantage of receiving orders from the Jacobin Club,—and perhaps from Assemblies more mysterious still. A curious statement gives us grounds for this supposition. Thomas Lindet a notorious free-mason wrote on May 5th, 1790, that while the Assembly was discussing an important affair, the Left, perceiving that they were in a minority, prolonged the session, and he added, increased their voting strength by giving "a signal of distress." And then these deputies of the Left were aggressors, innovators; they discoursed on sentiment and passion and, nine times out of ten, victory went to him who dared to stir, inflame and attack his hearers.

This explains how, owing to the mistakes of the advocates of law and order and the insolence of their adversaries, the revolutionary factions gained the day. This gave the sorry jesters the excuse to say, "that the Left was *adroit*, the Right had seemed *gauche.*"

The day came when these men who had spread ruin over the length and breadth of France perceived that the political system which they had constructed with an unstable Constitution and a feeble government was itself but a vast structure liable to collapse at any moment, creating havoc in its fall. The party of the Left meant simply to substitute a new régime for the old one; but already in 1791, the Extremists following in the wake of the Central Party, found themselves overrun and threatened by a group of substitutes and by the leaders of the "second Revolution."

Then they hoped to react against their own policy and remodel their masterpiece. They seemed disposed, under the leadership of Sieyès and till Lameth became their chief, to rely upon the support of the Centre against the extreme factions, just as the Centre had, in 1790, been anxious for the assistance of the Right against the Extremists on the Left.

Already Barnave was disturbed; he had found his road to Damascus. Having been entrusted with bringing the humiliated King and Queen back to Paris from Varennes he had journeyed in close company with them for three days. Flatteringly they took him almost completely into their confidence; also, being in reality only disaffected through personal ambition, his heart was touched at the plight of the bewitching Queen and permanently softened. He told the astonished sovereigns that he was anxious to react.

The Assembly seemed ripe to follow the now converted "tiger." "I assure you," Barnave confided to Malouet, his former adversary, "that I have grown very old during the last few months." And it was the same with a hundred of his colleagues who anxiously watched the rising tide of anarchy. The riot on the Champ-de-Mars on July 17th, 1791, which we studied in connection with La Fayette, caused not without bloodshed a breach between the Left and the Extreme Left.

It was the intention of the Left to examine the whole of the question before closing the Legislature. It was anxious to co-operate with the Centre and the Right in this matter, but, alas, neither of these parties was a force in itself. Cazalès from the Right and Mounier from the Left, the two outstanding men of these parties, had both resigned, followed by one hundred deputies. A member of the Constituent Assembly wrote on July 10th, 1791, that the Left regretted this. Besides, the recent disputes were still fresh in men's minds; feelings of bitterness went too deep, the lack of cohesion was only too apparent and fear, which was not to be trifled with, had them in its grip. The Clubs cried aloud at the many acts of treason: "Barnave! Barnave!" The traitor was joining the Right to fall under the influence of Maury and Cazalès and Lameth, Du Port, not to mention the "infamous La Fayette" were following his example. People held aloof from them and threatened them. Then, even in the Assembly, the Right which mismanaged matters to the very end, repulsed their advances. Wimpfen, a deputy from the Left, made them conciliatory proposals but Rivarol scoffed at "these worthy people" who "after being incendiaries came to offer their services as firemen." Alas, it is often necessary to submit to incendiaries becoming firemen—if they offer to do so—, because they know better than anyone where the fire was started. Wimpfen did not meet with a good reception at the hands of Maury's friends. He was discouraged and, on withdrawing said, "You are anxious to ruin everything and unhappily that is what you are doing."

The failure of these attempts to come to an understanding did, in fact, mean that all was lost. Almost nothing was done in the way of revision. The Assembly which was exhausted after a session of twenty-nine anxious months, did not ask for anything more than its dissolution. As a body, it had become unpopular, and was well aware of its unpopularity.

It is probably the knowledge of this unpopularity which caused the Assembly to commit its greatest act of folly. There were many deputies who thought that it would be a good gesture and a magnificent example of virtue to decide that no member of the Constituent Assembly could be re-elected to the new Assembly. This, I say, was their supreme act of folly, for this measure not only sealed the doom of the flimsy structure for which they were responsible but also meant the ruin of the State. At last these idealists came face to face with facts; therefore, seeing that dangers threatened within as without, they were already beginning, as their desire for revision shows, to be transformed into the most cautious of politicians. One of the new deputies wrote, "The workman having deserted his work, the Constitution was given over to men who would shake it vigorously and be crushed to death under its ruins." Exactly; these new men as will be seen later, were going to give vent to these new passions in all their virulence without having any of the experience of the retiring members. The Left had hesitated; the Right again did not understand that to hand over the State to newly elected members who were left with one thing to destroy—the throne—was to bring the Revolution one step nearer; it yielded to the absurd idea of bringing to nought an assembly which under men like La Fayette and Barnave, had continually humiliated it. One of its members declared, "There was only one great error left for us to make and it did not escape us." The great mistake, as could be foreseen, was to have terrible consequences, and it is doubtless for that reason that no other legislative body has passed a measure declaring its members ineligible for re-election; at any rate, it is better to think so.

The Assembly dissolved on September 25th.

Having carefully studied the characteristics of the Assembly in the foregoing pages, we will not find it necessary to say much in conclusion.

Three-quarters of the members in the Constituent Assembly were good-willed, well-intentioned men and were thus respectable enough. Many of them were highly intelligent and cultivated and considered themselves, rightly, as being citizens of exemplary character and devoted servants of the government and the country. The legislators, about three hundred in number, were a constant burden to the Assembly; they had inherited their forefathers' rather violent dispositions which marked the attitude of those servants of absolute monarchy. But they, themselves, put the fierce enthusiasm with which they did their work at the service of what they called "Liberty."

The people who elected them for their powers of oratory and high intellect only wanted them to bring order out of the chaos which had been rife in their weakly governed country for three-quarters of a century, and by abolishing the privileges, to re-establish a just system of taxation which should be the same for all; this would, moreover, bring about a restoration of the nation's finances, then in a critical state.

But they, immersed in the great ideas of a complete reform, had gone so far beyond the wishes of the people that, after the elections of 1789, there was much mirth when a deputy appealed to the popular desires as expressed in the "parish reports" as being against this wholesale destruction of the State.

The wishes of the nation which were expressed in these "parish reports" remained firm and, at last, prevailed. Even if the people who counted on their deputies defending them had been forced into a close connection with them by the necessity of saving the early reforms from counter-revolutionary movements, this war of words which in nearly every case hid the real issues from even the deputies themselves, conveyed nothing to the popular mind. There is no doubt that townspeople were intoxicated with the ideas of liberty which came straight from the Assembly tribune to a restless country, but the enormous mass still held to those which, in 1789, had seemed as being alone essential: order in the State, in institutions and justice in the allotment of taxes.

The Assembly had meant to put the State in order and had ended in creating a feeble form of government. Justice was theoretically established, but the creation of political freedom so upset the life of the nation that the people could not yet see clearly the benefits conferred on them by national equality.

These legislators had certainly allowed themselves to be carried away by and rather beyond their ideas. They were, by tradition, supporters of royal authority, but by this time, they had weakened it to such an extent that, according to a prophecy made in 1791, it only remained for their successors to destroy it altogether. And these sons of patriotic legislators, who had helped and sometimes forced the monarchy to bring about the re-establishment of the frontiers, went as far as to disclaim the work of their fathers by declaring that these frontiers, still unsettled, were as an age-long destiny appointed them to be. These men suffered from having two sets of ideas which clashed with each other; their temperament, inherited tradition, their method of facing realities, pulled them one way and their philosophical system dragged them another. They had built up the "Declaration of Rights" which ended in establishing a genuine democracy and, after having written this imprudent preface, they had formed a Constitution which closed the political arena to three-quarters of the citizens.

This inconsistency is shown most clearly by the struggle which raged in these men's minds. But if, momentarily, they lost touch with reality, events of a most dreadful character soon brought them back to earth. The constant disorders and the threat of a foreign invasion suddenly made them realize that a strong central authority must be reestablished and a barrier of natural boundaries fixed between France and a Europe that was always at war.

Many of these same men who, from 1789 to 1791, had talked of an unconfined liberty and peace at any price, appeared, one year later, firmly resolved to ward off the great dangers threatening the country by exercising an almost extreme authority and following an almost aggressive foreign policy. It was they who filled the benches in the National Convention and tried, while awaiting Bonaparte's approach, to re-establish in a quaking nation, the traditional principles which the Constituent Assembly, blinded by idealism, had completely disregarded.

CHAPTER V

MADAME ROLAND

CHAPTER V

THE GIRONDINS AND MADAME ROLAND

On September the 26th, 1792, the mob of Paris betook themselves for the second time to the Riding School in the Tuileries to witness the installation of the New Assembly: for new it was in its entirety, seeing that the deputies who formed its predecessor had of their own motion ordained that none of them should form part of it. The elections had, to use modern parlance, shown a marked swing of the pendulum in favour of the Left party. The supporters of La Fayette, as well as those of Barnave, now completely out of favour with the electors, found themselves thrown back on to the seats hitherto occupied by the Right. On the seats opposite, which had previously been occupied by Mirabeau and Barnave, there flaunted a Left party with views far more pronounced than their predecessors. All eyes were turned on this new Left: the counterparts of "Aristides and Cato, of Brutus and Cicero" as people called them.

In this Left party, now definitely committed to the policy of Revolution root and branch, we shall witness the appearance of differences of opinion: at first slight, but later on very marked indeed. The time would come when one division of this party would send the other to the guillotine: for the present they were apparently agreed on a policy of bringing the powers of the constitutional monarchy within the narrow limits of the statutes passed by the Assembly. There was however one small group among them, destined shortly to attract a large measure of attention: these were the representatives of the Department of the Gironde.

These deputies from Bordeaux—the Bordelais, as they were called first of all, were the original kernel of the Left party. The leading personalities were Guadet, very dark and thin, of fiery glance and atrabilious countenance; Gensonné, cold of temperament, cutting of speech, with a brain full of abstract ideas: Ducos, enthusiastic, steeped in literature, the type of a young hero crowned with a halo of light; Grangeneuve, full of audacity, violence and passion: finally Vergniaud, the shining light of the Bordeaux Bar, an orator of renown, always ready with a speech on the lines of a Philippic, gifted with eloquence of the grand classic style, which he employed to give expression to violent sentiments, the master of the rest, because where all were advocates he remained to the end the most thorough advocate of them all, a Cicero from Aquitaine. Around these "Bordelais" we shall soon see gather a regular band of admirers, consisting almost entirely of deputies from the south of France, of whom the most characteristic representative was the "Marseillais" Isnard, full of proposals characterized by the fire and extravagance of the Cannebière.[1] His adhesion to the party, it may be said, represented the miraculous fusion of the Rhône with the Gironde.

The attraction of this eloquent band was such that it even led a well-known Paris deputy named Brissot to join them. He was a man of established reputation, but with less sentiment and tenderness in his character than his colleagues from the south. Of Puritan type with austere countenance

[1] Main street of Marseilles.

and sober dress, he had journeyed to Boston and discovered America: and ever since it pleased him to pose as a French Franklin. With a profound belief in his own omniscience due to the fact that he had written much, he had previously, from 1789 to 1791, been the moving spirit of the Extreme Left: described by one of his colleagues as a "clever" rather than an eloquent speaker he was in the eyes of the young men from the south a great thinker, whom on occasion they looked up to as their chief: so much so that we shall see the Girondins dubbed on one occasion the *Brissotins*,— an unfortunate experience for them as (in the words of one of his former colleagues in the Legislature) he was really destined, "In a mixture of daring and rashness," to lead the party to its downfall.

Pagans in their extravagant worship of antiquity, these Girondins became, through their intense love of ancient Rome, the enemies of Rome of the Christian era and all it stood for. Guadet would never speak of God, but of "the gods." Most of them, though steeped in Rousseau's theories, differed from him on this point: for being almost all atheists, even pronounced atheists, they refused to follow the *"Vicaire Savoyard"* in his milk-and-water Deism. One of them, in fact, the Guadet mentioned above, one day bitterly reproached Robespierre for having in a speech dared to speak of *Providence*. Influenced more by the teaching of Plutarch than of Rousseau they were led to develop republican sentiments partly through feelings of extravagant idealism, partly from convictions derived from study of books. During this autumn of 1791, which saw their rise, they still "tolerated" the throne: some of them thought that it would be unwise to pull it down: but at bottom—even if it were only for the literary effect thereby resulting— their sentiments were republican and nothing else.

Above all, whether they were advocates or men of letters, they were slaves to historical phrases. The expressions which they heard and still more those to which they gave utterance intoxicated them; they swept them away and carried them off their legs. Vergniaud and Guadet would rise to speak with the full intention of not attacking the throne, but they were to demolish it; with every wish not to excite the people they were to rouse it to revolt; desirous of completing the Revolution in a spirit of brotherly love they were to stain it in blood. Vaublanc, who in this Assembly sat among the Right, has summed them up well. He speaks of the intoxication which overcame his colleagues as the result of the acclamations of the Assembly. "They often went," he says, "beyond their real feelings and often on leaving the hall were ashamed of what they had said." There was a Girondin expression of November 14, 1791, "It is imperative to cut out the gangrened part of the body to save the rest." It was this "tag" which was destined to give rise to the whole of the Terror and to lead the Girondins, who were considered to be smitten with gangrene, to the guillotine. At the same time Brissot and Gensonné, when denouncing the conspiracies of the Court party ejaculated, "You ask for proofs. Why proofs? There are no written records of conspiracies." Two years afterwards Fouquier-Tinville was to turn against them before the Revolutionary Tribunal their own deadly expression. Vergniaud, when he induced the Assembly to declare "the country in danger," never knew how fatal to himself this pathetic proclamation was likely to prove: he thought only of the aptness of the phrase. Vergniaud again was the man who said of the refractory priests whom Isnard was bent on expelling from France: "It is lawful for a nation to throw out from its bosom persons who remain there only to do evil": an expression which Desmoulins was to turn against Vergniaud's friends.

Some months later they began to meet regularly. Brissot used to collect them an hour before each sitting. But they did not form a homogeneous party until the opening of a salon, which brought them together at the feet of a woman. Romantic before their time, they felt the need of feminine interest in their politics; Madame Condorcet, and Julia Talma, the former a "grande dame," the latter a great artiste, had received and shepherded them to start with, but it was only when a little middle-class lady arrived in Paris from Lyons that the party actually took shape. This lady eventually became the Egeria of the party, for the simple reason that the Girondins found in her vibrating personality an expression of themselves, with all their ambitions, ideas, passions and illusions, reinforced, as far as she was concerned, by an ardent will and a managing spirit, of which all these poets, cast haphazard into politics, were totally destitute.

This little Marie-Jeanne Phlipon, wife of Roland de la Platière—her pet name was Manon—deserves some measure of our attention. For the men who surrounded her, this woman may be said to have represented Destiny. She was the first person in France to conceive the idea of a party regularly constituted, and in virtue of this her life formed a turning point in the history of French Legislative Assemblies. But in course of directing this party towards the achievement of her own aims and the satisfaction of her own private feelings she found herself bound to engage it in a terribly hazardous enterprise in which she became involved herself. Womanly though her character was in certain aspects, her influence over these twenty leaders of the Revolution entitles her to a place among the men who made the Revolution.

She was the daughter of an engraver, a Parisian of doubtful morals, and of his wife, a god-fearing woman of the middle class: she was born on March 17th, 1754, in the heart of Paris in a house in the Place Dauphin, which is one of the few buildings of the time left standing. She was brought up a true child of this terrible City, with a mind open, like every Parisian, to imbibe every possible idea and a heart, again like every Parisian, an easy prey to every possible passion. Madly fond of reading she had devoured everything. A study of Plutarch had inspired her with a spirit at once heroic and republican. Later she admitted that when she was eight years old she used to take to church the "Lives of famous men" in place of her "Missal." Later again she wrote: "In the first outpouring of my youthful feelings, when I was twelve years old, I used to cry because I was not born a citizen of Sparta or Rome. I had thought to see in the Revolution the application, hitherto unhoped for, of the principles on which I had been brought up." Then she came across the Divine Rousseau: she read him day and night: she read him through and through from the *"Contrat Social"* to *"La Nouvelle Héloïse."* He stimulated everything in her all at once, her brain, her heart, and her feelings. She borrowed from him his social and political ideas. She also took from him his peculiar conception of Love, which was to make her one day at the height of a political crisis the heroine of a strange domestic drama.

I have just said that she was inspired with a republican spirit. The fact is that in 1789, when the most advanced revolutionaries never even in their dreams went beyond the conception of a restored monarchy, this little Manon was devoutly praying for the advent of a Republic stern but

benevolent. "I hate," she wrote, "the kings of my childhood, and I have never without an involuntary shudder
seen a man abase himself before another." After July 26th,
1789, when she was disappointed in finding that the taking
of the Bastille had not led to a deeper upheaval she was
heard grumbling and abusing all concerned. "You busy
yourselves over Municipal questions," she wrote to politicians in Paris, "and you are allowing persons to escape you
who will plot new horrors against you. You are only children, your enthusiasm is a flash in the pan and if the Assembly cannot bring these two crowned heads to formal trial
(she is referring to Louis XVI and Marie Antoinette) you
are done for."

She was the more possessed by this overwhelming passion for politics, because of a disappointment in private
life: a disappointment which she had risked far too light-
heartedly. She had in fact contracted in 1780 a marriage
of a very peculiar kind. Being then 26 years of age she
had married an Inspector of Manufactures named Roland
de la Platière who was 46 years of age. He was devoid of
any qualities of character, which would have compensated
for the difference of age between them: with the outward
appearance of a Quaker he was stern and pretentious, stiff
and pedantic. Being always full of the need of proclaiming
himself "virtuous," he was of a type which would make
virtue detested everywhere. Being fully convinced of his
own capacities he was embittered at the lack of opportunity
to display them in a wider field. Manon married him in
order to escape from a home which the irregularities of
her father's life rendered impossible and vowed that, come
what might, she would remain faithful to the husband
whom she did not love. It must be noted that mediocre
though he was, while she did not love him she admired him

The fact is that he had been a contributor to the blessed *Encyclopédie* and had notable men for friends. She was more ambitious for him than he was for himself: and that is saying a great deal. But this young woman with her burning, one might say her frenzied, temperament, a woman in whom heart and senses and imagination were all on fire felt herself to be doubly weighed down by her life of obscurity and domesticity in the society of her uncouth and elderly husband. In a letter to her friends, the Mlles. Canet, she describes how she cooks her great man's meals and re-reads Plutarch at the same time: a method of work which must assuredly have led to very bad cookery. And all her life with her Plutarch in her hand, she continued to make a hash of what she undertook, burning her fingers at the same time.

All of a sudden the Revolution came to present her with an opportunity for realizing her ideas, with a big position and a burning love affair. Roland, who had been appointed to the Commune of Lyons and had been in communication with members of the Extreme Left in the first Assembly, took his wife to Paris. He there attracted to his house Pétion the future Mayor of Paris, Brissot the great publicist of the advanced party, Maximilien Robespierre the harsh orator of the Left. And one day it so happened that Manon saw the young deputy Léonard Buzot enter her salon: and she, who had conquered so many hearts was in her turn smitten by him.

It cannot be said that Léonard was very handsome: but he was young and eloquent, warm-hearted and full of inspiration. Though a Norman from Caen he was already in 1790 the prototype of those young Girondins whom I pictured to you just now; the men who in the next Assembly, a year later, were to expound a mass of wild ideas and in so doing to display the turgid eloquence dear to orators of advanced views. I said of them that they were romantics before the advent of romanticism. Listen to Léonard's words: "My youth was almost that of a savage: my passions concentrated in my burning heart were violent in the extreme, but limited to one object" . . . and so on in the same style. This savage youth of his—we are to hear the same story of René Chateaubriand at Combourg fifty years later. To Manon the man appeared sublime—the more so because he was married to an ugly woman with a hump. He was melancholy, a lover of storm and darkness, and sentimental in a dramatic way—a man of feeling as they then said. He seemed to Manon, steeped as she was in Rousseau, to be the incarnation of Saint Preux of *"La Nouvelle Héloïse"* come to life. She fell madly in love with him all of a sudden, though she vowed at the same time that she would never betray her husband, and wrote that she would remain obstinately faithful to her duty. When a woman has reached the point of making vows of this sort the husband is in parlous case. From that day forward, Madame Roland used to address her husband as "my worthy friend," nothing more intimate: which is a bad sign.

When the Rolands on their return to Lyons learnt that the new Assembly was fighting the good fight against the Tuileries, and, further, from Buzot and Brissot that a band of the undefiled, genuine Republicans of the Spartan and Roman type were leading the attack, there was no holding them. Roland had dreams of a big post and she dreamed that she had a big part to play. They returned to permanent quarters in Paris and she saw Buzot once more. The latter who was already in touch with the new deputies brought to her all those resurrected heroes of Plutarch, all those Romans of the Gironde, of whom I have been speaking.

Nearly all of these were at her feet after the very first visit, charmed by a glimpse of Manon with her piquant profile and frank smile, which, though so devoid of coquetterie, attracted them appearing as it did behind the disagreeable, pedantic personality of Roland.

But what was more charming even than her gracious ways was her passion, to which she could now give free rein, against "the tyranny."

I have said just now that though they were themselves full of this passion they were still, as far as their political views were concerned, somewhat undecided and that, though they had republican aspirations they had not reached the point where they wished to overturn the Throne. This tiny Manon arrived in time to fan the flame of energy and to force them to pursue their plans to the unavoidable end. All listened to her greedily: there were in her drawing-room Guadet, Gensonné, Grangeneuve, Brissot, Vergniaud, Ducos, Isnard and ten other representatives: also "beauty Pétion" as they called him, who had just amid scenes of incredible enthusiasm been elected Mayor of Paris, and a young Marseillais named Barbarroux, a fine figure of a man who while waiting for election to the Assembly represented the democracy of Marseilles in the clubs of Paris. Manon used to call him "Antinous," the most handsome of mankind. He had Marseilles at his feet: and Pétion secured for him the adoration of the capital. Everyone admired him; nearly everyone loved him passionately but none of them made Léonard Buzot jealous. The latter knew well that he was always Manon's special favourite. As for Roland, they told him that they would make him a minister at the first opportunity—and assurances of this sort made him think that these young people were charming.

There were signs that a fresh crisis was impending. Louis

XVI, in face of the somewhat arrogant attitude adopted by
the new Assembly and acting under the advice of the Constitutional Party of the old Assembly, seemed less inclined
to yield than he had been in the past: while the threats
of the *"emigrés"* engaged as they were in inciting Europe
to attack Revolutionary France, and the resistance of the
priests to the civil constitution roused the swarms of
political clubs to fury. The Assembly passed threatening
decrees against the *"emigrés."* Louis XVI sanctioned them
but refused to strike at the priests, whose only crime was
that of remaining faithful to the ancient church. Europe
was arming, while the Queen Marie Antoinette was strongly
suspected—and rightly as we now know—of intriguing with
the coalition through the agency of her brother, the Emperor of Germany, by whom she hoped to be saved; Louis
XVI, though he was more reserved, was nevertheless her
partner in her mistake. In the clubs it was said of them
that they were negotiating with the enemy who was making
ready to invade France.

At this point the Revolutionary movement seemed to be
swept into a whirlpool. The Left was anxious to create a
state of things which would precipitate the crisis and at
the same time provide a solution. Some revolutionaries—
though two years before they had given themselves out to
be strong pacifists—thought that war would be preferable
to this equivocal situation. War in their opinion would create
the national state of siege which would favour violent measures: war would force the King either to throw in his lot
with the nation or to cast aside his mask—and he could then
be overthrown and the Throne with him.

This was Madame Roland's idea and the whole of the
Girondin group who surrounded her declared for war. In
vain Robespierre and his like pointed out that far from

securing victory, war might lead the Revolution to destruction: it would in all probability mean defeat, because the people would be betrayed and liberty would be crushed by the foreigner: and if by some strange chance it resulted in victory, a military dictatorship was bound to ensue—another General Monk or Caesar. There was. on this point a division of opinion among the members of the Jacobin Club, and there ensued a bitter struggle between the two parties. But in the Club, as in the Assembly, the Girondins had at their disposal the persuasive eloquence of their leaders. From his wife's salon Roland breathed forth on to the Assembly a warlike spirit, which grew in intensity every day. Louis XVI in a moment of panic summoned to his council the Count of Narbonne, who declared himself ready to prepare for war. And then, just as he actually started preparations, Louis allowed the Queen's coterie to sweep him to one side. The Assembly protested vigorously against the dismissal of this "patriot"; Vergniaud openly denounced the plots of the Court party. "From this tribune," he said, "there is a view of the palace, where treacherous counsellors are leading the King astray; terror and fear have often issued from this palace; let them return there to-day in the name of the Law." "Let all who inhabit that palace know that the King alone is inviolable (this was a direct threat to the Queen), that the arm of the Law will reach all the guilty who reside there and that there is not a single head which if convicted of complicity will escape its devouring blade."

Everything bowed to this blast. Louis, who was alarmed, showed himself ready to accept a ministry at the hands of the Assembly. The latter, overawed by the Girondins, entrusted to this party the task of forming it.

It was in Vergniaud's apartments, 5 Place Vendôme, that the various combinations of ministers were first planned, and then upset, then finally completed. The first idea was to constitute a ministry of politicians belonging to the Left of all shades of opinion; there was talk of giving portfolios to Robespierre, to Danton and to other Jacobins. But the Girondins bore a grudge against these their erstwhile friends, whom they knew to be opposed to the war: they put their names on one side and concentrated on those who were obviously devoted to the principles of the group: thus General Dumouriez, whose supporter was Gensonné, was entrusted with the Ministry of Foreign Affairs; Clavière, whose supporter was his brother-in-law Brissot, with that of Finances; Ruranton, a magistrate from Bordeaux and friend of Vergniaud, with the Ministry of Justice. For the important Ministry of the Interior one man and one man only seemed marked out: Manon's husband, Roland.

His name was at once suggested and then turned down in favour of other candidates with more striking qualities and during three days of uncertainty the household lived in the same state of feverish excitement in which so many deputies' households, in similar circumstances, have lived during the last hundred years. These anxieties came to an end: thanks to Girondin support Roland's candidature triumphed. Late the same night a friend came to see Manon. She found her, she says, "with her freshness and charm fully restored, surrounded by a large circle of admirers, who were pouring out praises upon her." Roland was appointed minister—fully convinced in his own mind that he owed this position to his own merits, while in reality it was to their Egeria, his wife, that the assembled deputies entrusted the portfolio.

But already the Jacobins balked of office gave signs of dark displeasure, and none more so than Robespierre.

The entry of Roland into the Ministry was quite an event. No one was so sure of it as he. With his inborn love of giving lessons he contemplated astonishing the Tuileries by the Puritanism of his dress. "M. Roland," writes a royalist, "appeared before the King in shoes without buckles, a brown coat, a short red waistcoat, and his hair brushed smoothly down." The doorkeeper could not get over it. "Ah, Sir," said one of them to Dumouriez, who was leaving with Roland after the first council, "the gentleman has no buckles to his shoes!"

Manon took up her quarters at once not only at the residence of the Minister of the Interior (this was formerly the Hôtel du Contrôle Générale) but also in the personal office of the Minister. Barras tells us how, having gone to see the latter, he found by his side pretty Manon; as he waited for her to leave, the Minister said to him: "You can speak freely, my wife is fully conversant with the affairs of my Ministry." He was really more of a stranger there than she was. She managed everything, dismissing officials who were suspected of anti-revolutionary sentiments, appointing to posts the friends of her faction, all the time continuing to collect in her salon the whole of the party, with the addition of all the climbers, who always frequent the seats of the mighty. She presided over the formal meetings at which the ministers with the aid of ten or twelve deputies of the group and with the object of keeping a hold on the King, made preparations for the official meetings of the Council. It was she who incited them to keep the King dangling on the hook, to hold the hated Court in check. Through Louvet, the journalist of the party, she inspired the semi-official press: through Guadet and ten others she prevented the deputies from slumbering on their benches: at the end of the day Léonard Buzot came to join forces with his great friend and while Barbaroux maintained the liaison with Marseilles, Pétion placed Paris at her feet. The popularity of this new mayor was enormous; the first child baptized during his term of office received the names of Pétion-Nationale-Pique. They called him the Messiah, and this Messiah sighed for Manon.

No wonder that, living a life like this, she became overwrought to the point of frenzy. No wonder, too, that she made numerous enemies. While from the Right of the Assembly pressure was brought to bear on the King to dismiss the Rolandist ministers, among the Left and in the Clubs revolutionaries of another type considered that this little woman had far too much influence over "patriot" ministers. She remained a woman all the time, nervous, impressionable, inclined to be exclusive in her likes, downright in her dislikes. A party was formed from the extreme wing of the Girondins, which acknowledged that the man in the street was not likely to find any particular satisfaction in the fact that Manon Roland of the Ministry of the Interior was ruling the country. She mortally offended Dumouriez, Minister of War, whom she found "devoid of principles." The Court was carefully watching these signs of cleavage in the Left. When the King thought that the credit of the Roland household and its protegés was finally shattered, he struck his blow and dismissed his ministers. This event appeared to Madame Roland to be Royalty's death warrant. It was in the Roland salon, now thrown back into violent opposition, that preparations were made to overthrow the Throne. The party of violence were allowed free rein: it was Danton, who, we shall see, managed affairs with the bullies of the streets, but it was Madame Roland with devouring, fiery energy, who brought matters to a successful issue, seeing as she did only one possible conclusion to this new revolution: namely the return at the head of affairs of her friends of the Gironde and more especially of her husband.

The latter was in fact recalled by the Assembly as Minister of the Interior in the new executive Council. With Louis XVI and Marie Antoinette in the Temple prison Madame Roland was free to think that now at last, as her husband's shadow, she was going to rule without let or hindrance.

She was wrong. The Roland household had already been passed over. Danton had been elected to the Council, but with more votes than Roland. This had injured the self-esteem of the household. Manon already detested the man whom they called "the Titan of the Revolution." She was so impressionable that to her way of thinking a man's external appearance counted for more than anything: so that Danton's ugliness repelled and frightened her. Not content with dealing with this matter ten times over in her Memoirs she made this man the subject of a special study, in which she poured out her overpowering disgust even more than genuine hatred. Danton, whom I shall describe to you as a jolly, jovial person would have liked to dispel this antipathy: but Manon, woman-like, was as firm in her dislike as she was in her likes. So she turned him down, treated him as an intruder, one might say, a bounder. He was not a man who would let himself be despised and checkmated by a woman. Consequently with the support of Robespierre who could not abide petticoat influence of any kind, and Marat, who had also suffered under the snubbings of the Roland salon, he started to attack both her and her husband in his paper. Her good name was dragged in the mud.

Her friends, scandalized, irritated and exasperated, willingly rallied round her, but from that day forward there was war between her and the Clubs.

The massacres of September, which she did not hesitate to attribute to Danton, had revolted all that was noble and humane in her heart. She wrote, "You know my enthusiasm for the Revolution: well, I am ashamed of it. It has been spoilt by a lot of villains, it has become hideous." She urged her friends to make a stand against these "villains," to rouse the country against Paris, now in her eyes a town of blood.

The fact was that in September Paris had not only waded in blood, but simultaneously the capital had just rejected all the Girondin candidates for the Convention and elected what Madame Roland called "the execrable deputation," the principal personalities among whom were Robespierre, Danton, Marat and all those whom Manon called "the butchers." "In my eyes all Paris is accursed," wrote this furious woman. And it was hatred of Paris that this pure-bred Parisian was to breathe into her friends.

Though the latter were rejected by the capital a large number of them were elected to the Convention by the provinces: among them the former leaders of the Legislative Council, Vergniaud, Brissot, Gensonné, Grangeneuve, Guadet, Isnard and all their friends: Pétion, Buzot, Barbarroux, Louvet and over one hundred others. In short, the number of deputies in the Convention who allied themselves with the Girondin leaders is estimated to have been about 165: but they were only 165 out of 750.

The "Gironde"—the name is henceforward to be current coin—seemed to have gained strength but the changes made by the elections to the Convention were so sweeping that the supporters of La Fayette as well as those of Barnave were turned out: and consequently the "Gironde" took over the seats on the Right of the Assembly, which the others had vacated. The seats on the Left, which had previously been their preserve were to become the domain of the famous Mountain, and to be occupied by Danton, Robespierre and Marat, and the three hundred Jacobin extremists, who obeyed their orders: a party determined to secure the triumph of the Revolution, threatened as it was on all sides by measures taken in the name of Public Safety. At the head of the Mountain—the lightning-crowned Sinai—were the Paris delegates, "the execrable deputation" as Madame Roland called them.

The two parties confronted one another, as it was doomed that they should. It must not be thought that the Girondins were less keen on the Republic or less opposed to the Church than their adversaries. But disgusted as they were with blood shed in Paris during September by the Commune, they became by virtue of their views on this matter the sole hope of the party of order. Would that they had confined themselves to attacks on the Commune. But Madame Roland's friends joined her in abusing "this town steeped in blood and falsehood" and thus drew down on their heads the wrath of the City. Their opponents replied to them that ever since July 14th, 1789, Paris had been the principal author and defender of the Revolution; consequently those who opposed Paris were bad patriots, who wishing to appeal to the provinces were destroying the unity of the Republic, who were in short "Federalists." In the eyes of the supporters of the Mountain the dictatorship of Paris seemed the sole means of securing the national defence: it was the only manner of securing the formation of a government of Public Safety necessitated, on the one hand, by the war with foreign powers, which after a first invasion still cruelly threatened France and, on the other, by the Civil war, of which the rising in the Vendée was only the first stage. The Girondin dreamers, always boggling at the consequences of their own words, were hostile to this dictatorship of Public Safety.

It must be admitted that at this particular juncture the poor Girondins realized the position much less clearly than their opponents, who, owing to force of circumstances were brought face to face with facts. The Girondins had practically asked for war and now the whole of Europe was entering the lists against France: it would not have been possible for the country in its state of anarchy to stand up to this formidable coalition unless a strong central power acting in the interests of public safety had gripped it and held it together with an iron hand. A Girondin government, wobbling between lofty resolutions and stern action, would undoubtedly have exposed the France which they had embroiled in the struggle with Europe to the very greatest risks. Besides, events were to make this dictatorship daily more necessary; so much so that those who had been its advocates—from Danton to Robespierre—were bound to triumph, while those who had opposed it were equally bound first to be cast on one side and finally crushed. This is the history of this rivalry.

It is true that during the opening days of the Convention the Girondins seemed to have the upper hand. The fact is that between the Right, or Girondin party, and the Left, or Mountain, there stretched a Centre party—the "Marsh" as they called it later in contra-distinction to the Mountain. This centre party of three hundred who from Sept. 21st, 1792, to the 9th of Thermidor, Year II, were to remain in a continual state of wobble, were on the former date inclined to support the leaders of the Gironde, as being the defenders of the Provinces against Paris and enemies of the Commune and of its butchers, whom their electors feared and loathed. Thus the very first sitting saw the election of Pétion to the Chair of President and all the other offices placed in the hands of the Girondin staff. This roused the pride of the party and in the same degree the wrath of its opponents. It was clear from the beginning that a fierce struggle between the two was inevitable.

At that time Danton, as we shall see, full of ideas of combining against the foreigner, would have preferred to avoid this struggle, while Robespierre wanted it and Marat actually tried to bring it on. The mistake which the Girondins made was not to see that it was possible to attract to their side certain sections of the Mountain in order to ride roughshod over the less reputable sections of the party. Vergniaud was inclined to this line of action, but he was a poet lost in the wilderness of politics: and now that he enjoyed the society of a charming actress, Mademoiselle Candeille, he escaped from the influence of Madame Roland: being unwilling to embroil himself in the family quarrels, he saw further ahead than the others; a weak generous man floating down the stream without aim or object, he could never make up his mind to cut himself adrift from his friends.

These friends however shared in all Manon's aversions. We know that she hated Danton: the mastery which, as we shall see better in my next chapter, the "Titan" had secured in the Executive Council at the expense of that mediocrity, Roland, annoyed the latter and exasperated his wife. Marat and Hébert in their newspapers, "The People's Friend" and "Père Duchesne," dragged her name in the mud; they dubbed her "Queen Coco" (Lady Light o' Love): they indulged in the most coarse allusions to the attachments of this "Lucrece" to the smart young men who formed her following; they demanded that the Republic should be rid of this sham Roman citizeness. She on her part believed that these insults were due to Danton's inspiration and poured out curses on all and every one of his "villains." She incited Louvet, her pet editor, to launch a violent attack in the "Sentinel" against this leader of the Revolution then at the height of his power: while in the Convention, Buzot, her particular favourite, started a campaign against him and charged him openly with misappropriation of trust funds. The monster Danton, in whose character there was a strain of magnanimity which would ordinarily have led him to ignore Madame Roland's insinuations, found her outrageous attacks too much for his patience. He consequently, in his turn, broke bounds and from his place in the Assembly attacked not only Roland but also directly and by name his wife, charging her openly with interference in public affairs.

Then came the end. The Roland salon set out to rout the "villains" without distinction. But there was no organization in the attack. Instead of picking out the adversary, who was to be downed, they assailed all three leaders at once. The latter, although there was no love lost between them, made common cause under these violent threats, and repulsed the badly planned attacks. They then proceeded to have the Girondins expelled from the Jacobin Club with the result that henceforward they were dubbed traitors and excommunicated from the revolutionary party. It was said that Barnave, in 1791, had come under Maury's influence. Vergniaud was now called "Barnave the second."

I do not contemplate telling here the story of the eight months' struggle which occupied the sittings of the Convention from September 21st until the second of June, that disastrous day which marked the fall of the Gironde. I have told this tragic story elsewhere; to do so now would be to exceed the natural limits of this chapter.

It seemed as though the Girondins had a small majority in the Assembly. Danton for his part, notwithstanding their wild attacks on him, had no idea of 'proscribing them. In fact I will go so far as to say that he hoped at one time to be able to join forces with them, especially with the object of delaying action against the King and so saving his life. Why therefore did they take the opposite course and insist on action? Was it due to the persistent hatred of Madame Roland against the King and Queen? Perhaps, but more probably in order to prove that the edict of expulsion from the Jacobin Club was unmerited. The fact is that the Girondins, of whom everyone expected that in the proceedings against the King they should show themselves, if not his champions at least his fair and lenient judges, disappointed this expectation. Though in their hearts they were all opposed to the death sentence, in the divisions which preceded the terrible vote of January the 16th, 1793, they showed a want of unanimity. Most of them, denounced, as they had been, as traitors to the Revolution, were weak enough to hesitate to adopt a line of action, which in their opinion might have seemed to justify their enemies' aspersions. Consequently they allowed the trial to come to a conclusion. But even at that date, I am speaking of January 16th,—this conclusion might well have been different.

The Assembly were divided on the question and a number of deputies—I have noted this in speaking of Fouché —were uncertain which way to vote. Out of 721 who actually voted only 387 were in favour of the death sentence. The method of recording votes was for the roll to be called and for each deputy to vote in answer to his name. It was further settled by drawing of lots that the deputies for the Gironde should vote first. Consequently Vergniaud appeared at the tribune and to everyone's astonishment in a loud voice voted for death: sixteen other leaders of the Gironde followed his example. Now the majority in favour of the death sentence was exactly sixteen. In the list of those who voted for death we find the names of Vergniaud, Guadet, Brissot, Pétion, Louvet, Barbarroux, Léonard Buzot—in fact all Madame Roland's personal staff. When in the last resort the Girondins who were in despair raised the question of suspending the sentence, it was too late. The wobblers who always follow the crowd were by now tied hand and foot to the Mountain's chariot and the proposal for the suspension of sentence though supported by the whole Girondin party was rejected. The result as far as this party was concerned was to proclaim to all concerned their doubts and divisions: in the eyes of the "dyed-in-the-wool" republicans they had lost all the benefit of their "civic" gesture and they were henceforward doomed men. Robespierre was to be able to accuse them some time afterwards of having wished to spare "the tyrant."

Up to this point they had some advantages over their opponents. In fact they had to all appearances abused their position by managing to keep their enemies of the Mountain out of certain Committees, which were their exclusive preserves. But the King's death bringing affairs to a crisis with the adhesion of England and Spain to the coalition, the threats of war became most alarming: over and above this the Vendée was in a state of agitation and there was reason to fear that General Dumouriez commanding the army of the North was on the point of joining the insurgents. Every day made it more imperative to sacrifice everything to the policy of Public Safety: but it was the party of the Mountain who had been clamouring for three months for this to be done. The Girondins were to be the first victims of the policy.

The first sign of the latter's decline from power was the resignation of Roland. The Executive Council which had seemed after Danton's resignation to be inclined to follow Roland had become gradually estranged from him: the poor man struggled desperately to retain control but could not: Manon herself began to lose her nerve. "The sleuth-hound Marat," she wrote, never left her alone for a moment. Her cup of sorrow was now filled to the brim. She was beginning to realize in her own person how our actions here below recoil on our own heads. "The people," she wrote, "compare me to Marie Antoinette and call me the same bad names: they have published about me quite as many horrors as about her. And the market women are for treating me as they treated the Princesse de Lamballe." [2]

This unfortunate woman was gradually becoming a prey to acute neurasthenia as her strange behaviour was to show.

Ever since she had fallen in love with Buzot she considered that her life was one long sacrifice to the honour of her husband: for naturally she had now no illusions as regards the unlovableness of his character and the limitations of his intelligence. We find her still writing to Robespierre, "Roland is a rough diamond," but nevertheless she found him hard to live with. There is no doubt she remained faithful to him, "cherishing him," she wrote, "as a daughter would a father for whom she would make a sacrifice of her

[2] Friend of Marie Antoinette who was a victim of the September massacres (1749-1792).

love." But she could not keep from him the secrets of her heart. Roland began to show disapproval of the ardent devotion of all these young people and Manon thought it advisable to have a frank explanation with him. Like the Princess of Cleves of old she acknowledged to the poor man that she was madly in love with Buzot, adding that she had never been and never would be unfaithful to her duties as a wife. Roland did not take this confession in good part: Madame Roland remarks on this in her Memoirs with some surprise and in so doing shows us how naïve and unspoilt her character was: "My husband," she writes, "is extraordinarily sensitive both in his affections and his self-esteem and has not been able to bear the idea that he is no longer my absolute lord and master. His brain is full of black thoughts, his jealousy has put my nerves on edge, happiness has deserted us. He used to worship me, I sacrificed myself to him and yet we were unhappy."

In a fit of despair—and perhaps partly to punish his wife —he sent in his resignation and retired with poor Manon to a small flat in the Rue de la Harpe. Here life was one long misery. Their friends still came there to see them, though in decreasing numbers owing to the change in their fortunes and Roland's frosty manner. But she was so full of her troubles that she was no longer up to receiving them.

Besides they began to give ground. The Mountain had decided to set up a Government of Public Safety. They threatened to sweep away anyone who would not join in with them. Danton still had visions of a coalition with the Girondins: he made advances to and arranged meetings with them. But Madame Roland continued to look on this "Cyclops," as she called him, as the head assassin. Danton stipulated as the solitary condition of reconciliation, that recent events should be buried in oblivion; he was prepared on this understanding to ally himself with their party. Guadet retorted, "We will accept all your conditions except *the impunity of the assassins and their accomplices.*"

The epithet struck Danton like a blow; he grew pale and looking fixedly at him said, "Guadet, you cannot forgive; you will die."

The Girondins rejected the creation of the Revolutionary Tribunal as well as that of the Committee of Public Safety: it was in the teeth of opposition from them that these engines of the future Terror were erected. And they were not only put up without their approval but seemed to have been weapons forged for their destruction. Dumouriez was turning traitor: both the Girondins and Danton had, if truth were known, countenanced his doings but the latter in order to clear himself of a friendship, which Robespierre was ready to cast in his teeth, denounced the Girondins, describing them as accomplices of a traitor.

They denied the allegation but the excuse was there, and from that day forward they were doomed. People were writing at the beginning of 1793, "Brissot and Gensonné must have a taste of the guillotine: they must dance to its measure."

The feeling against them grew in intensity. Danton, exasperated by their obstinacy and feeling that if they were not done for he would be, allowed Desmoulins to publish his "Story of the Brissotins." In this the author, who was destined one day to regret his action most bitterly, demanded the expulsion of the Brissotins from the Convention. This was exactly what Danton and his friends wanted. "Let us get to work: when we have succeeded in saving France they will come back to enjoy the fruits of our labour." But Marat was not content: he wanted the heads of the twenty-five Girondin leaders. The Girondins, wishing to crush him, extracted from the Convention a Decree directing his prosecution before the Revolutionary Tribunal. But the Tribunal, which was entirely in Marat's pocket, acquitted him, and the crowd escorted him back to his place in the Assembly covered with laurels. All this was at the end of April.

The month of May was employed by the party bosses—Marat being their chief adviser—in making ready for the rising, which was to sweep away these new "enemies of the people."

On the evening of the thirtieth of May, the dread notes of the tocsin rang out from the belfry of the Hôtel de Ville summoning the populace to rise: they sounded again on the 31st at dawn. The Girondins, however, bravely appeared at the Assembly, and seemed by their bold front to disconcert their enemies. Danton held his peace: but Robespierre demanded that the traitors should be got rid of, wrapping up the request in his usual way in a mass of lengthy observations. Vergniaud interrupted him impatiently and called on him to finish. "Yes, I am going to finish, Vergniaud," he said, "and unfavourably to you." And he demanded the execution of 22 persons.

The Assembly were not yet in their hearts sufficiently hostile for this. Through fear of the increasing ill-feeling among the people they decided to abolish the Commission of Twelve, which owed its existence to the Girondins, and was still struggling to organize their defence.

But Marat had definitely turned nasty: that same evening he stole alone into the belfry of the Hôtel de Ville and with his own hands rang the tocsin. And at dawn on June 1st, all the forces which the Commune had organized in the metropolitan area sprang to arms under the command of the pseudo-general Henriot and with sixty guns surrounded the Tuileries.

I have described in all its details the dramatic session of the Convention, held while it was beleagured by this force. The Assembly, which shrank before no act of cowardice, would have preferred that those of its members who were singled out for attack should resign; they were told that in this way they would save their own skins. Those of the Girondins however, who were there—about ten in number—refused to resign. Barbarroux for instance, replied to the suggestion, "I have sworn to die at my post: I shall be faithful to my oath." The Convention, dumbfounded and aghast, would neither approve nor blame. Some of the deputies wished to leave the building; but they ran up against the cordon of revolutionary troops who surrounded the Legislative edifice. They fell back in a state of indignation. The Assembly then attempted to leave en masse. Hérault de Séchèlles, their president, walked at their head: when he reached the Place du Carrousel he found himself confronted by General Henriot mounted on his charger. He said to him, "What do the people desire?" The wretched general answered: "Hérault, the people have not risen in order to hear pretty speeches: they want to have the twenty-four criminals handed over to them." And turning round he gave the order, "Gunners! to your posts."

The Convention crowded back into the Assembly hall. There Couthon, who had recently become Robespierre's jackal, demanded the arrest of the "traitors." As he too, like the rest, concealed what was really a summons to the scaffold in a mass of hypocritical verbiage, a Girondin cried out, "Give Couthon his glass of blood, he is thirsty." As a matter of fact however he had given no names: it was Marat who, intoxicated with the joy of vengeance, came forward with the names of the twenty-two victims who were to be sacrificed to Moloch. He made jokes, started giving details, then stopped and after a pause went back to the beginning again. Gradually however the list of names filled up. There was not one person named in this list who had not helped to advance the Revolution in a certain degree. There was Lanjuinais, the founder of the Jacobin Club, Rabaud-Saint-Étienne who had stimulated the creation of the civil constitution, Vergniaud, Gensonné, Guadet, Isnard, who had all engineered the downfall of the Throne, Barbarroux who had harassed the King with his Marseillais, Pétion who as Mayor of Paris had supported the attack on the Throne, Brissot the great publicist of the Revolution, Buzot, one of the stalwarts of the first Assembly, and Abbé Fauchet the apostle of the Revolutionary Church.

The Assembly, terror-stricken, passed the decree for their arrest—or rather a microscopic minority of the members of the Mountain did so: for the great majority of the deputies sat head in hand, depressed and desperate and did not vote. This done, the mighty Convention received from General Henriot permission to leave: they passed out amid the plaudits, often ironical, of the populace.

Ten of the Girondins had managed to get away in time and escape from Paris: among these there were Buzot, Guadet, Isnard, Barbarroux, Pétion and Louvet. The rest with Vergniaud and Brissot at their head were arrested. The latter were put in prison, pending the initiation of judicial proceedings against them; these proceedings Danton was to endeavour to stay. But the deputies who had fled, in their determination to rouse the provinces against Paris, were destined to effect the destruction of the hostages who remained behind.

The fact was that the provinces disapproved of the coup d'etat which had been accomplished by the Commune of Paris and which had torn from their seats the flower of the representatives of the people. Thirty departments, in a line drawn from Caen to Marseilles passing through Nantes, Bordeaux, Toulon and Lyons, rose against the Government: it was a case of war for the Gironde. But here again the incompetence of the poor Girondins to organize anything became manifest. Buzot instead of betaking himself to Bordeaux, the centre of the insurrection and summoning there the deputies whom Paris had overawed, being a Norman dragged the whole band of refugees to Caen. It was impossible to direct affairs from this place: they wasted their time in discussions and denunciations, the only result of which was to despatch Charlotte Corday, Corneille's little niece, on her tragic errand which ended in the death of Marat. Morris, the American, noted on June the 25th, "They are *energetic talkers: nothing else."* Madame Roland herself wrote on July 7th that she was afraid that they were "dreamers." The Insurrection soon died down before the terrible measures of repression taken by the Committee of Public Safety, and, while it died away, the unfortunate fugitives, deserted by their friends, betook themselves to flight. My learned colleague, Gosselin Lenôtre, has recently, for the second time, sketched the tragic stages of their sad journeyings. Flying from Normandy to Brittany and from Brittany to the country near Bordeaux they were doomed to live for a year a life of misery, hunted from garrets to cellars, and from cellars to caves in the hills, stripped of everything, sometimes dying of starvation; some of them found means to write frequently and always eloquently of the causes of their failure: they really failed because they had put their faith in the power of those phrases which still soothed their sufferings.

But the insurrection in the provinces, which was severely criticized in Paris even by certain supporters of the Gironde, denounced by the orators of the Convention as well as by those of the Commune, considered, too, as a betrayal of the national interests at a time when "Pitt and Coburgh" were attacking the frontiers, it was this insurrection, I repeat, which actually led the Girondins arrested in Paris to their doom.

Four months elapsed before they were brought before the Tribunal. To make sure of their destruction documents were forged, false statements manufactured. When the statement of charges was ready they were sent on October the 14th to Fouquier-Tinville.

While they despaired of saving their own heads, they were anxious, being themselves advocates, to present an eloquent pathos in pleading their cause, and adduced such overwhelming arguments in support of it, that the whole structure of false statements built up by the prosecution seemed to be crumbling. The jury seemed overwhelmed: "Must we," wrote Hébert, "have all this ceremony to make short work of a lot of villains, who have already been found guilty by the people?"

The Convention which was by now voting in a state of panic passed a decree to the effect that the jury might, after the proceedings in court had lasted three days, declare itself sufficiently instructed in the case. This decree had no sooner been voted and forwarded to Fouquier-Tinville than the accused were refused further opportunities for speech. The unfortunate prisoners protested indignantly: at least all except Vergniaud. For some time past he had seemed to be indifferent whether he lived or died and had retired within himself, with an air of ineffable boredom. He only once dropped this when, during the reading of the sentence, he noticed that his next-door neighbour was trembling. "What is wrong with you," he said to him, "are you afraid?" "I am dying," replied the other. He had just stabbed himself and blood was pouring over his feet. The ten others, while they were being dragged off by the gendarmes, raised a last despairing cry: "Help us, friends," they cried to the crowd. "Help us, for the sake of the Republic."

Lamartine has described in dramatic fashion the events which took place the following day on the Place de la Revolution: it is a fine bit of writing but quite superfluous: there is no need here to draw on the imagination. It is sufficient to look at the spectacle of those young men (four were less than thirty and eight less than forty years of age) full of talent and virtue, in the civic sense of the word, dying victims of the most ignoble enmity, yet ever unwavering in their attachment to the principles which had inspired their lives. It is unlikely that they sang the "Girondins' Marseillaise," the song which its author, historian and poet, has handed down to us across his century. But they ascended the scaffold with a firm step. Vergniaud mounted last: he seemed thoughtful but cast an affectionate but fearless glance at the heads of his friends packed in the basket. There was one dreadful incident. Valazé, though already dead, was thrown under the knife. These are horrors which, if I may say so, dishonour crime.

Madame Roland had written in December, 1792, "Perhaps they want victims pure and unspotted to usher in the reign of justice."

She had been threatened since the end of May and could have fled; but she refused. She had her faults, but she had also fine qualities; there was no feebleness about her.

Besides, the events which had marked the latter months of her private life had left her, it might be said, without a wish to live. Buzot had fled and she scarcely hoped to see him again. With a perspicacity which was almost cruel she had been led to distrust the eventual success of all her fine poet-politicians, in whom she had formerly believed, in face of the machinations of their enemies; Roland, against whom a warrant of arrest had been issued, had fled and was now hiding in the neighbourhood of Rouen. She allowed herself to be arrested. From her prison cell she wrote her Memoirs marked by a depth of passion so intense that no romance yet written can equal them: a full and true confession of a daughter of the 18th century whom the century was to kill. On July 1st the Committee of Public Safety gave out that they had formed their conclusions "regarding the complicity of this sham Lucretia with her sham paragon of a husband in a scheme to lead astray the public mind."

This meant Death. Friends went to see her in prison: she astonished them by her charming coolness: but Riouffe—one of the Girondins who had not been proscribed—sometimes surprised beneath her wearied eyes the marks of tears which she had shed in secret. The only thing which worried her was the thought of the risks which Buzot was running, sometimes also uncertainty regarding the fate of her poor husband hiding in some obscure provincial retreat in constant fear of capture.

One day she received news of the death of Vergniaud and his friends. Henceforward her one idea was to leave this abode of sorrows. She appeared before the Tribunal, clad in white, stately, firm and calm. Riouffe wrote of her, "She exhibited the spirit of a republican in a winsome graceful person." Her enemies heaped abuse upon her in open court: she tried to speak in self-defence, but they cut her short. She was condemned to death. She replied, "You judge me fit to share the lot of the great men whom you have assassinated. I shall endeavour to mount the scaffold with the same courage that they have shown." On her return to prison, like a true pupil of Jean-Jacques Rousseau, she wrote the last line of her Memoirs, "O nature open thy bosom. . . . A just God receive me." But she added, *"At thirty-nine!"* I do not know if I am wrong, but it seems to me that in these three words written by one who might have been a heroine of ancient Rome we can read the expression of a sob which makes our picture of her even more beautiful. She was executed next day; she went to her death with astonishing coolness, "fresh, calm, smiling," wrote one who saw her pass on the tumbril. But she remained to the end the Egeria of a band of orators; when she passed before the huge plaster statue of Liberty erected in front of the guillotine, she could not, as you all know, refrain from apostrophizing it eloquently, "Ah, Liberty, what crimes are committed in thy name." She died as befitted a true Girondine, with an eloquent phrase on her lips. Some days afterwards her elderly husband Roland heard the news-vendors shouting outside the house, where he was lying hid. "Death of citizeness Roland, the accomplice of the Federalists." He at once left the house without a word, went outside the town, wandered about in the country for some hours and finally decided to kill himself. By this act the old man gave witness to the deep love which he still bore for the woman, notwithstanding the fact that she had broken his heart. Like his wife he remained the same until the end. After his death they found on his body a note with these words, "May my country learn to abhor all these evils and return to a more humane and sane way of thinking." He had always loved to lecture: he could not deny himself this sorry satisfaction even in the hour of death.

Meanwhile at the other end of France, his former companions were wandering, dirty and unshaven, aged, worn and ragged. Isnard and Louvet were the only ones who had gained a haven of safety. Guadet, Pétion, Barbarroux, Buzot and Salles were hiding like animals in holes in the earth. Both Guadet and Salles were in the end caught and guillotined at Bordeaux. One night, Barbarroux, Buzot and Pétion while wandering in the fields fancied that they had been tracked down. They pulled out their pocket pistols with the object of putting an end to themselves; Barbarroux was found later still alive, with his face half blown off and his beard caked with blood . . . a horrible sight. And this was the man whom Madame Roland called "Antinous." He was taken to Bordeaux and thrown under the knife, while still alive. Some days afterwards a shepherd found the corpses of Buzot and Pétion half eaten by dogs—Buzot the "adored" with the eagle eye, who had been Manon's last thought and Pétion the darling of Paris for two whole years, its Messiah, or Beauty Pétion, as they called him. Of the men of mark among the Girondins, three only survived: Louvet, who after Thermidor was to exact from the Robespierre "rump" vengeance for his friends' death: Isnard who was to join the royalist reaction: and Riouffe who was to become a Préfet under Napoleon, a transformation which would have startled the martyrs of the Gironde.

Martyrs; yes, they had earned the title but they had also been victims of their own illusions and imprudence. Their death excites our pity; but we know that they encompassed it with their own hands or rather with their own speech. Their eloquence inspired by extravagant ideas had aroused the storm: a tempest arose and swept them away. They regretted that blood had been shed, but it was their dangerous preaching in 1792 which opened the floodgates and let the streams of blood run.   Because, at the last, their own blood was shed as well as that of the woman whom they loved so well and because to the end there was nothing petty or mean about them, we remember with regret and nothing worse their part in the great debauch of phrase-making which against their will ended in the great debauch of death.

CHAPTER VI

JACQUES DANTON

CHAPTER VI

DANTON

On a lovely day in 1780, a young countryman who had come to seek his fortune in Paris, alighted from the stage-coach after his journey from Troyes in Champagne. He had only his spirit of adventure to sustain him. He was the son of a lawyer of Arcis-sur-Aube and grandson of peasants of Champagne so he was not well-off; his breeding showed in his hearty manner and robust constitution. He was of enormous height and even at that age very thickly built, but were it not for his eyes under his massive forehead sparkling with good-humoured intelligence and audacity, he would have been dreadfully ugly as his face was marred with youthful accidents and pitted with smallpox. He wanted to be admitted to the Bar and was on the look-out for a clerkship; so on the next day he started on a law-course, being engaged by Maître Vinot to whom he had applied successfully.

A month after, he was already popular in the little legal world which used to frequent the Café Charpentier in the Place de l'École. As he had plenty to say for himself, had a ready wit and an exuberant optimism, he soon won the love of the café proprietor's daughter who, as well as being a healthy, thrifty housewife, had quite a large dowry, which enabled him to buy the position of legal adviser to the King's

Council. Then he installed himself in a house in the parish of Saint-Sulpice, Cour du Commerce, and there also he soon became quickly popular. He had a pretty wife and soon a fat baby, an unpretentious though comfortable house, friends who dropped in to take "pot luck," several good cases which he won in the Council—all this satisfied a naturally pleasure-loving temperament full of jovial cordiality. He never passed a stall in that Cour du Commerce without shaking the hand of the shopkeeper or artisan; this was not to create a good impression but was the result of sheer good-nature. And everybody in the Court called him that "good fellow M. Danton."

No one—least of all that "good fellow" Danton himself—could have imagined even in the wildest nightmare that before five years were passed, he would have raised revolt in the streets of his Quarter, then of the city itself; that he would have toppled over a throne ten centuries old, raised armies, thus barring Europe's way, led a Royal Assembly and governed the country; and that he would finally perish on the scaffold. No one's life was more obviously turned upside down than that of the greatest of the Revolutionaries.

How and why did this loutish fellow become cne of the most riotous tribunes and most tragic heroes of this great movement? How was it that, after being one of the Revolution's most powerful leaders, he became one of its most striking victims? Some time ago I delved into his antecedents, his childhood and education. He came of very healthy stock, stolid peasants of Champagne who were peacefully prolific. His childhood he spent wandering up and down his River Aube, being a turbulent scamp but without any real viciousness. At school in the Collège des Oratoriens in Troyes he won the distinction of being classed *insignis*—remarkable. His education was that of the time, absolutely classical, with Greek and Latin, Plutarch and Tacitus. Their private reading was confined to the most full-blooded authors, such as Rabelais, Molière and, above all, Shakespeare—a fact to be noted. All this helped to produce a young barrister with a copious flow of words—altogether a smart fellow. That was all that was apparent from the outside.

What the frequenters of the Café Charpentier and the inmates of the Cour du Commerce had failed to notice was a kind of terrible hunger which unconsciously devoured him. This young man loved life passionately. "Happy the man," he said one day, "who has never cursed at Life." This form of eager, hearty sympathy was to burn with an even brighter flame under the stimulus of the tremendous events which were to enlarge his horizon. Unexpectedly he *loved* the Revolution, which swept away all sympathetic feelings, and because it brought him into contact with the whole of France, he *loved* the country with that kind of tumultuous, irresistible passion which was so apparent from 1789 onwards.

I have used the word hunger: as a matter of fact his loves were not those of a dreamer, idealist or philosopher. He was a materialist: whatever he loved he wanted to possess, guide and master. Although common to the point of vulgarity he had some unexpectedly noble traits. In his angry moods he was terrible but they never lasted more than a moment and he was equally ready with his forgiveness; he was quick to repent of his ill-humour and always ready to adopt a reconciliatory attitude. His displayed his feelings like a real Gaul, almost trumpeting them out aloud, being unable to cloak them under a mask for long, while, when need arose, he assumed far more dreadful responsibilities than he could ever have incurred. Although rather boastful on the subject of crime he really had a horror of it and wept enormous tears at the terrible misfortunes he helped to create. He braved the mightiest adversaries, found fault with the vainglorious, fought conquerors and sympathized with the conquered. Then, when he seemed at the height of his power, he became depressed, "fed up with men" as he said, because he realized he had been deceived and his heart was sick within him. Although naturally lazy he welcomed action, becoming intensely excited when confronted with danger and, if he was victorious, seemed to be able to stand aloof from his own victory. He was humane or atrocious according to circumstances. He liked leading movements then laying them aside as if to show his power. I am not sure that he had any principles at all; but he experienced every form of passion, especially that of managing men. If he had lived in the time of the Flood he would have wished to have been the Author who contrived and arrested that phenomenon. Such a man was Danton.

"Don't you see an avalanche is coming," he said in 1788 to one of the last Lord Chancellors of the old régime, Barentin by name, who wished, so it is said, to offer him a position in his cabinet. Foreseeing this avalanche he seized the opportunity to be swirled along with it. The very popularity he enjoyed in his Quarter urged him to share in the general agitation and suddenly made him the leader. That Quarter soon became the Cordeliers' district and there Jacques Danton made a kind of small Republic of which he was "king." In the confused state Paris was in, the Cordeliers, owing to Danton's leadership, became the advance guard of the city. Being both a trenchant and unruly speaker he showed himself at the tribune of the assembly of his district to be adept at arousing in men's hearts all the passions with which his own soul overflowed; in that little world he made sure that he owned the almost supernatural gift of winning over men's wills. But he won men by captivating their hearts with his cordiality; this quality of good-heartedness doubled the value of his terrific harangues and of his violence as an agitator. When once he left the tribune this ever-ready good-fellowship made him a gay companion and an obliging friend—always "that good fellow M. Danton."

From July, 1789, to June, 1790, with his strong personality he held the Cordeliers ready in battle-array. Against whom? The King? No. What I am going to say may be rather astonishing but I do not believe that Danton was ever a real republican. Like all his contemporaries his head was crammed with Latin and Greek and his eloquence sometimes showed its results; but as he believed in the necessity of a central authority one never saw him attack the throne from 1789 to 1791. As President of the district it was the Hôtel de Ville that he pounced on, threatened and held in check. Of the men installed there on July 15th he considered Bailly and La Fayette to be of very ordinary intelligence though these two were then the idols of the revolutionary bourgeois; he was annoyed that the Commune might be controlled by men whom he called "eunuchs" in his vigorous style. So masculine and virile himself he always had a horror of half-hearted, indecisive men. He led the campaign against La Fayette and Bailly and made them hold in awe his fortress of Cordeliers; he even made them withdraw by threatening them with arrest. Then he got himself sent to the Hôtel de Ville to fight them but seemed to fail in his undertaking because they were then at the height of their power; so shrugging his shoulders he returned to his briefs and to his old family life in the Cour du Commerce.

But because he had championed the people's cause against the bourgeois' leaders who were called "the eighty-niners," he was deemed to be a tribune of the Extreme Left from that time onwards. Therefore they came to look out for him each time a demonstration was prepared in favour of a further step in the Revolution. His Club of the Cordeliers was far more extreme than the Jacobin Club. Quite a staff of fanatics formed round him continually swelled by the most violent elements, from Camille Desmoulins, who had raised Paris in revolt on July 14th, to Marat; who upheld the extremest measures in his paper, the "People's Friend"; he became the centre of a band who would die for him and who would stick at nothing to help him. The Cour du Commerce, shut in by its walls like a citadel, was a hotbed of perpetual sedition in which one name alone was heard: *"Danton! Our Danton!"* while in some of the Cordelier writings occurs the phrase, "Our *dear* president."

Suddenly the King's flight became known. Up to this time Danton had never attacked him but as La Fayette was responsible for the guard arrangements of Paris it seemed to him to be a good chance of overthrowing his enemy. So the same evening the gigantic tribune rose to his feet in the Jacobin Club: "I summon M. La Fayette . . ." was the beginning of what was really a Catilinian satire. But La Fayette still controlled the Jacobins even though he was hated by the Cordeliers. He defended himself successfully and was absolved of the implication. Then Danton went back to his Cordeliers.

The district had been replaced by a section called the Théâtre-Français (the Théâtre-Français was at the Odéon at that time) and Danton still continued its king. To fight La Fayette who for some months had been suspected of anti-revolutionary tendencies and of being friendly with the King, Danton gave the countersign: *Down with Louis!* It has been said that ·Danton, really thinking a republic an impossibility, was working for the Duke of Orleans at that time. Since 1789 that wretched prince conducted a very precarious intrigue to place the younger branch of the royal family on the throne instead of the elder and employed the worst agitators he could find. But being as chicken-hearted as he was unintelligent he soon discouraged his agents and Danton thought him also an "eunuch." Moreover the Cordeliers surpassed even Danton himself by shouting for: A Republic! This word was bomb-like in its effects—and Danton loved explosives. Although the overthrow of the throne was not directly due to him he certainly forced La Fayette to declare himself its champion and so unmasked him. The section addressed a communication to the Constituent Assembly demanding that a Republic should be set up in France. The address bore Danton's signature.

Consequently he had definitely taken the plunge and when the skirmish at the Champ-de-Mars had resulted in bringing about a reactionary movement in the most advanced members of the Assembly it looked as if he would be made the scapegoat. One of the Left's deputies, Thomas Lindet, wrote that "all that had happened was that rascal Danton's fault and they could hang him quite safely and without the slightest scruple on his face alone."

As a matter of fact the whole Assembly hated him and it was decided to take proceedings against him, so he first took refuge in Arcis and then fled to England. This fact was the justification of a book called *Danton as an emigré*. Then he returned believing his persecutors to be pacified and hoping to be elected to the new Assembly. But the Royalists and Revolutionaries were at one in their agreement to exclude the troublesome fellow.

It is regrettable that he was then left high and dry, for the following reasons.

In connection with Danton I have used the word "materialist." A Champagne peasant by birth and upbringing, a bucolic strain was within two years to be his predominant characteristic. He had no principles at all; by this I mean that he was one of those men who reduce their principles down to the lowest possible number and then avow that they ought to give way before necessities resultant on circumstances. Although he was believed to be a republican he only approved of a republic so that he might create out of it a government stronger than the monarchy—which was overthrown—because a strong government was essential to save a country menaced by enemies. Though considered an extreme democrat his first move in the Convention was to reassure the property-owning class because the Revolution, if it wanted to prolong its life, must rely for support on the new property-owning class. He was supposed to be anti-clerical in feeling—if I may use such a modern word—but he showed his dislike for the destruction of Christianity because the priest—or the *man of consolation* as he said at the tribune—is a necessary factor so that people should not become demoralized at a time when an appeal was being made to the nation's spirit against a terrible danger. Then, after having toasted the abolition of frontiers in 1790, he undertook the work of national defence followed by the conquest of *natural boundaries,* because the work of national defence had taught him very thoroughly the unavoidable necessity of extending France's frontiers to the Rhine. I will return to this later. A few weeks in dealing with foreign affairs were quite sufficient to convert a hotheaded tribune into a cautious politician. That is why I said that it would not have been a bad thing if, deprived a year earlier of his rôle of a popular agitator and of the Cordelier Club, Danton had been confronted with the realities of France's plight.

It is true he was elected as deputy of the Commune's public prosecutor; but he distinctly lived in an atmosphere of distrust in the Hôtel de Ville because the General Council, who were for the most part moderate in their views, were very uncertain of him. However he endeavoured to learn wisdom in his position at the Hôtel.

But from that time onwards the situation at the frontiers worried him more than the happenings in Paris.

The war threatened to take a turn for the worst. The French armies were disgracefully beaten in the first battles in the April and May of 1792 with the Austrians, owing to the disorganization caused by the huge exodus of officers and the undisciplined state of the soldiers. Prussia was joined by Austria and with Flanders overrun by the Imperial forces it looked as if Lorraine would throw in her lot with the Allies. In support of the two Germanic Powers, Russia was calling the whole of Europe to arms and a strong national defence was necessary to combat this formidable coalition which was practically already formed. Was it feasible to contrive this defence in the critical state in which the country existed? It was said that the Tuileries were in negotiation with Austria. The Assembly, dominated by Vergniaud's men, in vain "proclaimed the Country to be in danger," for the Country could not be saved by mere words. More than any of these southern gentlemen, Danton, the easterner, whose natal province was directly menaced and soon invaded, realized that considerations of a national defence should come before everything else, but he also distinctly realized that before anything could be done, the abscess of internal trouble would first have to be lanced. He saw visions of a revolution

which would extricate France from her plight; he had visions
of "the Court's treason" and of the impotency of the Assembly and the King, each with a paralyzing hold on the
other. Indeed the abscess had to be opened and as a beginning
he overthrew the Throne.

Before the revolutionary tribunal he said simply: *"I paved
the way for the 10th of August,"* but he did more than that;
he actually brought it about. Everything was still in a state
of suspense: all the elements of a revolution were there but
they lacked cohesion. Danton realized that at the Hôtel de
Ville the Commune was the only obstacle in the way of the
overthrow of the Throne. Whoever controlled the Hôtel de
Ville could force the Tuileries to capitulate; the constitutional Commune would have to be replaced by a revolutionary Commune by means of an insurrection.

The details of this rising were prepared in secret. All instructions were issued by the Cordeliers, and when the great
evening came it was also the Cordelier Club that gave the
signal. On the evening of the 9th August the sections, having
assembled in a revolutionary manner according to the plan
laid down by Danton, elected new commissaries who were
to go to the Hôtel de Ville in the evening on the given signal
to form the new Commune. The signal for the rising was to
be the Cordeliers' bell.

I have related in detail the story of the night of the 9th
to the 10th of August in the Dantons' home where the Cordelier leaders debated anxiously. Little Lucile Desmoulins
has left us a picture of that tragic hour, gripping in its simplicity. The tribune was restless but silent. "Would the tocsin be sounded" was the question in everyone's mind. Suddenly the man got up; he was going to give the signal which
would result in the fall of a throne thousands of years old.
Then, some moments after, outside in the steamy hot night

the bell of the Cordeliers was heard at midnight calling into being the Paris of the second Revolution. At one o'clock the new Commune was installed in the Hôtel de Ville where Danton put in an appearance at dawn and, taking control of affairs, he summoned the leader of the National Guard, Mandat, who was devoted to the King, to the municipal building. This unhappy man, first dismissed from his post, was then beaten down on the very steps of the building. With all resistance thus disorganized, the bands were able to rush to the assault of the Tuileries. As is well known the King did not even wait for the Château to be captured before giving himself up to the Assembly; he was beaten before the battle had begun.

The Assembly realized that it was undoubtedly Danton who had managed and was responsible for everything. Although he was little loved and greatly feared it seemed inevitable that he should be the leader and his name was on everybody's lips. It did not seem though as if he wished to profit by his victory.

At nightfall he had returned to the Cour du Commerce and his bed, absolutely worn out. He slept till three o'clock in the morning of the 11th when his two great friends Desmoulins and Fabre d'Églantine shook him awake, shouting, "You have been made a minister." Fabre Églantine, who was nothing but a poet, introduced a comically human note into this tragedy by adding: "You must make me Lord-Keeper of the Seals." "And I must be one of your secretaries," said Camille. His adherents were already clamoring, "Give us appointments and quickly!" Thus roughly disturbed out of his sleep he murmured, "Are you quite certain that I have been made a minister?" "Of course," shouted both the youngsters very eager to handle the reins of power. Then he got up to take over his new duties, "the Seals of State," which high position he reached "like a shot out of a gun" as he described it later.

He was a good deal more than a minister. Although the King had only just been suspended from his duties the Assembly decided to appoint an Executive Council and also decreed that a predominant place in it was to be given to its principal nominee. Now by 222 votes out of an electorate of 285 it appointed Danton, first, as Minister of Justice. One hour afterwards he was installed at the Place Vendôme and Desmoulins, who was seated there in glory with him,—another rather funny incident,—wrote grandiloquently to his father: "The cause of Liberty has triumphed. Here am I in the palace of the Maupeou and of the Lamoignon." "Poor Camille," as Mirabeau called him.

Danton did not lose his sense of proportion among these trivialities; he was in office and thought less of making "Liberty triumphant" than of curbing it in the interests of national defence.

Here it is time to stop for a moment to make a careful examination of his physical characteristics. One day he declared: "Nature has given me something of *Liberty's athletic outline and rugged physiognomy!*" This was evidently not the calm, classic figure of Liberty as pictured in 1789 by the visionaries of the Revolution through their legal spectacles. No, but it was Liberty as he conceived it, all blood and muscle, flesh and bone, quivering with life, able if need arose to strike terror into the hearts of its enemies.

From that time onwards, it had, without a doubt, that "rugged physiognomy" which he had described. For a year, the jovial barrister in him disappeared; only the angry tribune with the additional characteristics of a kind of dreadful Titan remained. His hair grew straight back and crowned an always plethoric, prematurely wrinkled brow, which seemed to show the storms that raged within with its ever-present scowl. His broad, animal-like face was all scarred and out of shape; no smile, it seemed, could possibly brighten this curious countenance. Even the way he wore his clothes—and he was not untidy—gave some clue to his violent nature. There was something tempestuous about him from his knotted cravat to the lapels of his scarlet coat. This "Tartar's face," as a friend described it, was an important contributory factor in the terror which he inspired. He could say, with Mirabeau, "my ugliness is a great force." Besides was he not called "the Mirabeau of the rabble"?

Every feature proclaimed power and strength; his brow, his eyes, his breadth of shoulder, his arms which seemed made of iron, his right hand which he stretched out in violent gesture while the other "he pressed close to his left side," his "thundering, stentorian" voice which was much remarked upon in the papers of the time,—all these proclaimed his strength. He was called Cyclops, Atlas, Stentor, Titan and more often the Hercules of the Revolution; at one time or another he bore the names of all the giants in classical mythology.

This Hercules had his weak points; he was a waster and a voluptuary. Sensualist he certainly was, but he does not seem to have been so much of a roisterer as he would have liked to appear. My friend, Georges Lecomte, who has just produced Danton's love-story, has tried in vain to name his mistress, and has, like myself, come to the conclusion that there were only two women for whom he had any real affection. But how passionately he loved them, heart and soul, with every fibre of his being. His ideal seems to have been a comfortable home sweetened by the smiles of a pretty companion. When, after having literally howled with grief at the death of "his Gabrielle," he married charming Louise Gély four months later, it was, he said, "really because women were a necessity to him!" If he had wanted women, he certainly need not have married again; but it was a *wife* that he wanted. In both of these women his voluptuous temperament found full satisfaction and that caused his friends to say sometimes, "Danton is becoming less prominent." His passionate nature lost its fire when happiness of hearth and home engulfed him.

Affection was another of his weaknesses. He was artless, even if he was called "the cynic"; he believed in friendship and was always ready, hand outstretched, with his welcome. He was obliging and always anxious to prevent people from getting into trouble but his kindly actions taught him very little about men for he was not the kind to be a good psychologist. Some of his friends imperilled his safety when they had made the best use they could of him, as for instance, Fabre d'Églantine, the thief; mad Camille Desmoulins; debauched Hérault de Séchelles and twenty other friends, also unfortunately chosen. Others, like Billaud-Varenne whom he dragged up from the depths of misery and Maximilien Robespierre whom he looked upon for a long time as his "best friend,"— these were the men who by their treachery brought him to his death. Again this cynical fellow, pained and surprised at every fresh act of treason, wept bitterly. He does not seem to have hated anyone in particular,—or at least not for any length of time. Royer-Collard, who was evidently generously treated by him, was very emphatic about this trait in his benefactor. "Call him magnanimous," he said. It is indeed true that he was always ready to pardon any injury done to him, that he quickly forgot quarrels and only perished perhaps because he could never make up his mind to finish off an enemy, once he had laid him low.

Finally, there was his last and worst weakness; he appears to have been somewhat unscrupulous in money-matters. He was not really mercenary in character but, having no head for money and being generous and extravagant as well, he never had enough. I have long been doubtful whether all the accusations made against him on this point are justified, but it has been my duty to consider the revelations made by my colleague, M. Mathiez, who hated Danton as fiercely as Robespierre himself. I have carefully examined his trial from end to end and have come to one very definite conclusion: he certainly must have received money from many quarters. Like Mirabeau, he declared that, although he received payments in money, he did not sell himself. "The services of a man like myself cannot be bought," he told the Tribunal. He did not keep much of this money for his own use. His instincts were still those of the Champagne peasant stock from which he had sprung and he bought small properties one after another round about his ancestral estate. But the money spent in this way did not come to a large total; he really gave away almost as much as he received. He did not keep a tight hold on what he received and it soon dribbled away. Occasionally there was some left; the wonder is that there was ever any over for him because his friends were such sly, greedy creatures.

Those were his weaknesses and they were of a serious nature. His chief strength lay in his brain which was entirely materialistic and had all the fire of an impassioned tongue at its command. As I have shown, he was a materialist, a man who faced facts. I need not labour this point as the succeeding pages will make this abundantly clear. His speeches which were made extempore lacked method and preparation, and this at a time when elaborate, polished Ciceronian declamations were the rule rather than the exception. He could not be bothered to write and so there are scarcely ten letters in his own handwriting extant; and he had no notes to help him in the tribune. In making a speech, he started off with a rush, and, dispensing with any kind of peroration, quickly attacked his subject. His style was trivial and stately, affecting and bitter, all in turn; he was dreadfully indistinct in his utterances and vigorous almost to the point of brutality, but he put himself heart and soul into his speeches. They seemed like waves which, with here and there a foaming crest, come roaring, rolling down between rugged banks to rush, bespangled with a glorious tint of gold, through and over the muddy silt of the river-bed. Besides, his methods were direct and, amid the welter of extravagant, almost interminable, phrases—that was eloquence in those days—there was much that was worth attention. His style was daring, like himself, and pregnant with expressions startling in their crudity. His ideas were all alike and in formulating them he threw prudence to the winds.

For the moment, his whole attention, I repeat, was rivetted on the frontier. As a humanitarian, he had drunk in 1790 to the "happiness which would accrue to the whole universe" from the total abolition of frontiers but now, as a man with property in France, he had no hesitation in showing that he preferred his country to the universe. He would have liked to have seen quarrels, parties, and even the justifiable conflict of ideas given up if that would ensure France's safety from attack. *"Will all our altercations kill one Prussian?"* he cried one day. But if quarrels continued or parties and factions persisted in their disruptive policy, he was anxious to crush these elements with cruel and brutal violence, and was prepared, if need be, to plunge into the welter of blood that would be an inevitable result.

He was Minister of Justice but he paid hardly any attention to this Department. As I have shown he left everything to his cruel and dishonest "Lord-Keeper of the Seals," Fabre d'Églantine who singularly abused his position, even to the extent of forging his signature; and the affairs of the Department were allowed to fall into the hands of the latter's evil following in the Place Vendôme. In reality, he considered that he was head of this provisional government. Having prevailed upon his three colleagues in particular to leave the three departments of Foreign Affairs, War and the Navy to him, and, making his first appointments to the lower administrative posts, he busied himself with the question of national defence.

On August 19th a hostile army of 80,000 men crossed the frontier in Lorraine, took Longwy and Verdun, crossed the Argonne district, entered Champagne and threatened Paris. As early as August 11th, he foresaw that these disasters were inevitable for he knew that the French troops were undisciplined, badly led and that the army was, generally speaking, in an unsatisfactory condition. But much more than the state of the military forces, the state of the nation seemed to paralyze all the efforts made to prepare a defence.

For a long time now, the Provinces had taken no part in the Revolution; they only grudgingly accepted the fall of the Monarchy. Danton, accustomed to face difficult situations when they arose, was not slow to recognize this state of affairs. "The events of the 10th of August," he told the Council, "have divided France into two factions; one of these adheres to the monarchy, the other desires a republic. This latter group which you cannot but admit is *very much in the minority in the State,* is the only body upon which you may depend to fight." But the Provinces were almost beyond control: the Constitution of 1791 had weakened the power, now inherited by the Executive Council, of the Central Government, in order that the King might be attacked.

Danton relied upon the support of Paris for there he would be sure to find the might of revolution, a driving force still glowing with fierce energy but with an energy that created strength. In his opinion, the setting up of a dictatorship in Paris could alone provide the country with proper means of defence. But what was Paris? In his opinion, it was the terrible Commune which he had himself set up in the Hôtel de Ville, who were mad revolutionaries with horrible, dreadful passions. From that time onwards, he was himself obliged to follow a somewhat violent policy and submit to these acts of madness. He had fired Paris with hatred for the invading hordes but Paris would be threatened and lost if the enemy's advance was not checked. Thanks to the Commune, the ex-King's friends came in to some extent for the hatred that had been aroused; at the Tuileries proofs of the connivance of Marie Antoinette and her friends with Austria were found; but, even before that, the Royalists were considered as responsible for the enemy's onslaught. The volunteers whom Danton had sent off to the frontiers in thousands, were eagerly marching off, though filled with apprehension, for behind them, so they said, they had left thousands of traitors who would stab them now their backs were turned. Suddenly, the news of the fall of Verdun rang out like a thunderclap in an atmosphere which seemed already almost aflame.

The whole Council betook itself to the Assembly where Danton, as spokesman, delivered the greatest speech of his career. He declared, first of all, that the France that really mattered was Paris: the capital would assist the government in all its efforts. Commissaries were to be sent to the Provinces "to direct the popular movement, so lofty in character." He added, "We demand that any citizen who refuses to serve

in person or to take up arms, shall be punished with death.
. . . The alarm-bell that you will shortly hear is not an
alarm-signal, *but it will sound the charge against the enemies
of the nation.*" Already there was a burst of applause, and
then, with a gesture so impressive, according to an eye-witness, that not even a lapse of forty years could dim its glory,
he said: "In order to crush them, we must have *de l'audace,
encore de l'audace, toujours de l'audace,* and the victory will
be ours." One deputy wrote on this occasion that this dreadful man was ". . . beautiful."

To the listening Assembly, this policy of daring signified
that bold measures were to be taken against the Germans; on
the other hand, to the Commune it meant the massacre of
Royalists and priests in their prisons; and, for three whole
days, their blood was flowing in streams.

It will be necessary to study carefully the trial of Danton on this charge and examine the evidence, step by step.
Was Danton responsible for these massacres? Did he simply
permit them to take place or did he facilitate them? After an
examination of the facts, I have come to the opinion that,
without actually desiring or, more particularly, ordering this
butchery, he had without doubt the power to stop it; and he
allowed this outrage to be perpetrated,—which is a most
dreadful thought. He told the Council, "The Royalists must
be made to fear." He found that fear was a most useful
weapon in his armoury and, in his policy, he gave full scope
to the massacres of September. It is a ghastly blot on Danton's memory. With his usual custom of assuming responsibility, he said without any hesitation that the blame was
his. "It's I who did it," was his cry. He only put a stop to the
massacres when he saw that the Commune were trying to go

on from the Royalists to the Girondins; then he interfered and spared the latter—for a year.

Already he gave his whole attention to matters of war, and neglecting his Department of Justice, spent his time with Servan, the War Minister. "I have been just as much Adjutant-General to the Minister of War as I have been Minister of Justice." But he was more than that; soon making Servan entirely subservient to him, he urged and hustled that unfortunate Minister about, and had matters all his own way. He pressed for voluntary enlistments, he attacked the question of arms and munitions and sent agents, who were not "gentle girls," to the army to encourage generals to adopt bold measures and, if need be, frighten them if they were not bold enough.

Then he took Le Brun's place in the Ministry of Foreign Affairs and sent other agents across Europe. This was by no means the act of a madman; he was trying to negotiate the break-up of the Coalition. After Valmy, when the Prussian army, astonished by the resolute bearing of the French, turned and fled, people would have been better pleased if they had retired as far as the frontier. But what a glorious event it was and Danton was foremost in spreading far and wide the semi-legendary version of it. But he perhaps alone knew, with a few secret agents, how many millions of money the amazing retreat made by the Duke of Brunswick had cost his country. Two months later when the Girondins were determined to obtain the accounts of the Ministry from him, he shrugged his shoulders and said, "Are secret payments generally made public?" It would have been better to let the story, half true, half legendary, of the great victory of Valmy, a tale that inspired and excited the enthusiasm of his countrymen, remain current and complete.

As soon as the day after the battle the Convention met, though the parties were already face to face.

Paris had, as we know, rejected all the Girondins whom the Provinces had on the other hand elected to represent them. The capital had elected nobody that was not "pure"; first Robespierre headed the list with 338 votes only, while Danton was second with 638, which shows his election was almost unanimous. All the latter's subordinates were likewise returned. It was thought that the election of the Duke of Orleans, now known as Philippe Égalité, was due to his influence and, later, before the Tribunal, there was an attempt to heap the blame for it upon him. He had possibly other projects in mind but the delegates from the Provinces were not men who were capable of great decisions.

It is interesting to notice with what uneasiness the Convention decided to agree to the term "Republic" which was not proclaimed but simply *acceded* to as inevitable.

The Provinces, in the main, disapproved of the disorders in Paris: the Convention, composed of sober-minded bourgeois, was elected to oppose the policy of massacre. The first committee, as I have said, was entirely Girondin, but the first orator to appear in the tribune was Danton. To the astonishment of everyone, he asked that first of all, the doctrine of the inviolability of the "age-long" rights of property should be declared in order to remove any fears that might be entertained in the Provinces of a social revolution. "Let us renounce once and for all any extremist policy; let us declare that the rights of private property shall be recognized for all time."

According to his enemies this was hypocrisy, but they were wrong. He had many faults but this was not one; the materialist in him was uppermost when he made this declaration. He expected that after censuring what he called "the feverish attack of September," the whole nation would unite in re-establishing order at home, for otherwise the defence of the country would be impossible. He also meant that all sections of the community, even the conservative element, would support the policy of boldness which he had advocated.

As I have already shown, the Girondins, who, much embittered especially by his attitude to them in Madame Roland's salon, were ranged against him, rejected his offer of an alliance. This exasperated him. "Your debates are futile," he cried, *I am aware of only one thing,—the enemy. Let us beat him."* Having made the right of private property unassailable, he was anxious that there should be no meddling with religion. On November 30th, he made his famous speech about the priest as "the man of consolation" who, he said, "was regarded by the husbandman as a saint, for to him (the priest) were due those fleeting moments of happiness in childhood, youth and old age." He already dreamed of a stabilized policy: "I shall hitch on," said he, "to the chariot of the Revolution." He was anxious that no untoward events should occur. To Lameth who came in November to beg him to save Louis XVI, he said (and he knew the whole conversation would be reported), "Without being convinced that the King is blameless, I think it is just and fitting that I should extricate him from his predicament"; he would do his best, he added, to put off, adjourn or prevent the trial's taking place, because once it was set in motion and the issue raised, the Sovereign's death was certain and he would vote for it. On this point as well, he hoped to reach an agreement with Madame Roland's party, to wrest the King's head from the Robespierre group who claimed it. Louis XVI paid with his head for the Girondins' stubborn refusal to unite with Danton, he to whom they gave no other name but "the Massacre-Chief."

I have described how a struggle had commenced between the Girondins and the chiefs of the Mountain. Danton was incensed by the violent attacks of both Marat and Robespierre and even more so by that offensive and embarrassing question of the accounts. This stirred the Roland faction to oppose him actively; they thought that they had found in it their enemy's great mistake. He disputed and resisted the charges made against him, and then, taking the offensive, he strove furiously to clear his character; finally he came back to his original proposals for a union.

His only really serious preoccupation was still for national defence. If he emphasized the necessity for a united front, it was because he sought to intimidate the enemies of France. "The news of this hallowed alliance is certain to make the Austrians quake with fear; then I swear that it will mean the destruction of our enemies." He did not include the Prussians in his prediction, for he had a great respect for them.

But attacks on him continued and the dispute became daily more bitter. Anxious to appear none the less straightforward than those they were attacking, the Girondins hurried on the trial of the King which soon began entirely against his wishes. Danton was heartbroken and wanted to withdraw from the scene of action; he obtained a place on the mission which was starting first for Belgium which Dumouriez had entered at the head of his victorious troops and afterwards for the Rhine district which was being overrun by the armies of Custine.

Danton's journey through the eastern borders is a noteworthy event in French history.

In my, perhaps, rather critical examination of the Constituent Assembly, I have remarked how extraordinary it was, in my opinion, that the legislators who were its masters should be so deluded by their vision of perpetual peace that, in order to make their dream a reality, they declared the frontiers of France to be determined by age-long destiny and any aggression interdicted for all time. But fifty generations of legislators with their kings and ministers had, for a thousand years, laboured to obtain for France her "natural boundaries." They were not prompted in this policy by an arrogant, vainglorious imperialism but by the very common spectacle of their country continually in peril from foreign invasions so long as the barriers escaped her grasp: the Pyrenees, the Alps and more particularly the Rhine. The Constituent Assembly, by an action unparalleled in the history of France, appeared to abandon the famous project and, even after another invasion by the Germans, the new Assembly did not seem anxious to break altogether with the new pacifist doctrine.

It was a solemn moment when Danton arrived in the Rhine district. At the very moment when the last of France's kings was being cast upon the scaffold, Danton, the great revolutionary, now a witness of the situation as it really was, picked up the threads of the plan which the monarchy had had in mind for a thousand years. He went from Brussels to Aix-la-Chapelle, as a kind of *missus dominicus* of the new Republic. The question was whether Belgium now in Dumouriez's hand was to be united to the left bank of the Rhine now occupied by Custine's troops. He came to a very definite opinion on this point but, when he returned to Paris, all attention was rivetted on the King's trial. The Right hoped that he would vote against the Sovereign's execution but he had told Lameth quite openly what his course would be; if it was found impossible to put off the trial, he would vote for the extreme measure. When he declared himself in favour of the King's death, exclamations of surprise were heard from the benches of the Right which proved that they had counted on his generosity. Being determined to fight Europe to the death, an inevitable consequence of the victories already won, it is a question whether he did not intend to strike terror into the hearts of France's foes by this fresh outrage.

On the morrow of Louis XVI's execution he appeared in the tribune. No longer was the point in question merely the denunciation of a few private citizens; the matter of the moment was the problem of national defence which he interpreted in a much wider sense. The people of Liege, Savoy and soon of the Rhine district begged for reunion with France but the Convention was hesitant. It could not blind itself to the fact that if these reunions were effected, there would be no end to war. The pacifists in the Constituent Assembly, even those in the Convention of 1793, were not yet quite prepared to abandon their cherished dream of perpetual peace.

On January 31st, 1793, Danton went up to the tribune to make the famous speech, so long awaited. It was a magnificent dissertation, and in course of it he came to these striking conclusions: "In my opinion it is useless to have any misgivings about extending the territories of the Republic. Its frontiers are marked by Nature's hand. They lie north, east, south and west and we shall reach them all: the sea, the Rhine and the Alps. *Those must be the boundaries of our Republic and no power in heaven or earth can prevent us from attaining them.*" Perhaps a man of his stamp was lacking in 1918 or history would have been different.

He carried the Assembly with him and, resuscitating the past, he began at once to prepare the future. He left once more for the eastern frontier to arrange for the reunion with

France of those peoples who had demanded it. It was noticed that he was more violent than ever, harsher and more cruel. The death of the King for which he had certainly voted with great reluctance haunted him. During his sojourn in Belgium, he seemed restless, and more than usually ill-natured. His soul was already in anguish; but he returned to Paris on February 7th only to find his home rendered desolated in his absence by the death of his wife.

He seemed literally frantic with grief. Although the wretched woman's body had been already nearly a week in the grave he had it exhumed so that he might cover it with his kisses and have a cast made from the features. Then he gave her back to the tomb but, during the weeks that followed, he seemed stricken with a kind of madness.

The Gironde continued to attack him but it was not so much their aggressive policy as the discord which it sowed that caused him anxiety. Spain, England and the Italian States were now allied to the Germans. The war to the death (as he had described it) broke out with the whole of Europe. Danton was elated but soon his happiness was dimmed. Unable to obtain assent to his proposal of a united front against the invading armies, he hurried forward the Committee of Public Safety to lay siege, as it were, to the State. In this way he hoped that it would intimidate those opposed to his scheme and, if need be, would destroy all resistance. He therefore voted for the establishment of the Committee of Public Safety, for the Revolutionary Tribunal and, in fact, for all those measures which were to lead up to the Terror. If he took no active part in the overthrow of the Girondins, he did not interfere with Marat and his men in their destruction of them; and we have already seen in what circumstances this came to pass.

At this juncture, he was returned to power and threw himself enthusiastically into his new duties. On April 6th, he had been elected to the Committee of Public Safety with all his friends; it was really *Danton's Committee*. He saw that in his new rôle discretion would be very necessary. "To defeat the enemies of France, to re-establish order within and frame a good Constitution"—such were the heads of proposals in the programme that as spokesman of the Committee he laid before the Convention on April 10th. He did not feel bound to employ force only in "conquering the enemy"; Albert Sorel has shown how Danton was engaged in difficult negotiations with the whole of Europe which was united against his country. Neither did his plan for "the restoration of order" in France imply an undiscerning repressive policy: in even the most violent proposals there was an evident desire to avoid extreme measures. And this policy of moderation alarmed and irritated the "chaste party" now that Danton and his fanatical supporters were in possession of the New Committee; Robespierre and his party, displeased at the Tribune's omnipotence, were already secretly conducting a campaign against him. Even in the Commune which up to then had been a staunch supporter of his policy, it was said for the first time that he was "moderating." He was making every effort to save the Queen: he thought that it would be one step nearer peace with Austria if Marie Antoinette was released. He made proposals which showed Europe that he was attempting to inaugurate a sober policy. He became much softened and tried to save those Girondins who were in prison or had been forced to flee. As was evident to everyone, his over-strained mind began to relax, and this caused universal astonishment; from foreign cabinets down to the Jacobin Clubs, everyone was amazed.

The explanation for this sudden change was that this

extraordinary man had, in a new setting, regained his domestic happiness. Four months after Gabrielle's death, he married one of her young friends, Louise Gély, who was sixteen years old and a very charming, attractive girl. A man of deep emotions, he loved her passionately. She demanded that not only should the marriage be blest but that it should receive the blessing of a Catholic priest. He made no objection and, at a moment when Christian worship was on the point of being destroyed, the Abbé de Keravenant heard the marriage-vows of this singular couple. It was even rumoured that, the evening before, he heard (I dare not say his confession), but his intimate secrets,—and these must have been far from common-place. Thus, under the influence of this regained happiness and the burdens of his high position, his peaceful outlook became more and more marked.

But he was again attacked, this time from the Left. Robespierre still hesitated to break with Danton but Saint-Just goaded his master into action. It will be more convenient to describe this handsome, odious young man in the chapter dealing with Robespierre and his circle. But having mentioned him, it is important to state clearly that, implacable in his hatred, he had always loathed Danton. Even his veneration for Robespierre made him bitterly jealous of his idol's rival. It was Saint-Just who, with Maximilien's sanction, conducted the campaign against *Danton's Committee* and charged it with adopting a feeble attitude towards the federal conspirators. The political writers of the Extreme Left described it as "The Committee of the public ruin."

Blissfully happy in his married life, Danton was passing through one of those phases in which his inherent indolence proved too strong for the energy which generally marked his actions as a statesman. The Committee which he now scarcely ever attended, made but a poor defence when attacked in the

Convention and was held responsible for the reverses in the Vendée. It was decided that a new Committee should be formed, and, so thoroughly was it remodelled that, in a few hours, Danton and his friends found themselves no longer members of it. Robespierre and his party became its masters and, under them, it became the terrible Committee of Public Safety of the Great Terror which will figure so prominently in the succeeding pages.

Danton was a good actor; he affected indifference in the face of the carefully laid intrigues against him. He thought that he was still powerful and his surmise was correct. On his reappearance in the Convention, he was elected President and declared that as he no longer belonged to any Committee he would be "the goad of all." He was often seen in the tribune and his famous speech on national education dates from this time. "Next to its daily bread, education is the primary need of the people," and this was greeted with much applause. The hostility of the Robespierre group, which daily increased in intensity, caused him no anxiety; on the contrary, he loudly proclaimed his disapproval of the whole of their dreadful policy.

Soon the Terror got into its swing and the guillotine began to function daily. The Tribunal still made some pretence to a form of trial but Fouquier-Tinville was already starting his celebrated "expeditious" methods, sending people in batches to the guillotine. The whole system of the Committee of Public Safety seemed to Danton much more adapted to crush the French people than to roll back the Germans for, in the meanwhile, the war was standing still and the newly conquered frontiers were being feebly defended: France was only saved for the time by the lack of unity among the Powers. But, as an offset, the régime of horror which was beginning to disgust him, started upon its hideous way; yet it was he who had made this system possible.

Moreover, the disgrace which he had suffered in August, 1793, had affected him more deeply than was generally believed. He was anxious to attack the new Committee but on the other hand he was frightened of causing fresh quarrels. Besides, his life continued to be one long honeymoon, which made him languid and cut him off for the time from politics.

Suddenly, he disappeared and for two months the Assembly saw him no more. Leaving Paris with his family, he went to Arcis where he tried to forget everything.

In times of crisis, the adage concerning the absent who are always in the wrong rings doubly true. The Convention was, like many assemblies, variable and easily influenced. Danton had suddenly obtained the mastery over it but his presence was now very necessary and he was asked to return. He was, however, very happy to be once more in his charming house at Arcis, to row his boat on the River Aube and live, his mind at rest. In answer to the demand for his recall, he replied that he was "fed-up with men." But from afar he followed all that was taking place; the actions of the gang in power, the Queen's death and the execution of the Girondins—a calamity which caused him the bitterest grief. His nerves seemed shattered and all he said from time to time was, "Danton will awake." All the same, at the end of November, his friends, much alarmed, informed him that Robespierre was undermining his position and that, already, he was in mortal danger. He shrugged his shoulders. "You are too confident," said the messenger. "Go and tell Robespierre," he answered, "that I shall yet be in time to crush him and his following." Nevertheless, he decided to return to Paris.

He immediately took up a most determined attitude and demanded that the Terror should come to an end. "He wanted a pardon for the guilty, therefore he wished for a counter-revolution," so Robespierre said later. Actually, he was trying to influence his own party so that there might be some show of "leniency."

Camille had always been his newspaper-man. Danton urged him to found the *"Vieux Cordelier"* and now this young writer was able to defend his master's policy through the medium of its pages. "Take your pen," Danton said, "and ask for clemency." He upheld the same policy on the tribune and thereby risked his life. He spoke as if intoxicated: "It is a hundred times better to be guillotined than to be the executioner." In the Assembly, he made the same powerful speeches and scored the same successes. He did not as yet blame Robespierre; he had been on terms of warm friendship with him, and it caused him the greatest grief to enter into mortal combat with a man who, besides, to all appearances, was not fighting him. Quite the contrary, Maximilien began again to treat Danton as a friend and seeing his irritation at the excesses of demagogic rule, made use of him in his attack on Hébert's extremist group which he intended to destroy before turning his attention to his rival's party of moderates. The tribune launched attacks in the Assembly against the disguised attempts made to destroy Christianity in France, against the doctrines of equality and against the imbeciles who semed anxious to make the Revolution an object of hate and ridicule. But when Hébert had fallen before the onslaughts of Danton and Desmoulins, Robespierre suddenly turned on them. He summoned Saint-Just from the Army of the Rhine to his aid and entrusted him with their overthrow, for he felt that, alone, he was not strong enough to overwhelm them.

Danton seemed unassailable and Desmoulins was under his wing. Desmoulins will be remembered for his work on

July 14th, and Danton by August 10th. But their followers were troublesome as I have already remarked. The tribune was the leader of a very compromising gang: Fabre d'Églantine was a thief who had been mixed up in about ten fraudulent cases of contracting; Hérault de Séchelles was merely a lewd braggart and there were seven or eight of that kidney. Robespierre meant to ruin them by ruining their master: one by one he knocked away his "enemy's" supports and each time one of his friends was arrested for some unfortunate affair Danton's position was doubly weakened.

I have related in detail the clever scheme which resulted in Danton's death so I will not refer to it again.

However the rupture with Robespierre was an accomplished fact; an interview brought about by their common friends ended badly and he went out slamming the door.

Robespierre still hesitated to strike but his friends were clamoring for the Titan's head. Vadier said, "We will empty this fat stuffed turbot!" Saint-Just got ready his report composed of material given him by Robespierre who, as a friend of the Dantons, had taken notes for the past five years of the man's life and had stored up his remarks, all carefully recorded.

When Saint-Just's speech was ready it was decided to move his arrest. There is no doubt that if the Convention's sanction had been asked it would have been refused; but it was decided to confront the Convention with the deed as an accomplished fact. Danton was warned of their intentions on the day before the event and he was given the option of taking refuge abroad. He made the celebrated reply that "One cannot carry away one's country on one's shoe-sole." And besides he still believed himself too powerful to be arrested. "They will not dare," he kept on saying. "Have a look at my head; it is firm enough on my shoulders, isn't it?

And why should they wish to kill me? What good would it do? What would be the point of it?"

However on 9th Germinal at the same time Danton and Desmoulins were arrested. The Convention was badly frightened: Legendre, the butcher, one of Danton's oldest friends, tried to protest but he was timid and alone. Robespierre went up to the tribune: "We shall see during the day if the Convention knows how to break up a false idol, long since decayed." Then fixing his gaze on Legendre he added: "Anyone who wavers is guilty also." The butcher made his excuses but he was so terrified that he left shortly afterwards. The Convention, though really disgusted, was silent and passed on to the day's routine work with the eternal cowardice of assemblies.

The trial should really have a chapter all to itself. One ought to follow each minute of these fabulous sittings in which every precaution was taken to confine the defence, though the Titan burst the bonds with which they tried to enmesh him. The public prosecutor, judges, jurors, who were all devoted to Robespierre and who were determined from the very first to kill his enemy, were dumbfounded. The crowd which besieged the Palais de Justice heard "the rumbling of Danton's thunder" behind the walls. Saint-Just even had to force the Convention to pass a law for the occasion so that the president of the tribunal could brusquely declare the proceedings closed when the examinations had scarcely finished. "Closed," shouted Danton, "Closed! How can that be! They have not yet begun! We haven't read the documents! There is no evidence at all." The defence was not even heard and they were all condemned thanks to this coup of Jarnac.[1] Danton realizing Robespierre's presence behind the

[1] See page 80.

cloaking figure of Saint-Just, who had provided the bow-strings with which to strangle them, cried, "Cowardly assassin. . . . Infamous Robespierre. The scaffold will get you yet! You will follow me, Robespierre!"

In spite of all several jurors hesitated: Danton! the man of the 10th of August! They were told that "if Danton is not guillotined, Robespierre will be." They were all friends of Robespierre and their verdict sent Danton to the scaffold.

On the 16th Germinal (April 6, 1794) the tumbril came for the condemned men: never had a similar batch been despatched, for it consisted of Desmoulins, Fabre d'Églantine, Hérault de Séchelles, Danton and eleven others, all famous under different headings in the history of the Revolution. "Big game," said a gendarme to the executioner who came to the Conciergerie prison to make the sinister preparations.

Although for the previous year it had been the usual practice of the crowd to insult most vilely the condemned wretches during their journey it allowed the fantastic tumbril to pass by in silence, almost sorrowfully according to a witness. Danton was superb: "With his enormous round head held proudly erect he gazed at the stupid crowd." He encouraged poor stricken Camille, who despairingly murmured the name of Lucile, with heartening and jocular words.

The procession passed in front of Duplay's house where Maximilien was living. Once more Danton cried out, "You will follow me!" He was fuming with rage. The Abbé de Keravenant, who was disguised, followed the tumbril praying for the man about to die so sinfully proud.

When they got down from the tumbril Danton wanted to embrace his friends but the executioner's assistant separated them. "Idiot! Will you prevent our heads from kissing in the basket?" He was still the old Danton.

He went up to the scaffold the last as had Vergniaud.

"Although he was about to die he still seemed to issue the law," wrote an eye-witness.

All the same he had a sentimental moment when, face to face with the knife, he thought of his little Louise who was to be made a widow at seventeen by the guillotine. "My beloved," he sighed, "so I shall see you no more!" But taking hold of himself: "Come, come, Danton, no weakness!" and once more the tribune turned round to the executioner and said, "You will show my head to the people; it will be worth the trouble." A moment afterwards that forceful head rolled into the basket.

At the Conciergerie prison he had said, "A year ago on a very similar day I instituted the revolutionary tribunal. *I ask the pardon of God and man for that deed.*" But above all he ought at that time to have asked pardon for the September massacres. Perhaps he did so in the privacy of his soul. The great misfortune was that all those men only saw their mistakes when they no longer had the power to correct them.

Danton certainly committed many serious, unpardonable mistakes; he was responsible for all the blood that was shed before his own. But he regretted his faults: he tried to avoid fresh crimes and he even died because he had made a stand for mercy. And then, once, amid great mistakes and great crimes he had saved his threatened country. This cannot be forgotten.

So one hesitates equally to wither him or to praise him with a word.

I have not concealed any of his faults or virtues. He was a strong character with all the dangers present in this type of man whom revolutions inevitably lead astray.

In summing up, having studied him afresh I will end as I ended a dozen years ago: a saint he certainly was not: but he was a man.

CHAPTER VII

MAXIMILIEN ROBESPIERRE

CHAPTER VII

ROBESPIERRE AND HIS FRIENDS

I<small>T</small> is now time to discuss quite the most difficult man to understand in history—certainly the most difficult of the Revolution.

When questioned on Robespierre at St. Helena Napoleon shook his head and replied: "He was made a scapegoat," and thus in a few words raised a point for discussion about him.

In the course of my career I have tried to understand this peculiar man's character on three occasions: I encountered him while dealing with Fouché, I met him in conjunction with Danton, I found him in every stage of the Revolution. No other man has given me more trouble, and risking the accusation of exaggeration, I will add, has caused me such serious doubts.

Posterity overwhelmed him with disgrace: he was indeed made the "scapegoat." He succumbed after having brutally flung aside all parties and in most people's opinions having created the dreadful Reign of Terror. In order that his assailants might justify their coup de Thermidor, they, though hardly his equals, heaped ignominy upon him. And, as his party was almost entirely exterminated along with him, for several years, he had no defenders. Historians usually distrust such cases of disgrace. I have studied his trial three times with great care to find out the truth of the matter. For twenty years my colleague Mathiez has thrown into this trial a mass of documents, arguments and new facts out of which he hoped Robespierre would arise with his name cleared—I might almost say, glorified. And I have read M. Mathiez. Also have I read Henri Béraud's charming book *Mon ami Robespierre* through which runs an undercurrent of sympathy. And for the fourth time I said, "Now! what was this man really?" But I have been unable to change my opinion. Maximilien was an honest man, upright and sincere, chaste and with an unimpaired faith; nevertheless to France he was a Divine scourge. I can think of nothing more terrible than the way this sincere man, through his imperturbable, boundless vanity, shed blood without any scruples and almost callously.

Even his friends noticed this vanity which was his dominant characteristic from his youth onwards.

His childhood was a sad one and is the key to his character. Maximilien was only seven when his mother died and his father, who was a barrister at the Bar in Arras, disappeared, stricken with hypochrondriasis, leaving no trace of his whereabouts, to die of a broken heart. The four children were taken care of by their grandfather on their mother's side and brought up in rather a joyless atmosphere. Their grief which found no outlet embittered them, and at the age of seven Maximilien was hard. He had a scholarly brain and was one of those pupils over whom masters enthuse. He was one of the cleverest boys at the College des Oratoriens at Arras and even more so at Louis-le-Grand, where the Abbé de Saint-Waast nominated him for a scholarship. He completed his studies by a course of law as a clerk in company with his future adversary, Brissot, in the office of Maitre Nolleau, a solicitor, who was my great-grandfather. Though he seemed mean and serious-minded he was capable of enthusiasm. He adopted Rousseau as his teacher but treated him rather as a saint. As he knew the unfortunate, embittered old philosopher had taken refuge in Ermenonville he made a pilgrimage there at the age of nineteen and he came away from this interview a fanatic. He had been bullied and flattered by Jean-Jacques in turn and received from the latter a definition of virtue. From that day Virtue was his creed and it may be that the greatest misfortunes were the result of that interview because he became Virtue's disciple.

Because he had gained so many prizes in examinations, because he had been blessed and consecrated by Rousseau he considered that, at twenty-four, his name would live forever. He returned to Arras to become a member of the Bar and he found that his reputation had preceded him there—always rather a dangerous circumstance. But on February 27th, 1782, this one-time brilliant pupil came to grief in his first case in which he showed himself to be bumptious and mediocre and he was considered clumsy and tiresome. In the end he won some cases but without gaining the glory which he had claimed too quickly. Dissatisfied with this state of affairs he was just ripe for an aggressive political career. Politics called to him, so taking his opportunity he entered the arena.

He continued to read all the philosophers from Montesquieu down to Raynal, although Rousseau remained his favourite; he knew hundreds of pages of the latter's works by heart. Until his death he kept the *Contrat Social* on his desk, which makes one shudder. His legally trained mind led him to reduce into a digest all this extravagant literature fated to intoxicate men's minds but not to govern them.

On the day that the convocation of the States-General became known in Arras he wrote the *Avis aux habitants des campagnes;* in it he drew a picture of the ideal candidate who before everything else was to be—already!—"incorruptible" and who resembled him as one pea another. And as early as this he confided his wishes for France to "the Supreme Being." He was understood. On April 26th, 1789, he was elected the fifth deputy of the Artois bailiwick fully convinced that if the Revolution, which was beginning, went far on its way he would pretty soon play a big part in it and to begin with in the Assembly. And in this he was again to receive a great disappointment.

He was small and slender with a massive forehead sparsely covered with curly hair always carefully powdered; his blinking green eyes were terribly myopic, so he was obliged to use spectacles which he continually raised to his pale face; his nose being slightly thickened at the top and his pouting mouth gave rather a mean expression to his square face,— the face of a spiteful cat, several witnesses said. In spite of his slenderness he was well-built and restrained in his gestures. He always wore high heels, thus making the most of his height; he was affectedly elegant and always wore a close-fitting coloured coat, his legs being encased in thin stockings after the fashion of minor lawyers. His perpetually frozen, pontifical expression prejudiced people. His rather naïve vanity shone through this portentous gravity which, in a young man of thirty, was dumbfounding by reason of its constancy. Whenever he went up to the tribune in the assemblies or the clubs he always looked like some Mount Sinai from which the law came forth.

On the other hand, his eloquence neither justified nor redeemed such blatantly displayed pretensions. The Arras judges had considered him dull and the deputies were very prompt to acquiesce in this estimation of his oratory. He found it difficult to elaborate his style and had difficulty in giving his thoughts any precise expression; as he was practically incapable of speaking without notes he wrote out all his speeches with much labour in the evening of the previous day, thus tiring himself. If one reads these so elaborated speeches nowadays one soon stops, exhausted; one feels the style to be too much polished, scratched out and written over; his ideas, nearly always borrowed from philosophers, are expressed in pompous formulæ in which even his aggression was tempered with noncommittal phrases. He was very long-winded and, if he felt that he was not being followed, he excitedly tried to force home his meaning, simply displaying by gestures his impatient irritation.

His reserved expression, his spectacles, his feline appearance, his face of a "spiteful cat" and his markedly provincial accent were all the subject of jests at first. Mirabeau—temperamentally his opposite—held up the young man's characteristics to derision and was amused by his imperturbable gravity. In fact he said: "Robespierre will go far; he believes all he says," but a friend, a political writer, pointed out that the deputies complained of the "irascibility" of his energy. He certainly believed all he said and what a faith it was; in fact he was the only one who had a complete creed and who championed its infallibility. Jests and, to a greater degree, indifference, only served to irritate him and he returned in kind the contempt which the Assembly members, whom he hated, had for him. However, in spite of repeated checks, he continued in the exposition of his doctrine.

All his conclusions tended to the ideal of democracy and he considered himself to be the people's champion. The People! The word recurs a thousand times in the fifty speeches of this little precise "bourgeois." Maximilien never got a picture of the real people often warm-hearted, sometimes savage, capable of enthusiasm and cruelty, of the worst follies and most generous gestures. He did not even wish to see it. He never went down into the streets to mix with the crowds as did Desmoulins, Danton and a hundred others. He feared their contact even when they cheered him. The people he loved and vaunted was an ideal, almost conventional, people. "If you wish to calm the people speak to it about Justice and Right." This was from Rousseau. "O good, warm-hearted people. . . ." he wrote unceasingly, and to show his love for it, although he hated familiarity, he only used for a long time the second person singular when talking to the people, as the English do in their prayers to God.

Being a good pupil of Rousseau he deemed the people exemplary. For already references to "virtue" appeared in all his sentences. He evoked it so frequently in all his speeches that even the idealists in the Assembly smiled.

He carried idealism to the point of absurdity. His work was not constructed on a fundamental realism but on philosophical theories. As I have already said, he was to have only his one triumph and this occurred on the day when, defending a completely pacific policy, he contrived to get the famous principle of eternal frontiers passed even in the face of Mirabeau's opposition. Right up to the end he retained his antipathy to the Assembly, although he never gave up the hope of forcing his opinions on them through the medium of more than fifty studiously polished speeches. Both to the Left and the Right he seemed very boring and he was irritated by the fact. But because finally he appeared to be alone in the fight for democratic ideals the people declared that he was the only sincere man among them. Marat described him as "the Incorruptible," and the nickname was then so popular in the clubs that a portrait of him in the *Salon* of 1791 bore as a title only the words "The Incorruptible."

Was he a republican? It did not look like it in 1791. Because he was an unfailing supporter of the Left he was compromised in that unfortunate affair at the Champ-de-Mars, which I have already mentioned. In the brief reactionary hours which followed it he thought—as everyone else did—that he would be arrested at his house. One evening, receiving a mixed reception as he came out of the Jacobin Club, he felt a hand on his arm. A citizen was dragging him along. It turned out to be an unknown supporter, a joiner, Duplay by name, who lived in the Rue Saint-Honoré. Hoping to avoid the imminent possibility of arrest he pushed Robespierre into his house where the latter passed the night, and finally stayed altogether. His vanity always craved adulation and in Duplay's household he found a family of fanatical adorers who surrounded him with an atmosphere of flattering homage and eager attention—worthy people whose affectingly constant love was touching and rather pitiful. Only great egotists know the devotion of blind partisanship. He was fascinated; he was pleased with his barely furnished room because his tastes were simple and he was not fond of ostentation; besides it was an advantage for a political personage to be seen living in the intimacy of the household of an artisan who planed his planks in the courtyard below, while up above the politician polished his sentences. The family of Duplay, the joiner, lent colour from that time onwards to his halo of democracy, of his friendship for the people, of his sincerity.

This halo was already visible around him. He was certainly popular but inspired respect—this young man!—rather than enthusiasm. Madame Roland in July, 1791, referred to him as "this worthy man" as if he was a man of fifty; he received all applause with the expression of a graven image, only thanking the crowd in flattering, carefully thought-out phrases such as "a good, warm-hearted people."

The Assembly came to an end, and he was elected Public Prosecutor on the criminal tribunal. It was evident that such a widely recognized virtue ought to be used against crime; he accepted unenthusiastically, because it was not his real métier. He wanted to follow up his real career in the club where he continued to act the part of a high priest rather than that of a debater.

However from September, 1791, to September, 1792, he worked on the tribunal.

There he came face to face with the newcomers of the Legislative Assembly. Those young men had at first hung round him and regarded him with veneration like the rest of the world. But they were more eloquent and brilliant than he. Robespierre, although only thirty-two, treated these newcomers as hotheaded, crazy youngsters; and they soon had enough of this youthful pontiff, of the pedant who was everlastingly taking them to task, and grew restive under the rod. He considered them shallow and vain, without any steadfast aim or resolution. He foresaw the Girondins as fancy revolutionaries and as men with whom virtue would carry no weight. They used to contradict him and actually got Brissot, his friend, over to their side and—what he never forgave them—even turned the latter against him.

The serious question of war which, as we know, cropped up in the spring of 1792, fired people's minds, revealed and deepened their differences. Robespierre was in opposition to Brissot and his friends who supported the war; they got the

better of him even in the Jacobin Club, and he felt deeply
resentful about it.

After some days war was decided upon and Maximilien
received another disappointment when the King allowed the
Left to select a "patriotic" ministry for him. At Vergniaud's
house the question was raised of giving him a portfolio; but
the Girondins threw out the motion. He noted the insult and
took his revenge in biting words which threw a suspicion of
a lack of patriotism on the whole group, both deputies and
ministers even at that early date.

He grew embittered, and, what was worse, being unappre-
ciated and humiliated by Roland's friends and by Brissot,
he was also rather overwhelmed.

He was not a man of action and in those warm July and
August days of 1792 deeds were the order of the day. While
he argued over the events Danton, the man of deeds, overthrew the throne with the agreement of the disgraced followers of Roland. Then in the evening of August 10th, a provisionary government was set up. Danton and Roland found
places in it but no one in the Assembly gave a single thought
to Robespierre, who seemed to be discarded—worse—forgotten, and he the Incorruptible!

Nothing annoyed him more. Indeed, Robespierre did not
think that Danton wanted to get rid of him. If he had
wished to banish him, thus losing the strongest influence in
Paris, Maximilien might never have recovered from the blow.
But on the 5th of September Robespierre was elected first
as a deputy of Paris by 338 votes against the 136 obtained
by his rival, Pétion, the Girondist candidate. Danton was
only elected the second on the next day—by 638 votes it is
true. There is no doubt at all that the "Titan" stood aside
on the first day in order to stage a triumph for his danger-

ously disgruntled friend. All the deputies elected on the following days were friends of Danton; Robespierre therefore only entered the Assembly thanks to his friendship with the powerful tribune who was master of the situation at the time. Madame Roland wrote at this period that Robespierre was only "Danton's lay figure."

On account of this fact his position in the Assembly was rather difficult. From the very first he was eclipsed on the one hand by the brilliancy of the Girondist staff and on the other by the powerful tribune. Robespierre was all alone on the Left while the Girondists and Danton were the champions of the Right and the Centre. In addition Madame Roland's friends were there with their hatred of the Jacobin high priest and as for the Mountain of which the majority was of the Danton clique, it could not stand the arrogant airs of little Robespierre and distrusted his "vehemence." Even Marat who formerly had championed his cause came away from an interview with his *Incorruptible* with his ardour much damped. "He has the knowledge of a wise senator and the integrity of a man of property but he lacks both the outlook and courage of a statesman." This was Marat's opinion of him.

As this Assembly was so distrustful of him, was it going to be the old story of the Constituent Assembly over again? He had then to set out his plans. He would be more than ever the man with the uncompromising doctrines; he would have nothing to do with materialists or men opposed to theoretical principles. Whenever the Revolution, being exasperated by the war, gave way to unbridled passions he, as the man who had never compromised, would be there to act as its mentor, leader and master.

But till this day arrived he felt rather isolated, and he might have continued in this state if the Girondists, who reckoned on crushing him incontinently, had begun by attacking him. But as I have already mentioned the Girondists assailed first Marat and then Danton even before Robespierre. This resuscitated the Mountain faction, as I have said. From the first Marat's and Danton's friends were at the disposal of Robespierre, so he was the last of the trinity to be attacked.

Not only its intended victim but the whole Assembly were terrified by a violent attack in Louvet's famous Catilinian satire of the 29th of October starting, "Robespierre, I accuse you. . . ." The victim appeared to be discomfited by the accusation that he was—already!—aiming at a dictatorship. Deeply disturbed he demanded a week in which to prepare his defence. On November 10th he arrived with a whole book and for once he comported himself very discreetly and humbly. What a fantastic idea that he, one of the most significant of the Revolution's soldiers, should aspire to a dictatorship! The Assembly went on to discuss the day's routine work. But that same evening in the Jacobin Club he raised his head and tore his slanderers to shreds even hunting down his former friend Brissot and the "virtuous" Roland together with the "infamous" Louvet.

He had already condemned them all in his own mind. It seemed to him that he ought to take advantage of the King's trial. His attitude in it was no longer only incorruptible but also pitiless. It was said that they intended to bring in a verdict against the King. But had they the right to judge him? Legally speaking no discussion on the case was possible as the King was covered by the 1791 Constitution which had declared him inviolable. "You are not judges at all; you are, and only can be, statesmen," he said, meaning that the King's death, legally just or not, was a political necessity. More than any other leader of the Revolution this man of virtue constructed the King's scaffold. And he took advantage of the fact that the Girondists had voted for the delay in the execution to use it as a weapon to bring about their downfall.

He succeeded in this on the celebrated days of May 31st and June 2nd, 1793.

Robespierre was not a labourer. He allowed the street leaders to do the work. He had left the 10th of August to Danton; the 31st of May and 2nd of June he entrusted to Marat. On the occasion when Marat launched the troops of the Commune on the Convention, Robespierre simply meant to go up to the tribune to announce the arrests but ended his long dispassionate speech by demanding their execution. When his request was conceded he took care that they did not slip through his fingers, no one being more energetic than he in their trial. Since he was master of the situation the result appeared to be a foregone conclusion—the death of Louvet's friends.

The master! He had not yet attained this position at the time when the Girondists were only under suspicion. The Committee of Public Safety, which had been instituted to concentrate the Convention's powers into a smaller body, was only composed of Danton and his friends of the Assembly.

I have already discussed the relations existing between Robespierre and the tribune. The interests of the two men seemed to be very closely knit; on Gabrielle Danton's death Maximilien wrote a letter to the broken-hearted husband in which he declared that he was "a loving, devoted friend, . . . until death." Nevertheless he became irritated at the excessive influence exerted by the "Titan" and felt a puritan fastidiousness at this coarse man's truculent ways. Perhaps, however, he would never have dared to attack him openly if it had not been for his companion, Saint-Just, who fanned the embers of his hate into a flame.

One day in August, 1790, Robespierre, then a deputy of the Constituent Assembly, received a letter from a young gentleman, the Chevalier Saint-Just, in which the author protested that he was his devoted adherent. *"The wonders you perform make me think of you as God."* Maximilien was very susceptible to flattery and this flight of fancy pleased his vanity; he received this bigoted partisan whose fanaticism never gave way even when put to the proof. When he threw in his lot with Robespierre he was twenty-one: there is a portrait of this terrible young man by Greuze. He was handsome with pensive, almost compassionate eyes, under a brow covered with fine curls; he was well built and dressed elegantly. Behind this attractive exterior burned an awesome soul and behind that brow a still more terrible brain. This young man from Nivers was temperamentally fanatical from his birth and he idolized Robespierre to satisfy his need. He loved him with his single-minded soul, passionately, being atrociously cruel to anyone who tried to impede his god's triumphal progress. He used his clear, cold intellect teeming with clever powerful ideas and altogether much superior to Robespierre's, in the latter's service because of his love. His stronger will enabled him to be more daring and decisive. Maximilien was not easily dissuaded from a theory but in a plan of action he had the vacillancy of the politician who, although pursuing a definite end, seeks about for ways and means, sounds them, hesitates and sometimes postpones the moment. As for Saint-Just, he followed a direct course to the end, sweeping aside all obstacles,—"a straight line," as someone said of him. "Remember, Robespierre," he said, "worldly power is only won by the calm, undisturbed personality." His own indifference in the midst of those horrors is monstrously abnormal.

This handsome, awe-inspiring young man won Maximilien's affection by his boundless devotion. When he had joined Maximilien in the Convention by the 1792 elections he had almost dominated him owing to his obviously superior gifts. But, jealous as he was of all his master's friends, he particularly loathed Danton, who used to make this "dandy" a butt for his witticisms. In consequence the "dandy" urged on the crafty but cautious Robespierre to enter the field against the man of audacity, and he also undertook the leadership of the campaign, being chiefly instrumental in the overthrow of Danton's committee. The ever-prudent Robespierre obtained the election, on July 10th, 1793, of his men, with Saint-Just at their head, to the new Committee, not entering it himself till the 24th, when he was sure of finding his friends there.

There they evolved the policy of the Terror. The rebellious provinces were subjugated—eventually if not always immediately; Commissaries were sent first to the towns in actual revolt and then to those which might follow their example with power to inflict the severest penalties; the grim framework of the guillotine rose up everywhere. Even in Paris the number of executions, at first low, began to increase rapidly immediately after July, 1793, when Robespierre began to feel himself firmer on his throne. I have written many pages on this massacre of a whole nation in which blood flowed like water.

I wrote just now that Napoleon said "a scapegoat." Evidently Robespierre must have disapproved of certain outbursts of cruelty and crime. But nevertheless he provided the executioners with their weapons, for they only put into practice the theory of the Terror created by him. "Virtue is powerless without Fear." This phrase of Robespierre's is heard above the tumultuous uproar; it clears the names of the vilest executioners and stifles the cries of their victims.

By its aid he had arrived at the position he sought— adding moreover: "Terror is calamitous without Virtue."

Virtue: this is the key-word to Maximilien Robespierre's character; he was the man of virtue.

He was the living representation of it in all its forms. Scrupulously honest he was "afraid of money," as Danton mockingly said. Except for a tendency towards elegance in his dress he had simple tastes and lived frugally, drinking water only and being quite content to spend his evenings with the Duplay family. He hated the power of money of which he stood in no need and was pitiless towards those who intrigued to get it or benefited by it. Indeed there was some reason for his "fear of money," as a group of robbers were already trying to bring off a colossal "financial deal" out of the Revolution. And not only was he simple in his tastes, he was also chaste in his morals; but, in this again, his chastity made him harsh and almost disliked. It was one of his peculiarities, over which all are agreed, that he seemed to have an instinctive antipathy towards women. Although he had formerly been a visitor at the houses of Germaine de Staël, Manon Roland and Lucile Desmoulins, he hunted down these three, who knew how to manage men, with a particular virulence. And, perhaps, he was to die for having cherished the idea of sending, by his own efforts, Thérésia Tallien—after Manon and Lucile—to the scaffold. Of course he was surrounded by Duplay's daughters, Elizabeth and Éléonore, but as a matter of fact he accepted their homage as his right as a god. He had no love affair; not even a flirtation. In his relations with women, as with money, he was "the Incorruptible," and this double dislike heightened the public estimation of his character. It is a remarkable fact that the French nation, so Gallic and sometimes so volatile, often allows "men of virtue" to force themselves upon it.

In his own opinion his almost affected simplicity was a guarantee for his virtue. In the midst of all this indecent, civic disorder, he maintained the correctness of his behaviour, for this leader of roughs wore thin cloth breeches which was rather hard on those who, in an effort to please him, wore red bonnets and displayed their filthy jackets as if they had been flags. His room with its blue Persian coloured curtains and tidy desk was always kept very immaculate. But his most characteristic trait in the room was displayed by the number of reproductions of himself in drawings, paintings and sculpture—"in every form," as a visitor said.

This was because he was primarily self-centred. No one carried egotism to such a pitch and his flatterers (from the age of four he received thousands of ridiculous letters of adoration) merely increased his vanity. He finally came to the conclusion that he was divinely inspired in his mission: that he was the man chosen to establish the reign of Virtue. It was France's terrible misfortune to be under the control of one of those prophets who, like Cromwell, appear from time to time to stamp out "impiety" and "corruption." Those who think their despotism is divinely inspired consider any means justifiable and make far and away the worst tyrants.

Everything was to be sacrificed in the interests of the divine mission and friendship was the first thing jettisoned: all his childhood's friends, from Brissot to Desmoulins, were guillotined by Maximilien's orders. Madame Roland wrote: "A ferocious being who lulled his conscience with lies." She

was wrong. No: quite to the contrary, the most terrible thing
about him was his implicit obedience to his conscience which,
impregnated with his conviction of a Higher Mission, bade
him sacrifice what he called, in Rousseau's feeling phrase-
ology, "Humanity," and even veracity. He used any and
every means, such as disgraceful—and often false—slander,
with which he overthrew Hérault de Séchelles. All these
doubtful methods were necessary to get rid of Virtue's enemies—"the reprobates."

Being the embodiment of virtue he had a strict regard for
truth and obtained from this a calm serenity of manner like
"that of a priest" which struck all those who from 1790
came into contact with him. "Robespierre is a priest," was
written over and over again. He was a High Priest and very
nearly a prophet. "There was something of both Mahomet
and Cromwell in him," said Thibaudeau, but his devotees
called him a Messiah. He certainly had the impassivity of
a high priest and in his theoretical ideas, which were the
guiding factor of his life, he was immutable. As he considered himself the incarnation of Liberty, of the Republic and
of the Revolution, he thought quite frankly that all his own
personal enemies were also inimical to them.

He was naturally very dogmatic, being a high priest.

His three main doctrines were that Fear was Virtue's
mainstay, the existence of a Supreme Being and the equality
of rights, with a rider to the effect that social inequality must
be respected. Everyone at all times had to submit to this
teaching. Such men as Danton, who indulgently preached
the aim of Terrorism, or Barras and Tallien, who practised
Terrorism without Virtue, he considered as *bad citizens*.
In the same case were Chaumette, who denied the existence
of a Supreme Being, and Fouché, the disbeliever in the soul's

immortality. Under the same heading came the wretched Jacques Roux, the first "leveller," and, once more, Chaumette, who both attacked, with many others, the rights of ownership and claimed that the distribution of wealth should be proceeded with. But, if this was the case, out of so many reprobates what a few chosen ones there would be! He acknowledged this and his gloom increased in intensity. He developed the inquisitorial spirit, the fanatical puritan's disgust when confronted with this *non-conforming mass* of whom, according to Rousseau's advice, the city ought to be cleansed. In this high priest's eyes all personal enemies were heretics and schismatics.

The only "conformists" were the little group of friends who surrounded him and who were strengthened by this state of mind.

Of these, two stood out as being especially devout in this conception of Robespierre's divine guidance: Couthon and Saint-Just.

The others, amongst whom were Philippe Le Bas and little Augustin Robespierre, his brother, were only his friends: although of course, devoted to him body and soul, they were young men whose love for Robespierre was that of juniors for an adored senior. They only adopted their master's ideas because of their rather light-hearted, though sincere, devotion to him. But in the case of Saint-Just and Couthon it was their master's theories which were food and drink to them, which exalted and armed them.

Couthon, a lawyer from the Auvergne, was a singular personality. He had a pleasing, noble face and a clear, bell-like voice, but from the age of four suffered from a disease which had left his legs twisted. In consequence he was only able to get about in a small invalid chair and he used to be carried to the tribune where they put him on a high seat; it was from this sick-chair that he launched his anathemas. Even more than Robespierre he possessed an inquisitor's religious spirit which inclined him to use the power of excommunication rather than that of benediction. Although more tender-hearted than Robespierre, he had retained more than the latter Jean-Jacques' belief in a duty, but he carried this belief to the borders of fanaticism. While hating Catholicism and its priests he intended, by way of compensation, that, far from destroying Christianity, the Revolution should take it under its wing and even impose it on the unbelievers, using force if necessary. In his opinion religion was the sole mainstay of morality and he considered it was the duty of all decent men to see that virtue should triumph over immorality. His speeches were imbued with an ever-present religious atmosphere: the Revolution was to render to the State "the rights usurped by the priests"; if he destroyed statues of saints in his missions, he also composed a kind of republican Lord's Prayer. On several occasions he invoked "God's blessing on us" and the whole refrain of his speeches is "the need in sincere men, of recognizing and adoring a Supreme Being." But anyone not experiencing this need was a scoundrel to be banished and suppressed; he was even more extreme than Robespierre in demanding the execution of the nonconformists. Such a man was his master's greatly respected adviser.

Robespierre did more than listen to Saint-Just. We already know the relationship existing between these two. Couthon extolled Maximilien's religious theories; Saint-Just raised to a pitch of enthusiasm Robespierre's hopes of a dictatorship of the Public Safety founded on the triumph of Democracy, for he, alone of the whole group, pictured the complete application of the Rights of Man. Saint-Just was the outstanding adherent to the principles of Terrorism. Levasseur, a friend of his, wrote: "His enthusiasm was the result of his mathematical certainty in the correctness of his views," and he added: "He would have given his head to found his cherished Republic and a hundred thousand other heads as well as his own." Another of his colleagues said that "in every dissenter from these views he saw a criminal" and so flattered Robespierre's idea on the same subject.

The latter had more confidence in him than in anyone else. I have already said that in spite of his powerful, though limited mind, Robespierre was rather vacillating when faced with the need for action. Whenever he thought that the time was come to strike he invariably dispatched his young dev-otee on the mission; he it was who advanced to the fray and struck while Robespierre remained behind the scenes. "Robespierre's squire," someone wrote of him. It was through this medium that he killed Hébert and then Danton.

Hébert and Danton, both overthrown in a few days! With these two great blows the master's path was cleared of two "sentries" who sadly impeded his progress by their powerful positions in the winter of 1793-1794.

Hébert with his paper, *Le Père Duchesne,* held Paris in his grip. Placing himself at the head of the Cordeliers whom he had taken over from Danton he soon became the most prominent figure of the Revolutionary extremists. Amongst his followers the institution of official atheism and the land laws were spoken of as being the first step to a general distribution of wealth. The establishment in the Paris Cathedral of the religion of Reason was a momentary triumph for them as was their institution of a completely socialistic policy at the Hôtel de Ville, if I may use the word which was not then coined. Now Robespierre, with Couthon's approval, did not merely condemn these pagan debauchees but also, to use his own words, "the system which resulted in the people putting everything on an equal footing." For on this subject he was not so downright as Saint-Just and remained a good radical who would only give verbal concessions to this precocious democracy while Saint-Just might quite easily adopt nationalization at least. Already Robespierre had struck hard, in Jacques Roux' case, against communism which began to show its face.

With great glee he saw Danton launch his attack on Hébert and his followers and thanks to his assistance the latter group was defeated and incontinently hurried off to the scaffold. Then, having seized their forces for himself which the unfortunate men had prepared a long time before—the Commune, police, revolutionary army—and as he already controlled the tribunal as well, he waited no more than a month to strike at Danton. I have narrated the circumstances in which he sent him with his party of *indulgents* to the guillotine.

Thenceforth, for the three months from Germinal to Thermidor he was absolutely master of the situation.

Everything and everybody made obeisance to him: the Convention, by giving up Danton, became his slave, measures were passed without discussion and the members tried hard, so Baudot said, to look satisfied unless, as he added, they wanted to be "the object of Saint-Just's attention as in Nero's time." A man could not afford to appear even as a visionary in the Convention. A deputy, while lost in a day dream, observed Robespierre's eye fixed on him and cried: "Good Heavens! he will believe that I am daring to think of something."

In the large Committees everyone seemed to be well trained "to heel." The new mayor of Paris, Fleuriot, who was supported by the fresh Commune, was quite devoted to the Master and gave up the Hôtel de Ville to him. Robespierre controlled the tribunal through its president Dumas—Red Dumas as he was called—and also the jury, through Fouquier-Tinville, the Public Prosecutor; he had packed it with his subordinates, with Duplay, the carpenter, as foreman. The Paris army was also in his pocket, commanded as it was by the wretched Henriot—"Robespierre's donkey," as the markets nicknamed him.

The Year II was certainly that of the dictatorship of Virtue. It was the fashion in the Parisian and provincial clubs to boast of one's morals. A popular society called the Provins imprisoned—to quote only one of thousands of regulations—"anyone guilty of not having immediately regularized his mistress' position." The Committee of Public Safety closed all the brothels, and guillotined their prostitutes. Robespierre's sole topic of conversation was virtue. "It is a Salente [1] we are founding," he said to Robert Lindet.

While waiting for this day the Reign of Terror increased its orgy of cruelty. Blood was shed so liberally that the guillotine was removed from the Square of the Revolution to the Throne Gate and every evening bodies were thrown pell-mell into an enormous ditch dug out behind the Picpus building. Everyone, from the worthy Malesherbes and the venerable Bailly to Hébert's grossly debauched crew, from Madame Elizabeth to simple domestics, was considered to be "a scoundrel." For in this way was Virtue vindicated. In full tribunal Fouquier styled the Beauvais nuns "foolish virgins."

The provinces simply wallowed in blood and it threatened to become even more of a massacre. The prisons were filled

[1] A city of virtuous people in ancient Italy; it is described in Fénélon's "Télémaque" (Book X).

to overflowing: on the 7th Thermidor there were a thousand people in the Arras prisons, three thousand at Strasbourg, fifteen hundred in Toulouse and more than seven thousand in Paris. They were nearly all condemned to death on the charge of "having depraved morals."

It was necessary to ratify Virtue's triumph by some dazzling display. Couthon urged Robespierre to authorize the worship of the Supreme Being for the public; Tallien on the 11th Thermidor sneered that "this little Robespierre would like to take the Almighty's place." On the 17th Germinal, all unbelievers being guillotined, Couthon announced that the Committee was preparing a holy feast in honour of the Supreme Being. On the 21st he wrote that "all sincere men felt the need of a superior intellect which they could avow and adore." On the 18th Floreal, Robespierre also made his famous speech on "the harmonious intermingling of republican ideals with those of religion and morality," as they were conceived in the same spirit and ended by instituting the worship of the Deity. Thus it became law. The goddess of Reason was officially expelled from her altars.

The fête of the Supreme Being was organized for the 20th Prairial and, in order that Robespierre might preside at it, he was elected to the Presidential chair on the 16th.

This fantastic ceremony has been painted at least ten times. Maximilien officiated as high priest dressed in his famous sky-blue coat and wearing his enormous tricolour plume which—at last! made the little man look taller. On the platform, which seemed to convey some hint of a throne, he gave vent to a long rhapsody and a hundred thousand voices sang Gossec's hymn to the Supreme Being. Then climbing an artificial mountain on which incense was burning he was enveloped in its wreaths. This all helped to make him esteem himself higher than God's vicar: a veritable **god** himself.

But when he walked in front of the people to return to the Tuileries at the head of the deputies he heard some disgruntled murmurs and even some insults arising from their ranks. He had exceeded his limits; an undercurrent of revolt was abroad.

For such a man as he there was only one conclusion to be drawn from this incident: another display of blood-letting was necessary. On the 22nd Prairial, Couthon proposed in the Assembly to pass an act with the object of wiping out his master's remaining enemies. By a part of this act the tribunal, already so unencumbered by ordinary rules of justice, was to be allowed to try and condemn suspects in a body and not one by one as had been the case up to this time. By another part of the act the tribunal was to be allowed to arrest deputies on the order of the committees alone without the Convention's sanction. Hundreds of the deputies felt the chill of the guillotine-knife at their throats in anticipation, and strongly protested. "If this act is passed," cried Ruamps, "I might just as well shoot myself; I demand an adjournment." But Robespierre rose to his feet; he wanted his act passed, he wanted his heads. He only said three biting words and the act became law. The next day the Assembly meant to recover their immunity by reconsidering their opinion on the last part of the bill. Maximilien dared to come and demand his heads over which the struggle waxed so desperate. "Some plotters," he said, "are trying to entice away the Mountain with the object of recruiting leaders from them for a party." "Their names!" shouted the wretched men. He ought to have named them, because, in the state of terror in which the Assembly was, it would have handed them over to him. However, he made the mistake of allowing their apprehensions to be aroused without reassuring the mass. He said coldly: "I will name them when it becomes necessary." They bowed to his will. The article was re-enacted as law but everyone felt himself to be marked, tried and condemned—which was an exceedingly dangerous state of affairs.

Seven frightful weeks followed that meeting on 23rd Prairial. In forty-nine days the tribunal, armed with its new powers, sent 1,376 victims to the scaffold. Sometimes sixty persons were executed a day. Terror reigned in a dismayed Paris. About a hundred deputies no longer came to the Assembly, but, like Fouché, were in hiding and changing their lodgings each night. However, public opinion veered round quietly. The war was being carried on successfully; the enemy was being beaten and, besides, the civil war had been almost suppressed. What on earth was the good of all this butchering when the nation's safety seemed assured? And so the suspected deputies, feeling that public opinion was with them, tried to bring about the tyrant's downfall in the interests of their own safety.

Even so soon as the day after Danton's fall he began to miss the desire to please him in the Committee which he had been wont to expect. I have described elsewhere the violent scenes which occurred when his colleagues came to grips with Robespierre. Moreover, that harsh, unaccommodating man, Carnot, who was in the throes of "organizing victory," lost all patience with the superior airs affected by Robespierre and Saint-Just. Billaud-Varenne and sometimes Collot d'Herbois indulged in furious outbursts under the dictatorship of this high priest, who prescribed laws in the name of a Supreme Being whom they had rejected. Robespierre thought to end this state of affairs by crushing them;

but Saint-Just was with the armies, so on the 10th Messidor he recalled him so that he might arm himself for the fray. But the suspected deputies, Tallien, Fréron and, above all, Fouché, sought out the others. "You are lost. Either he must die or we shall."

At the beginning of Thermidor all the strands of the conspiracy were knotted. The Mountain, influenced by those who wished to avenge Hébert and Danton or to escape a similar fate, mobilized its forces against Robespierre. But it needed the support of the Centre who distrusted Collot, Tallien, Fréron, Billaud and Fouché even more than Robespierre, and who hesitated to lend its aid to these survivors of Hébert's régime at the expense of the latter. Robespierre had at least led the Marsh for a year and, as he had tried to instill some authority into the Revolution, he had leant on the terrified bourgeois for support. For fifteen days, the Assembly, outwardly so calm and morose, shook with a fierce fever.

On the 8th Thermidor, Maximilien, quite unconscious of what was in store for him and completely immersed in his ambitious dream of absolute power, went up to the tribune. For some days in the recess he had polished up a long speech or a form of manifesto in which he disclaimed all responsibility for violent measures, denounced the bloodthirsty ideas of some of the Terror's missionaries and begged the Assembly "finally to wipe out authority and to establish the power of justice and liberty on their ruins." This speech placed the onus of the crimes on the shoulders of his colleagues of the Mountain and was intended to reassure the Centre from whom indeed came the applause—so much so that Couthon was able to pass a measure ordering it to be printed, which implied more than mere approbation.

But the Mountain, although stiff with terror for a mo-

ment, regained control of itself. Robespierre had said that
the Committees ought to be "purified." But the men on the
Committees did not wish to be "purified." For a week Fouché,
who felt, more than anyone else, the proximity of the guillotine, went from one to the other effecting reconciliations between Robespierre's lately separated enemies, approaching
Hébert's and Danton's old friends and fanning exasperation
and fears to a pitch of frenzy. But he did not dare show himself in the Assembly and he needed someone to give the
signal for rebellion.

The man to fill the breach was Cambon, who had been
accurately described by Robespierre as a dishonest, luckless
financier; he hurled the signal of freedom at the tribune.
"Before being dishonoured I will appeal to France. A single
man paralyzes the Convention's will; that man is Robespierre!"

A shudder ran through the Convention and, the word having been given, there was a concerted rush to the tribune.
From there, with his revolutionary prestige of a "straight
line" behind him, Billaud-Varenne declaimed his philippic:
"It is time to take off masks. I would prefer my body to
serve as a throne for a tyrant than that by its silence it
should become an accomplice in his crimes!" Then accusations poured in from all quarters.

Robespierre did not yet realize his danger; he remained
quite unmoved, thinking that he would regain control of
the Assembly. Paris having said that a list of suspects had
already been drawn up, many anguished looks were thrown
at the dictator: "Give us the names of those you accuse!"
they cried. He refused. Accusations again rained down and
the decree ordering the printing of his speech was revoked—
the first stroke of the alarm-signal.

But he could still rely on the Club—*his* Club, which had

never yet failed him since 1792. He had just hounded Fouché out of it, so lately elected its president. When on the 8th he appeared there in the evening he was carried in triumph and attacked Collot d'Hérbois and Billaud-Varenne by name this time; as they were present they had to withdraw under a hail of insults. "À la guillotine," was hurled at their backs. This merely decided these men, who were not lamblike at the best of times, to adopt decisive measures.

But the Duplay family were amazed at his cold optimism when Robespierre once more returned serenely to their house with his mind at ease.

As always, he relied on Saint-Just. He suggested that his master's enemies should be subjected to a deadly attack and he got ready for the next day a vituperative report against the Committee's "criminals" and "bribe-takers," which took him the whole night to write.

The dawn proclaimed the beginning of a hot day; at midday the temperature in the open was 104° and the sky was lowering with dark clouds.

At nine o'clock the members of the Committee, once more reunited after a dreadful night, learned that the tribune was already occupied by Saint-Just. The Assembly was seething with excitement. During the night negotiations had taken place between the parties; the Mountain had tried to win over some deputies of the Centre to help them against the tyrant.

Robespierre was there; he had put on the sky-blue coat so prominent on the 20th Prairial, his hair was always well powdered and his face as expressionless as ever. It was noticeable that he sat down in the first row of benches in the Centre and not in the Mountain. Perhaps this was only to be able to follow the speeches the better but it was also possible to read into this act an indication that a new policy was going to be established on the ruins of the old Mountain. Not knowing how to decide between these terrorist enemies, the Centre was non-committal.

One most unfortunate circumstance for Robespierre and his friends was that Collot presided; another (unknown to everybody) was that Tallien, whose activities had been curtailed by fear for some days, had received that very morning a letter from Thérésia. In this letter, his wife, who was imprisoned and condemned to death in the batch of victims of the 10th, laid the responsibility of her inevitable end on her husband's cowardice. Tallien adored this woman and his love changed a poltroon into Robespierre's first daring assailant. Scarcely had Saint-Just begun his arraignment in his biting voice when Tallien actually climbed up to the tribune and pushed him off it, crying: "I demand that the veil be torn away!" The Mountain applauded delightedly. "Quite right! Quite right!" they shouted. Billaud was the third to ascend to the tribune, from which coign of vantage he denounced the meeting of the evening before in the Jacobin Club, where "the intention had been to cut the Convention's throat." "The Convention will perish if it is weak now."

Robespierre's friends tried to speak but could not make themselves heard above the din and Collot drowned their voices by loudly ringing the presidential bell. The Centre was motionless; on the nearly empty benches of the Right a few very pale men thought of their guillotined Girondin friends; but all these men of the Left—attacked as well as attackers—were their assassins.

At last Robespierre dashed up to the tribune but a terrific clamour which he had not expected to be so great drove him back to his seat on the bench in the Centre. "Down with the tyrant." Tallien again took possession of the tribune. In a bellowing voice, he spoke of "this new Cromwell" and, drawing a knife from under his coat, cried, "I have here a dagger to stab him to the heart if the Convention hasn't the courage to decree his accusation." This melodramatic gesture produced the intended effect. Straightaway the Convention decreed the arrest of Henriot and Dumas, thus raising their hands first against Robespierre's devoted general and judge.

Barère and Vadier went up in turn to the tribune but they were windbags who might perhaps save Robespierre by attacking him more temperately and, therefore, badly. Tallien returned to the charge, once more reviled the tyrant and overwhelmed him with abuse.

The latter rose once more. He was no longer calm; on the contrary, his face was purple with rage, his eyes starting out of his head; he walked unsteadily towards the tribune and spoke, threatening the Left with outstretched arm. As Collot was already worn out, Thuriot had taken his place in the presidential chair. But he was only another enemy who with fresh vigour continually rang the bell so that not one word of "the accused" could be heard. It was like the sound of a tocsin. An obscure deputy, Louchet by name, yelled above the din, "Let's have his arrest!" With a supreme effort Maximilien made himself heard and requested Thuriot, who kept on ringing: "For the last time, will you let me speak, *you president of assassins?*" There was an outburst from the Left; the tyrant insulted the Assembly. "Put his arrest to the vote," they yelled.

Then came a pathetic moment when he turned for help to the Centre who up till now had been silent. "Honest men! virtuous men! I appeal to you! Give me the permission to speak which these assassins deny me."

Assassins! However, who had been the very first to demand the Girondins' blood and had eagerly urged that they should be executed? Who had sent Danton to the scaffold? And who had been responsible for proposing and forcing on the Convention that act in Prairial which resulted in 1,400 heads falling in six weeks? Who—if not Robespierre? The "honest men" of the Centre knew perfectly well that at that very moment the tumbrils were rumbling along to the guillotine carrying innocent victims who had been persecuted by Fouquier and condemned by Dumas, both Robespierre's tools. Suddenly, led by Sieyès and Cambacérès, the Centre rose to its feet under Robespierre's despairing eyes to vote in favour of the decree of arrest which was then passed.

The arrest of Saint-Just, Couthon and Robespierre was decreed. At once young Augustin Robespierre demanded the honour of being included in his brother's proscription, and warm-hearted, devoted Le Bas also wished to join him. Quarter of an hour afterwards all five of them were sent off to the prisons.

I cannot describe the events that followed in detail, as that day's work would require a chapter all to itself.

It was indeed far from being crowned by the Assembly's vote. The Commune, distinctly in favour of Robespierre, rebelled and called Paris to rise in revolt; they seized the five victims from their prison and took them to the Hôtel de Ville.

Maximilien raised several difficulties. I have mentioned that, although he was a fluent, eloquent speaker, he was not a man of action, fearing all responsibility and being frightened by anything that had the appearance of illegality. The very idea of encouraging and, worse still, leading an uprising in Paris caused him great anxiety. The Mayor, Fleuriot, literally had to drag him to his feet to conduct him to the municipal building, where he rejoined his friends. The Place de Grève was filled with a huge crowd, which at heart was rather irresolute and overcome by the heat of that stormy evening. However, the Commune's call to arms was bruited abroad throughout Paris; it was read at the crossroads by horsemen and the crowd before the illuminated Hôtel de Ville swelled in numbers.

Although at first startled by this resistance, the Convention, thanks to Robespierre's vacillation, had time to recover their equilibrium. It had appointed commissaries who were to go to the Hôtel de Ville to draw attention to the decree which had been passed against the rebels. Barras, who was placed in command of the public forces, would support them with his loyal troops.

At 10 o'clock in the evening they were still arguing in the Hôtel de Ville where Robespierre refused to sign the appeal to the people. The jurist and lawyer in him had the upper hand; he was the man of whom Danton said: "He is afraid." The remark he made on the appeal to arms was, "In whose name?" So for two hours a tumultuous struggle raged within him. Suddenly a torrential downpour came on, dispersing the crowd so that Barras' troops were easily able to approach the Hôtel. Robespierre had just decided to sign the appeal as the troops entered the house. We still have the paper on which, in his tiny scrubby handwriting, he wrote the first two letters of his name, *Ro* . . . There is a large drop of blood on the paper. The door opened and the Convention's gendarmes entered.

Whether Robespierre, letting go of his pen, then seized his pistol and tried to blow out his brains, or whether one of the gendarmes laid him low, is not at all clear. One of them, Meda, boasted of having fired the shot and founded a fine career on this statement.

Whatever may have actually happened, Robespierre was wounded, his jaw being broken. When he was arrested his cheek was in ribbons. Le Bas did not fail him; he was dead when they picked him up. Augustin was arrested all bruised and broken as he had fallen while trying to escape by climbing along the cornice outside. Couthon was thrown down a staircase, at the bottom of which the unhappy cripple was discovered the next morning with his limbs broken. Saint-Just allowed himself to be captured; his behaviour was coldly correct and his clothes were not even ruffled.

Robespierre spent some frightful hours in the hall of the Committee of Public Safety, where they had carried him. His wounds had been dressed with the idea of preparing him for the guillotine, but he lay on a table, bleeding, dirty and unconscious. Perhaps he only pretended to be unconscious through pride, so that he might not seem to hear the foul insults heaped on him by the cowards.

At four o'clock they were dragged to the scaffold as outlaws. With them went thirty-five "accomplices" and first amongst them President Dumas.

The crowd hurled insults at the tumbrils at the top of their voices and the whole of Paris went mad with joy; with Robespierre dead they foresaw the end of the Reign of Terror.

The unhappy men only got to the scaffold at seven o'clock. Couthon, absolutely livid, and poor, broken Augustin were carried on to it like corpses. Saint-Just went straight to the machine, outwardly unmoved, silent and expressionless. Maximilien was twentieth on the list. "The executioner," according to a witness, "having tied him to the plank and before making him bend down, roughly tore away the dressings on his wound. He uttered a roar, like a dying tiger, which was heard in every corner of the square." So said an inimical eyewitness.

The people were shown three heads: those of Robespierre, Dumas and Henriot—"the dictator," his "judge" and his "soldier"—as if to say: "Good riddance!"

Then from a hundred thousand throats arose a huge shout of joy: "Long live Liberty."

Nevertheless, the very fact that the Terror seemed to be over with his death was a condemnation on him.

He was laid low by men who were far worse than himself as we shall see when we discuss the wretched Thermidorians. Robespierre was an upright, honest, terribly sincere man; he was rather narrow-minded and not very strong-willed. As a speaker he was too rhetorical and he was more a talker than a man of action. The one thing that sustained, guided and perverted him was his inordinate pride. Owing to the flattery he received his pride convinced him that he was a man of exceptional truth and virtue and that, consequently, it was his duty to see that others obeyed these virtues. To enforce this view he considered any means justified—whether deceit, murder or massacre. He was certainly not wicked, cruel, or bloody-minded. This makes his case all the more diabolical. He killed people in Virtue's name.

How right the Catholic Church is to hold spiritual pride as the most damnable sin of all.

CHAPTER VIII

CHARLES FRANÇOIS DUMOURIEZ

CHAPTER VIII

SOLDIERS OF THE REVOLUTION

THE last three chapters necessarily dealt rather pitilessly with the scaffold, which after the 9th Thermidor, was not finally abandoned until it was deluged with blood. When reviewing this dismal narrative, one experiences the feeling, so exactly expressed on the 9th of Thermidor by the universal cry: "Enough of this bloodshed!" We look for more attractive sides of the Revolution. Is it possible for the history of a warm-hearted, kindly nation to have contained three such horrible years of misery?

But the reader knows that this history has a happier side. From 1792 to 1795 France showed heroic qualities and, during the Reign of Terror, the Revolution gained posterity's esteem by reaping on France's extended frontiers what one may call, in imitation of the style of that period, the laurels of glory.

It is not only to escape from the stifling atmosphere of the terrorist policy (which would be rather difficult) that I have hastened to introduce another chapter of this tragic story. No. It is really because the impression obtained of the Revolution—even in its most bloody crises—would be false. Any judgment passed on it would be unjust if the story of those dreadful years is separated any longer from that of the

period which dominates and explains—though not excuses—
nearly everything: the War.

"Virtue was found in the camps," wrote a contemporary—
but not that "virtue" in whose name Robespierre guillotined
thousands of victims including Vergniaud, Brissot and Danton. This was the virtue that inspired young soldiers with the
faith, ardour and love with which to protect, from 1792,
their threatened capital. By saving the country they saved
her honour and if we follow them to the frontiers we shall
form a better conception of the great crisis.

"The Republic is nothing more than a great town closely
besieged. . . ." So cried the Convention on August 22nd,
1793, when it organized the national defence forces against
the whole of Europe. From the time that Vergniaud proclaimed the country to be in danger—July 11th, 1792,—
France was truly in a state of siege. The country's upheavals
are explained to some extent by this danger which remained
a constant menace from the summer of 1792 to the summer
of 1794.

This danger was all the greater inasmuch as, since 1789,
the army had been in a state of dissolution caused by the
fiery breath of new ideas which found a positive breeding
place in it.

The army of the last of the Bourbons consisted of a mediocre type of man—being pitifully recruited. The recruits, who
were obtained by force—by blows on the head, or seized during drunken bouts by ingenious recruiting sergeants—tended
to produce an army of scoundrels. In fact one of its former
officers, the deputy Dubois-Crancé, described it without contradiction as "an army of brigands."

Above this military rabble the officers were, for many reasons and apart from several brilliant exceptions, a poor lot

and had no influence on the troops. They were gentlemen for whom their parents had bought a company, even a regiment, so young that some of them were qualified for the nickname of "bibbed-Colonels." Separated from their men by an immeasurable distance they were shown to be not up to their work by the eighteenth century wars—brave, certainly, "but usually incompetent."

The non-commissioned officers—or lower officers, as they were called—alone held the army together. Such sergeants as La Tulipe, La Fleur, La Grenade, Risque-Tout and Sans-Souci, who were both jovial and fearsome, made the soldiers laugh and quake in turn. It was thanks to these men that this army of scamps, so badly commanded, was fairly strong.

The zeal with which these non-commissioned officers carried out their work for two hundred years was partly the result of a faint hope of achieving officers' rank. For "officers of fortune" had not been rare since the seventeenth century.

But the unfortunate edict imposed on Marshal Ségur, the War Minister, in 1781 by the privileged class not only closed the door of promotion to even the lowest officers' ranks to every plebeian, but even denied the higher ranks to young officers who could not show the four quarterings of nobility. A Bernadotte, sergeant in 1789, could no longer aspire to a lieutenant's stripe; a Bonaparte—of rather dubious noble birth—could certainly not get any higher than a captain's rank. Some of these non-commissioned officers, Oudinot, Masséna, Murat, had just left the army discouraged by these conditions; the others remained but murmured.

Officers of the minor nobility, Davout, Berthier—even a Bonaparte—were no less disposed than they to welcome any event which would open a career to them.

Therefore the army was ready to welcome the Revolution. From the very first the soldiers were tempted with the idea of revolt; the mutiny of the French Guards had even preceded and facilitated the taking of the Bastille; during the fateful evening of 9th October at Versailles the soldiers who were supposed to be guarding the approaches to the Château laughingly showed the rebels that they had not loaded their muskets with bullets.

Kellermann later wrote that "the Revolution owed its existence to the army of the line" meaning that the army could perhaps have smothered it, but, not wishing to do so, helped it when need arose.

The nobly born officers were not reactionary.. My friend Pierre de Vassière has published, under the title of *Lettres d'aristocrates,* hundreds of letters which lay bare these dissolute officers' souls and they certainly do not show a prætorian spirit. They disclose a bitter sadness caused largely by a justifiable feeling of impotence.

Besides they knew they were always liable to be dismissed. La Tour du Pin, the first National Convention Minister for War, had proved himself a brave soldier in the Seven Years' War. He was an honest man, courteous, sensitive and weak, one of those men we all know and who, when in power, always meant to put out fires with a sponge. His efforts to put the sponge on the French Guards' exploits on July 14th are common knowledge, and after August 12th, 1789, Noailles, who was hardly unsuspected of holding slight reactionary views, had timidly drawn attention to the lack of discipline which developed everywhere as the outcome of similar causes. The Assembly had replied by appointing a Committee entrusted with the task of making "a new army" —another reason for the former to dissolve.

After October, 1789, the sedition had continued to work

and until June, 1790, had broken out here and there, disclosing its presence by mutinies which always went unpunished.

I have mentioned elsewhere the long series of outbursts which finally ended in the great rising of the Lunéville and Nancy garrisons—a real insurrection which was only prevented by the energy of Lieutenant-General de Bouillé from turning into civil war.

At each outburst the Assembly would declare itself, "sorrowfully surprised." It groaned but took no action and the officers who tried to resist were deemed to have acted wrongfully. On June 4th Robespierre attributed the "justifiable" irritation of the troops to the counter-revolutionary attitude of their officers. "They want to force them into a collective resignation," wrote a deputy of the Left.

As a matter of fact many did resign and emigrated, and soon the number of resignations increased. In the Assembly they spoke already of allowing the men to elect their officers, thus following the method that prevailed everywhere. The military committee again suppressed the measure as being "subversive of all discipline." But on February 28th, 1790, the highest ranks were declared open to all candidates. This proclamation spread a kind of intoxication amongst the ranks of the non-commissioned officers and, as the soldiers' pay had been augmented by thirty-two farthings a day, the army, already favourably disposed to the Revolution, conceived a violent love for it.

But the army was melting away. These resignations caused gaps which, to tell the truth, were largely in the higher ranks and, with reference to the various arms, in the cavalry and infantry; the more specialized arms, the artillery and engineers, retained three-quarters of their staff of officers as they were less popular with the nobility. But even in the ranks of the soldiers other gaps appeared. Breaking their contracts, many rascals ran off to Paris in quest of adventures. Thus during 1791 the Royal Army was reduced to the moderate total of sixty thousand men.

This situation was very serious, because in the midst of all this, Europe was obviously preparing to make war on France.

Europe has always kept an eye on France. For three centuries that great country, so rich in men and glorious deeds, had aroused, together with Europe's admiration, also her envy by her solidarity, her strength and her prosperity. From Charles V to William of Orange they had envied and feared her whom this same William called the "insolent nation." Often victorious over the most formidable coalitions, for three centuries she had waged war on those who had meant to break her, and, though sometimes beaten, she had, thanks to her marvellous power of recuperation, soon taken a dazzling revenge. Because her kings, helped, sometimes deputized for, by ministers of genius, had appeared to lead the nation's happy endeavour towards its reconstruction and on from strength to strength Europe had concluded that the monarchy was France's sole support.

So there was great rejoicing in ministries and among princes at the French King's downfall because in that they saw the country definitely weakened. When the Assembly on May 22nd, 1790, had solemnly proclaimed that it repudiated war, renounced the idea of conquest and considered as "eternal" frontiers which every French statesman since Richelieu had deemed incomplete and merely provisionary, Europe, as Albert Sorel has so well shown, concluded that she had deduced correctly and that it was high time to think of the spoils.

Europe had just, if I may say so, tried her teeth on

Poland. It might be possible for France to be another Poland only a thousand times more rich, and if she could not be shared out she might be partly devoured. The nation, being distressed by anarchy—as Poland had been in 1770—could not possibly defend herself. Her army was in an obvious state of dissolution and the Assembly had repudiated its kings who were considered by all the foreign courts to be its essential support.

As we know Europe was wrong. On the contrary the French nation, founded in the fifth century and perhaps before, had been the strength of its kings—and of its ministers who, originating from every class of the nation, were only the representatives of a whole people's wishes to the King.

I have attempted, in a large volume called *History of the Nation*, to trace the course through three centuries of this unique collaboration of a faithful nation with admirable advisors.

Even more than their leaders the French people had always been set on the great idea of the completeness of France. In any case, nationalistic as she was to the marrow, as we say nowadays, she was ready to leap up before these menacing foreigners whom she had so often beaten. The fact that, included in their plan for breaking her, was a design to stifle her newly-recovered liberty, now the nation's idol, was added fuel to the country's wrath.

The threats became more definite in January, 1791, when the Constituent Assembly at last aroused itself out of its pacific attitude. They spoke of restoring ruined fortresses and remodelling the army. The two Germanic powers, Prussia and Austria, until then hostile, approached each other, urged on by Russia; Sweden offered to swell their forces, while the King of Sardinia mobilized and the Spanish and Italian Bourbons assumed an hostile attitude. England kept an eye on the situation—wanting her revenge over the American War. An army was needed; for the sixty thousand men of the Royal Army would be quite insufficient to bar the advance of the three hundred thousand men whom the Germans alone could throw on the eastern frontier. It would be necessary to find at least two hundred thousand men. But the Constituent Assembly, always afraid of annoying the people, rejected the idea of conscription. By the decrees of the 11th and 13th of June the Assembly appealed for volunteers who were to be paid well,—15 pence a day,—elect their own officers and only serve for one campaign. They reckoned on two hundred thousand men, but it was too much to hope for; they got one hundred thousand, which was good. But what was also good was the spirit revealed in this first outburst of patriotism on the part of the nation.

In a book which had its momentary recognition, Camille Rousset set out to destroy what he called the *volunteer legend*. It was commonly said that they had saved France from invasion! Rousset proved conclusively (and all I have read since has tended to confirm the view) that, without the old Royal Army strengthened by years of service and firmly held together by its solid non-commissioned officers, the volunteers would have done nothing. On the contrary it seems that these newly-joined, excitable soldiers, who were ill-trained in the use of their arms and ill-disciplined, had, from 1792 to 1793, thrown the army into confusion and nearly jeopardized the situation. As we shall see, this was perfectly true *of the 1792 volunteers*, who were inspired with revolutionary zeal, one might almost say delirium. But this was not true of the *1791 volunteers*.

The majority came less from the lower classes than from the bourgeois who were sustained at that time by the enthusiasms of 1789. They—unlike the later volunteers of 1792—had no need of inflammatory appeals, rolling drums and tricoloured platforms. The flame was within them; lawyers' clerks and students, doctors and well-to-do farmers, shop assistants, office employees, they all enrolled because their hardly-won liberty was, it was said, menaced by despots. Their enthusiasm knew no bounds but they did not shout about it: they were all in agreement with one of their number, young Belot, when he wrote to his father, a small bourgeois of La Brie: "You have sent me to fight against the privileged classes. 'Go,' you said, 'fly to the frontiers and frighten the cowardly tyrants who dare to threaten them! Depart and if fearing for a life which is only useful inasmuch as it is useful to society, you shrink from it, then stay; and learn from me how one should serve one's country!' Oh! I will fight for it; remain where you are and always believe that your son will never disgrace you! Soon with his companions on the frontier he will prove to the enemy that they cannot strike so easily as they think a people who wish to be free!" One may be inclined to smile at the grandiloquent style; it is not the one we used in 1914 when departing for the frontier, but it is only the exhilarating mode of expression of a stirring call to action. Thirty years after, having become marshal, then duke, one of the Lorraine volunteers of 1791, the ex-drummer boy, Victor, used the same style to express himself: "O sublime enthusiasm of 1791, would that I could sing your praises worthily! O most magnificent sight that ever any nation has shown to the world! O days of patriotism and glory! warm both us and our children with your unquenchable fires."

So great was the enthusiasm that a hundred young girls slipped in amongst these hundred thousand young men. The two young girls, Fernig, alone became famous as Dumouriez's aides-de-camp a year later. A commissioner of the convention wrote of them—quite wrongly as it happens: "The monarchy has had only one Joan of Arc and we have two." There has never been more than one.

Nearly all these 1791 volunteers were sensible, and were intelligent men as well as patriotic, because, when called on, rather rashly, to elect their officers they often made choices amply justified by future events; indeed they elected as battalion-commanders such men as Bessières, Championnet, Davout, Jourdan, Laharpe, Lecourbe, Marceau, Moreau, Oudinot, Victor, Suchet, who in three years were to become Generals of the Republic; six of them became Marshals of the Empire.

When they presented themselves so full of ardour, the military leaders augured well of the future from the first. "These are Frenchmen and a good type of them," wrote one of them, and judging them more zealous than disciplined, they expected them to make, nay, they would make, good soldiers of them.

But there was so much trouble in assembling, in organizing and in training these hundred thousand young men that, although the crisis became more acute, they were certainly not yet capable of standing firm before the enemy. Even the Royal Army, which was inexperienced in real warfare owing to the fact that there had been peace for thirty years on the Continent, still suffered from the ravages in their ranks caused by the first Revolutionary wars.

So one cannot be surprised at the singularly shameful events which, at the end of April, 1792, were the prelude to the war. But this war, which lasted twenty-three years from Valmy to Waterloo, became a hero's war.

When, on April 28th, 1792, Rochambeau's army on the

march to the Belgian frontier—then an Austrian possession
—came up with the Imperial army, a most unexpected stam-
pede took place without a single shot having been fired
except at a general who, having thrown himself across the
path of the panic-stricken men was, with several officers,
struck down by the fleeing soldiers. The astounded Austrians
said jeeringly the next day that the French motto was "Con-
quer or run." Moreover they were so surprised by this
peculiar victory that, fearing a trap, they fortunately stayed
several leagues from the frontier leaving Lille and Valenciennes, in which our terrified men swarmed, unattacked.

Naturally Paris ascribed its cause to treason and the
startled Assembly appealed to the country; there was a new
call for volunteers and forty-two new battalions were raised.
And all over France the country was proclaimed to be "in
danger."

There was a new agitation, more feverish, perhaps more
disorderly, most certainly more noisy.

At the first sound of the tocsin appeared a volunteer sortie
"from under each cobblestone," as the expression of the
period has it. Then Brunswick produced his manifesto. When
it was known in Paris that the Commander-in-Chief of the
Prussian army had threatened to exterminate anyone who
had had any part in the Revolution the resulting indignation
caused the enrollments to increase rapidly. Gouvion-Saint-
Cyr later wrote that the manifesto was the means of increasing the defence force by a hundred battalions. Madame de
Marolles, "an aristocrat," wrote: "Volunteers sprang up
from under the ground." Great platforms were built, draped
with the tricolour: a plank laid across drums served as a
table, and behind it, a municipal official received the enrollments. All the young men rushed to join with a kind of wild
"abandon."

The throne having foundered on August 10th, Danton, as I have already said, had added his fuel to the furnace. The enrollments redoubled and the crowd besieged the Parisian platforms. In the meantime in the smallest villages the little French peasants enrolled. Their letters are still extant, touchingly enthusiastic; some would return one day to the villages without any rank, sometimes lacking a limb, but proud of having served their country; others, after the campaigns of Liberty, would be the soldiers of the Empire, little volunteers turned into Napoleon's grumblers; all would keep that wonderful vision of their own heroism and moving departure. They tore themselves from the arms of weeping parents. "The rolling of the drums," later wrote one of them, the future general Lejeune, "the cheerful shouts of the crowd, which ran up to see us pass, singing the Marseillaise, drove away all sadness at parting and we would all shout joyfully, 'Now we are soldiers!' "

They were bad soldiers. Excitement does not make a warrior. They ought to have kept them in the rear. Unfortunately the Assembly, by its decree of July 22nd, had them thrown into the armies where they sowed disorder. The generals protested against this rapid influx of brave lads. A section of them, drawn from the madly enthusiastic lower classes, was only a troublesome and undisciplined element in the army which, at that time, they were trying to remodel. Dumouriez and Kellermann had been appointed army commanders, one at Sedan, the other at Metz. The first was a clever old stager and very wide awake; he was untroubled by scruples and not more hampered by tradition; he was intelligent, venturesome and a rugged character. Kellermann was a rough Alsatian who was promoted under the old régime for good service. He remained plebeian and so was in a position to understand the new France but a born soldier who worshipped discipline—an army's chief strength. Both considered that the former Royal Army needed to be taken in hand and that, moreover, the volunteers, even those of 1791, constituted a dangerous supply unless, on the other hand, they were to become very precious. That was the great merit of these two men; the success they achieved was only the result of a proper estimation of the situation. They were not discouraged but gave credit to the new spirit; the old Royal Army was a stiff dough which only required re-kneading and the volunteers would play the part of the yeast. By their slowness to act, the Austrians and Prussians gave these leaders the time to create order out of disorder and, in the camps, to turn the fugitives of Mons and Tournai into the future soldiers of Valmy and Jemappes. Before long they would be tested in the furnace of battle. They were called "blue pottery" by the enemy on account of their new blue uniform. On its first appearance under fire the pottery had seemed to crack; but "the type is good" as one of the chiefs said. It would harden in the fire and in a little time that blue pottery would become like bronze. We also have known after 1915 the strength of another lot of blue pottery.

"They must be calmed and purged under the enemy's fire," wrote the Minister Servan. "Excitement must be replaced by patriotism and fanaticism by discipline." Kellermann had replied more practically: "The only way to get an army is to fill up the line troops with volunteers and to incorporate old battalions with the new. Otherwise France is lost." It was this idea of amalgamation that the two commanders conceived and practised before it became the subject of a famous Conventional decree eight months later.

Thus in six weeks these generals managed to reconstruct some sort of an army after a fashion. From the moment discipline was established their enthusiasm could only have happy results. "Enthusiasm makes up for everything," Gouvion-Saint-Cyr said later. No: it did not make up for everything, but, as exploited by Dumouriez in clever speeches, enthusiasm made easy the acceptance of the roughest work and of the severest disciplinary measures. Soon the stage was reached of persuading these young men that courage consisted, while waiting for great deeds, in strict obedience. "With courage most things can be brought to a successful conclusion," wrote the volunteer Fricasse on this subject; and he only echoed his comrades' thoughts.

One can hardly imagine the mysticism which was their support. "God of Justice take under Thy protection a warmhearted nation which only fights for equality." This was also Fricasse. Davout, eventually to become a battalion commander, said later, "They went into action shouting, 'Long live the Nation! Long live Liberty and Equality!'" Marmont was to say that "We lived in an invigorating atmosphere. At fifty-five I felt I had the strength and impetuosity of a boy." Kléber, who also commanded a battalion, was enthusiastic over the Alsatian volunteers: "It is quite impossible to depict their joy and eagerness when the order to march came. Not one of them thought for a moment of leaving the colours. Why, even the sick demanded to be allowed to go with the battalion. . . . If French generals only knew how to make the most of the worth and courage of these brave soldiers, to what heights of glory and success could not the Republic aspire?" Dumouriez at Sedan and Kellermann at Metz had not waited for the appeal, as is known: in a few weeks, although still with many gaps and much disorder, the troops were already immensely superior to those who in the spring had given way.

It was just in time. The Austrian army was advancing on Lille which was to put up an heroic resistance and the great Prussian army had been launched on its campaign. It had crossed the frontier at Redange with an army corps composed of emigrés and consequently marched with an unheard of presumption not expecting to meet any obstacles. As later, in August, 1914, the German officers, declaring themselves the instruments of the All-Highest against the Revolution—"the old German God," does not date from yesterday—made a rendezvous in these days of August, 1792, for the first day of September at the Palais-Royal, then the centre of Parisian pleasure-seekers.

So great was the prestige of Frederick the Great's army that it sufficed to make Longwy capitulate, and then, on September 2nd, Verdun owing to the lack of foresight in 1791. That was a serious matter. The Germans again forced the Argonne approaches and the road to Paris seemed open.

In the meantime Kellermann came up from Metz with his army by Bar-le-Duc and on September 8th he joined Dumouriez behind the Argonne at Sainte-Menehould. Then the army, thus reinforced, advanced on to the Valmy plateau. The Prussians reckoned on but an ephemeral resistance and their presumption, when faced by the slightest check, brought about an extraordinary demoralization. A severe cannonading and some cavalry charges were sufficient to stop them. But it is certain that the resolute attitude of the infantry massed round the mill, the fiery, impassioned yells to which this enthusiastic mass gave tongue and the bold front displayed by all the troops impressed Brunswick's army. Goethe never forgot the bearing of those "little black men."

But this does not entirely explain the Prussians' discouragement and headlong flight to the frontiers. I have mentioned elsewhere what were the real causes. But this weird, almost miraculous, victory—ever the French miracle—sufficed to create a victorious spirit in the new army. From that moment their enthusiasm was transformed into confidence and, in spite of reverses following greater victories; that confidence of victory never afterwards forsook those men. From the Valmy Mill through twenty years it carried them through Vienna, Berlin, Cadiz and Moscow.

The 1792-1793 campaigns were made up of successes and reverses. Dumouriez conquered Belgium by the single battle of Jemmapes, while Custine, commanding the Rhine army, planted the tricolour in Mayence and even in Frankfort. The French had now taken the offensive which only served to raise the soldiers' spirits still more by strengthening their first great enthusiasm with a justifiable pride. Then they were checked by the German counter-offensives in Belgium and the banks of the Rhine. Neerwinden was followed by the loss of nearly all Belgium to France; Frankfort was recaptured by Brunswick and the Rhine army retreated quickly towards Landau while isolated Mayence was besieged by the Prussians.

Certainly these reverses were the result of Dumouriez's irresolution followed up by his startling treachery and also of the new confidence the discomfitted Germans received by the entry into the coalition of England, Holland, Spain and all the Italian States. But the French commanders' reports also told of damage done by the influx of the new 1792 volunteers who were sent into battle without material or moral preparation; they gave way at the first hint of panic, broke their ranks to pillage and were disobedient. Beurnonville, commander of the Moselle army, wrote that "he lost a third of his men through desertion of volunteers." At Neerwinden they had thrown the firmest troops into disorder by their flight. When attacked by Brunswick on the Rhine they had "run like hares" as he himself said. And so the French forces had been beaten back to the old frontiers. After a three months' siege, heroically sustained, Mayence capitulated on July 28th although Kléber's soldiers came out with honours of war. French Flanders was invaded, Condé and Valenciennes were occupied by Austrians on the 15th and 27th of July, and, right up to October, 1793, the French colours were without a victory. The situation was exceedingly serious with the whole of Europe in arms against France. Civil war was rife in the country requiring still more troops while the French armies in the northeast, on the Meuse, in the Alps, in the Pyrenees, in fact everywhere were inferior in numbers to the enemy corps.

But, at this moment, the government of Public Safety was instituted in Paris and from April onwards Danton took the reins.

The Convention had not waited for that moment to face the situation. On February 24th it had passed a decree which, by making another appeal for volunteer recruits, was the first step towards requisitionary methods. The decree at least stated the principle.

The principle was forced on the country by the fall of Mayence, of Condée, of Valenciennes, the reverses of La Vendée and the provincial risings. Never had the country been in such a dangerous position even in 1792.

On August 21st a report, of which Carnot was the author, was brought forward by Barère. It contained among others these arresting sentences: "The Republic is only a huge beleaguered city and France must be nothing but a vast camp with Paris as its arsenal. . . ." And Barère read a proposal which was then and there enacted as a decree amid indescribable enthusiasm. One must not smile at this decree of August 24th in spite of its emphatic style because it was to beget victories.

"From this moment till the time when every enemy has been swept out of Republican territory every French person is permanently conscripted for service under arms." This was the principle. Article VIII stated: "The levy will be general, unmarried citizens or childless widowers of from eighteen to twenty-five years will join the colours first. They will present themselves without delay at the chief town of their district where they will practice the use of arms every day until the time of their departure." Article XI: "The battalion, which will be organized in each district, will be assembled under a flag bearing the following inscription: *The French nation in arms against tyrants.*"

It is difficult to imagine the effect produced by the decree in the country in which the fear of a new invasion gave rise to the deep emotion of 1792. Carnot, who had been elected to the Committee of Public Safety, had said that it was necessary "to organize the popular fury for military use." The "fury" was so great that the Convention, which had decided, in order to obtain the four hundred thousand men they needed, to call up the second batch after the first, were able to dispense with it. The first class, augmented by numerous volunteers, provided four hundred and twenty-five thousand men who, right up to the Directory's last years, supplied the French armies. Barère cried that this was "Liberty's requisition." All those conscripts did not consider themselves so free but not one would have dared to evade it. "These men, sent in their thousands to the frontiers, went trembling to make Europe tremble," later cried Rivarol. It was a pithy saying—worthy of Tacitus—but the remark of a malevolent Royalist; many also went trembling with righteous anger.

A measure had just rendered this new levy efficacious. The Revolutionary government, learning from experience, certainly did not intend the 1792 volunteers—more particularly the conscripts of 1793—to fall into their erroneous notion of discipline. All the new soldiers—both volunteers and conscripts—were to be absorbed into the old line army. This was the *amalgamation* formerly advocated by Kellermann. Monsieur Chassin has told us, with Camille Rousset, the method which they used and how two volunteer battalions mixed with a veteran's battalion formed the *demi-brigades* which became so famous.

This system is indicative of the practice of the time. According to M. Chassin, "A member of the National Convention, a commissioner of recruiting, went to each army; two volunteer battalions and one of the line were paraded. He declared their amalgamation and made them take an oath to uphold Liberty, Equality, and the Republic as one and indivisible or to die at their posts. He appointed the most deserving of the three battalion-commanders to lead his country's defenders to victory. The new commander dismissed his men all of whom embraced each other saying 'Long live the Republic!'" Then they reformed and the demi-brigade moved off before the commissioner singing the Marseillaise. That is how they moulded the army which, when it had been tested in the fire, was before long to make the whole of Europe tremble. The small peasants and artisans were now the Republic's soldiers—carefully distributed among the brigades, reinforced by seasoned troops and launched on the path to glory.

Discipline and a tactical sense had been infused into the army. "The way to win battles is to attack," as Richelieu said one day to his marshals. Dubois-Crancé, one of the

Convention's military advisers, said the same. He was all for "massed warfare" and bayonet charges. They were to concentrate the greatest possible number of troops on the selected points of attack, then to attack the wavering enemy at the point of the bayonet, "which form of fighting," he added, "is suitable to the Nation's character and impetuosity."

The generals should be soaked in these tactics and there would be no excuse for defeat. One of the Committee's members stated that "it is time it is realized that a heavy responsibility rests on those for whom there will be no excuse for even an involuntary mistake. The Convention desires the general to obey the orders of the Committee of Public Safety. Each man's head will depend on their execution." It was not an empty threat; Dumouriez, Custine, Beauharnais, Houchard, Flers and ten others were to pay by their dismissals and deaths not only for their troops' reverses but also for the most imaginary wrongs or even the ill-will of army commissaries. Even Kellermann and Hoche were dismissed and arrested on the eve of Thermidor. These terrible commissaries were now attached to the armies virtually to oversee their commissariat and their work but in reality to control the army commanders. These commissaries were "armed with thunderbolts," and "mightier than a king," as a member of the Convention said. Some of them abused their powers and sometimes tried—a civilian weakness—to force generals to accept their plans, inflicting their ill-humour—and even baser feelings—on them. However, the majority collaborated actively and cordially with the military leaders, displaying, when need arose, like Carnot, Saint-Just, Merlin de Thionville, Levasseur de la Sarthe, a courageous example by exposing themselves to fire. Again some denounced sagaciously not only the real incapacity of some old generals but also defects in discipline and a faulty system of supply. In fact they were links between the Convention and the armed forces and far from betraying the commanders sometimes saved them from falling foul of the Convention.

Rather naïvely, the Convention, unable to escape the lure of figures, had expected "the fourteen armies" suddenly to appear, fourteen armies of an hundred thousand men! It was a childish idea. It was Carnot's cool brain that materialized Barère's high-sounding words. He despatched to the frontiers and to the interior in unequal lots the seven hundred and fifty-two thousand men whom the Convention had at its disposal after the 1793 conscription.

Carnot! He was the Revolutionary whose thoroughly practical genius was responsible for the efficiency of the country's defence.

Albert Sorel called him "the great Staff Major-General of the Revolution"; he was just the man to organize all that bubbling, grandiloquent enthusiasm which, without him, might have made the most horrible mistakes.

In 1793 at the age of forty he was only a captain. He was a native of Burgundy with strongly marked characteristics and powerful brain, and, although sprung from a race of lawyers, was attracted by the mathematical sciences while still quite young. So he had entered the specialized arms and turned his attention to the difficult science of engineering. When elected a deputy of the Legislative Assembly he sat in the Left; for, as an ardent patriot, he wanted to combine his desire for a powerful France with the aims of the Revolution. He then specialized in military affairs and so, when he entered the Committee of Public Safety, matters relating to the war were entrusted to him.

He was tenacious to the point of obstinacy and not very

easy-going, being rather dictatorial; unable to bear contradiction, he was hard, sometimes even harsh and always stiff; he seldom smiled and never flattered. As he distrusted politicians he did not follow Danton, he contradicted Robespierre and later on annoyed Barras. He was upright, disinterested and scrupulously honest. A story can be cited of twenty-four thousand francs which had been entrusted to him when he had been sent on a mission to the armies. The fact, that on his return he had brought back half the sum, was so unusual that they did not know under what heading to place this unprecedented return. He was coldly courageous, leading the troops at Wattignies where this civilian-sapper headed the attacking infantry right up to the cannon's mouth. He also showed his courage when he dispersed by threats and blows the soldiers who pillaged or got drunk near him. Although he seemed cold and reserved he was really an enthusiast. "All greatness must have a soul capable of deep feeling," he said later. And those words embody exactly the spirit of his own enterprise. He has been unjustly criticized on the score of not being able to judge men although he had a methodical, balanced brain. How can this be so when one looks at the men he placed in command of armies when he was first on the Committee and then in the Directory. "A man with a wonderful divination of patriotism," later said Michelet in his efflorescent style, "he *sensed* heroes. He discovered first Jourdan, then Hoche and then Bonaparte."

By temperament a hard worker, duty was only another urge to work. "No one worked harder in Committee; the others often arrived late because they had been to a play or to the Jacobin Clubs. Carnot, morning and evening, arrived the first and was the last to go." So wrote one of his adversaries.

Bent over his reports and his indexes he really scarcely ever left them except just to "bolt down a crust." Thanks to his many solid harmonious qualities he was the dispassionate organizer of victory amidst this effervescent nation, because in spite of his deep passions he had methodically arranged his work. All the grandiloquence and bloodshed of the Terror which in the opinion of some would have sufficed to produce victory, would far more likely have ended in disaster on the frontier if all that red-hot lava had not been led by this stern engineer through channels to positions of usefulness. In conjunction with many others I repeat that it was Carnot working in his green portfolio-lined office who saved France from invasion and preserved the Revolution from disgrace.

However a lot remained to be done in the way of arming, feeding, clothing and paying the famous "fourteen armies." Money for war purposes was found by taking the confiscated wealth of emigrés. Powder factories were set up: Carnot was not one of those who said, "The Republic does not want chemists." He commandeered all of them, his future colleagues in the Institute: Fourcroy, Monge, Berthollet, Guyton de Morveau. The latter created the art of balloon-flying which so astonished the armies at Fleurus. Chappe was enrolled with the rank of lieutenant-telegraphist. The sciences made great advance profiting by war experiences. As for clothes and food, the commissariat departments provided it partly from Marseilles, where Barras and Fréron suddenly required twenty thousand well-to-do citizens to hand over their shirts, and partly from Lyons where Fouché by taking all the boots condemned the whole population to walk in clogs. Then for food for the soldiers, "an eighth of the Republic's pigs" were requisitioned.

The wholesale sacrifice of the old generals—from Custine

to Houchard—often cruelly unjust, allowed the young men, who had just become known and who were more conversant with the new methods of manœuvring and fighting, to be placed in command of armies; I shall say more of these men; Hoche, Kléber and many other brigadiers all imbued with the same remarkable spirit as that General Chancel who replied to the complaints of his starving soldiers: "You must learn that it is only by suffering and hardships that the honour of fighting and dying for one's country can be won."

He knew the type he was speaking to. After two years of war the Revolutionary army was in a transitory stage, its soldiers becoming experienced warriors, but still keeping alive their rather mystic faith, which they had as citizens.

They had several rude shocks from Neerwinden to Frankfort but their faith in the ultimate triumph of their soldiers of Liberty over the tyrants never wavered. Since the amalgamation of the old soldiers of the Royal Army and the soldiers of Liberty, the latter had had their lessons and experiences like good soldiers. This faith was confirmed by the fact that defeat was turning into victory. Jourdan's victory at Wattignies on October 16th, 1790, drove the Austrians out of the Low Countries; Hoche after a series of successes in Alsace defeated the Imperial forces at Wissembourg on December 26th; and after six months of successful fighting on all frontiers, Jourdan, taking the offensive in the north, on June 26th, 1794, was victorious at Fleurus—the greatest success of the Revolutionary armies. Brussels was entered a fortnight after. The war of conquest went on. The French armies were to threaten the marches of Spain and Italy, to penetrate Holland, to reconquer the left bank of the Rhine, raising the tricolour flag on Cologne Cathedral where it flew for some time on this occasion, to reach the natural boundary from Basle to the sea, to force Spain and Prussia to abandon the coalition, to cross the Rhine on two occasions, once with Jourdan and once with Hoche, and threaten the Danube, to cross the Alps with Bonaparte's army and, after eighteen months' memorable fighting, to force Austria to surrender—thus re-establishing peace on the Continent by an unprecedented series of victories.

The volunteers of Liberty had become the conquerors of Europe.

At the head of affairs, all the staff helped to lead them to victory: this staff had itself risen out of the great rush to the colours in 1791 and 1792 and was composed of young men of whom the majority were sprung from the people. The former non-commissioned officers, Marceau, Masséna, Augereau, Murat, Moncey, Soult, Lefebvre, Oudinot, Bernadotte—formerly sergeant Belle-Jambe—whose careers had received a check from the Ségur edict, had their revenge. They became brigadier and divisional commanders, but the young volunteers, who had started their careers in jackets and after three years already wore the general's braided coat, had won quicker promotion. Lazare Hoche, a Versailles greengrocer's nephew, was the most characteristic figure of that shining constellation. He had enlisted at twenty-one and in three years had climbed up through eight ranks to the position of Commander-in-Chief of the Mozelle army. Paul Louis Courier relates that he went to visit the young general. His chief of staff was older than himself, being twenty-five, and all around him he saw generals and brigadiers the eldest of whom was not twenty-six. "He seemed as young as the Revolution and as strong as the people," said a visitor. "His glance was as proud and searching as an eagle's; let us hope, my friends, that he will lead us as the French ought to be led." And as a matter of fact he did. Knowing how liable they were to pillage and become undisciplined, he said to them: "If such patriots as you are, have discipline, anything undertaken is bound to succeed. You fight for Liberty and, in spreading its doctrines, you ought to love it. . . . Be orderly and disciplined and the country will be saved." Firm and dignified when need arose he spoke to them as a young elder brother who, knowing their faults and virtues, only corrected them by appealing to their better nature. The herculean Kléber, who, with his rough joviality and strongly impetuous Alsatian courage, bubbled over with patriotism, seemed a patriarch by reason of his forty years. Mention must be made of the chivalrous Marceau and Masséna of Nice whose fiery glance already betokened genius, while the dreamy Breton, Moreau, with his amazing coolness and unshakable courage —a general at thirty-one—was also to command an army. "With young commanders taking their share in the dangers of war, discipline is easily bearable," wrote Lavalette. Indeed discipline was maintained chiefly by the rise of very courageous, strong young men. They were generally cordial and light-hearted, often inspired; besides they were burning with love for their country, of the Republic and of the civic revolution. Hoche mourned for Marat as "that unfortunate apostle of Liberty" and right up till 1795 their only claim was to serve France to the best of their ability without for a moment making any distinction between Country, Revolution and Republic.

In all these characteristics they were very similar to their soldiers—except in intelligence.

The latter—whatever their origin—were patriots of the 1792 vintage. The "virtue"—using the word in its old sense —which had urged them to the frontiers in the defence of their country still remained the same.

Their hearts were still in the principles which had triumphed in 1789: Liberty, Equality, Fraternity. They adopted the likes and dislikes, the enthusiasms and prejudices of the Revolution, using its catch-phrases such as "the crimes of tyrants" and "the fanaticism of priests." Some of them still retained their religious beliefs, although being violently anti-clerical in feeling; so much so that the fusilier, Joliclerc, withered "these scoundrelly priests" in a letter in which he bemoaned the loss of his scapulary. As they loved Liberty they hated the royalists who had joined the enemy and against whom they had fought. On the other hand they made no distinction between the parties disputing over the Republic or, rather, they were always on the side of the successful party deeming it always the most sincere. In this way they hailed and reviled in turn Brissot and Marat, Danton and Robespierre. There was a time when they considered Hébert's paper, *le Père Duchesne,* which was everywhere in the armies, as the Gospel of the Revolution, according to Barras. They thought that the Committee of Public Safety saved the country and, knowing that Barère had been ordered, after October, 1793, to tell the Convention of their victories, these worthy men charged the enemy shouting, "Barère! Barère! Send Barère to the tribune!"

But they made no distinction between their love of the Republic and their Country. They always thought of the dear Motherland. Undoubtedly the majority hoped in their hearts to return to their own homes. "We cannot think that the War will last very long. . . . Here is some good news that will surely bring peace nearer—Pray to God it may!" said one of them; but they would remain under arms as long as there was the necessity. Some of them, although only enlisting for one campaign, remained under arms, sixteen, sometimes twenty years. "One must make some sacrifices to save the country. I hope to return to the country only when there is peace," wrote one, and in another letter I read: "Either you will see me return covered with glory or you will have a son worthy of the name of a French citizen . . . who will know how to die in his country's defence," and in yet another, "As long as the country needs me, I shall continue to serve it."

Revolution, Republic, Country—they loved them all with the same sense of exaltation which vibrates in every note of the Marseillaise. It is impossible to convey what the Marseillaise meant to these men. "It is worth ten armies," Napoleon was heard to say and he scarcely exaggerated its importance. When they were worn out, discouraged and beaten it stiffened them. It was the signal of attack, an encouragement under fire, the enemy's knell and a hymn of victory. "Send me a thousand men and a copy of the Marseillaise," wrote a general at the beginning of the wars. "We fought hopelessly outnumbered," a soldier said, "but the Marseillaise fought with us." In the camps, when they reached the line *"the sacred love of the country"* men sometimes fell to their knees.

They were brave and inured to hardships through long experience. In spite of efforts to feed and clothe them they were nearly always half-starved and without a rag to their backs. "A third of the soldiers marched barefoot," writes Gouvion-Saint-Cyr, "and the only vestige of their uniform they had left was the belt." Joliclerc, whose charming letters my friend Funck-Brentano has published, went through a whole campaign with a pair of trousers cut out of a woman's apron which he had found in La Vendée. They went hungry nearly all the time: "We often went six days without receiving any rations," writes Joliclerc. But they suffered patiently and even joked about it. "I am your much overfed son,

. . . but to-day is an Ash-Wednesday." "I am suffering from hunger, thirst, heat and cold; I have no tobacco or white linen. . . . Badly shod and still more badly clothed. Strangely enough I have no fever nor colic, my appetite is always good, but I have nothing to satisfy it with." What did it matter! "There is no hardship the soldier cannot endure for the sake of the Republic." They thought, with Chancel, that it was only by a long series of privations that a soldier could win the honour of dying for his country.

They brought the same humour to their aid when confronted with worse sufferings, being careless of danger, joking about wounds and jeering at death. "I have been wounded by grape-shot in the nose," writes a soldier, "but as it was too bulbous before it has only taken away the unwanted portion." And Fricasse, who was in the siege of Mayence, writes, "All those who were killed in that siege never complained once amidst all that misery. Their faces were calm and serene; their last words were 'Long live the Republic!'" "Those fighting for Liberty bless the bullet that strikes them down, because they know their blood is only shed for Liberty!"

Valiant and resigned, not always easy for their leaders to handle, sometimes pillagers and immoral, but good fellows when all is said and done, they won all hearts. And as they deemed themselves Liberty's missionaries they boasted in front of the Germans, Belgians, Dutch and Italians of the virtues of the Revolution which "broke off the shackles of slavery." The delightful story *Madame Thérèse* by Erckmann-Chatrian is the best historical picture I know of these soldiers who were, at one and the same time both hairy and bombastic, ragged yet alert, wide-awake fellows though ranters. They combined in them the qualities of rough plebeian warriors and the exaltation of apostles entrusted with the task of spreading abroad the doctrines of faith and even love.

Victory was the result of the soldiers' efforts just as much as Carnot's strenuous vigils in the Committee of Public Safety. This victory of France seemed to Europe like a miracle brought about by the denizens of the underworld. It is only another proof that Europe was (as I have said at the beginning of this chapter) absolutely wrong, when seeing the country in the throes of civil war, she had considered the time ripe to crush her. In the Ministries of Europe, the French kings and their ministers had acted as a cloak for the nation which, for centuries patriotic to the core, had blazed up yet once more with the warlike genius of the race. The foreigner should have remembered that a girl of the people had saved the country a century before. These thousands of young men, all of the same people, despatched to the frontiers, after two dramatic appeals of their country in danger, what would they not do for her!

Little by little, between 1796 and 1799, the leaders and the soldiers began to change their attitude although without changing their principles. Becoming conscious of the services they had rendered they intended to put an end to political troubles. I have drawn a picture of these Directory soldiers over a period of some years and I will refer to them again briefly in the last chapter. The Republic, driven into a corner by the great war, was to undergo the fate which Saint-Just already predicted: "One day some ambitious man will arise from their ranks and kill our liberty!"

Meanwhile, trying to save the country, they had moreover saved, in those times of internecine strife, the nation's honour and had shown the astonished foreigner what this time can truly be called France's real character.

CHAPTER IX

CHAPTER IX

THE THERMIDORIANS

THE Revolution of Thermidor—the eleventh month of the Republican year—had been a tragic misunderstanding. The significance attached to this movement by the public and by the originators of it, differed widely.

For the most part these men were terrorists, who had held the extremest views for three years, and who, for a year, had taken part in the most terrible massacre. Not for a moment had they dreamed of a reaction against the Terror—still less against the Revolution. Menaced by Robespierre, they had killed him to save their own necks and for no other reason, like jackals rushing upon the "tiger"—as they called him—caught in a cleverly contrived trap. "A seraglio-revolution," wrote Thureau-Dangin, and before him Joseph de Maistre had called it, "A family quarrel."

The chief actors and players in the tragedy are well known: in the background Fouché and perhaps Fréron; Collot d'Herbois and Billaud-Varenne in the Committee; in the fateful sessions Vadier, Amar and above all Tallien; then in the evening of the 9th Thermidor, Barras had delivered the final blow to the "tyrant." They were definitely the worst elements of the Mountain. Collot d'Herbois and Billaud-Varenne, who had formerly deserted Danton for Hébert, had always been great champions of the Terror in the heart of the Committee. When they had been entrusted with the correspondence of members on missions they had always urged them to use very severe punishments thus assuming responsibility for the great massacres. It was under their ægis that the big butchers, Carrier of Nantes, Le Bon of Arras and twenty other savage executioners had worked.

In the Committee of Public Safety Vadier and Amar had been the most eager to use their powers of proscription. They had been Danton's real assassins. Amar once even wished the entire Convention to go to the foot of the scaffold to participate by its presence in "the great red Mass."

Fouché was one of the worst of the provincial "executioners." He had shown himself of the Revolution's way of thinking, which he had called "entire," by his attempt to apply Hébert's doctrines in the departments of the Centre; in the Cathedral pulpit of Nevers he had upheld the official atheism. By his decrees he had tried to propagate almost communistic doctrines and, if he did not actually organize, he certainly presided at the notorious massacre on the des Brotteaux plain at Lyons where people were mown down by grape-shot. He did not leave Lyons, the second town in France, until he had caused the destruction, at the lowest estimation, of two thousand persons of whom he wrote: "Their bloody carcasses thrown into the Rhône presented a terrifying sight, and an impression of the people's limitless power." And Fouché was one of the most active promoters of the "coup [1] de Thermidor." A member of the Paris Commune, Tallien, is said to have actually taken part in the prison massacres during the dreadful days of September. He did at Bordeaux what Fouché achieved at Lyons sending thousands of victims pell-mell to the guillotine—both royalists and republican Giron-

[1] Robespierre's overthrow.

dists together. And Barras and Fréron continued this kind of work in the south of France, at Marseilles and at Toulon, using in their own words "the Cordelier [2] bludgeoning." Fréron boasted of having shot eight hundred people of Toulon, and Barras, having decreased the population of the same town from 29,000 to 7,000 was hailed in Marseilles, according to his own writings as "the Saviour of the South." In the group of men which overthrew Robespierre there were many such "saviours," and indeed the Thermidorians, far from stopping the reign of Terror, would sooner have thought of increasing its intensity. In any case they would have laughed at the idea that their efforts would eventually cause a reaction to set in against the Revolution. But public opinion took a totally different view of the case.

By this time the French people, worn out by the Revolution, which had always distorted its wishes by going too far, was sickened by the dreadful riot of blood which had lasted a year. It was because the people were so ruled by terror that the outbreak of this "riot of blood" had been possible: still it is only fair to say that this régime, which resulted in the system of Public Safety, had its supporters. The great dangers threatened to the country from the formidable coalition of the spring of 1793 had convinced a number of men of its utility while they deplored its dreadful excesses. But this usefulness was no longer apparent. Defeat had been changed into victory; instead of being attacked France was now the aggressor. Belgium had been conquered at the battle of Fleurus; plans were made ready for the occupation of Holland and, as the left bank of the Rhine had been seized again, preparations were made for crossing what the soldiers boastfully called "the big stream." Robespierre well realized what

[2] A club founded by Danton, Marat and Desmoulins in 1790. It soon amalgamated with the Jacobin Club.

consequences these reassuring successes would have for the régime which he had created. Later on Barère wrote that *"the victories eventually dragged Robespierre down."* Saint-Just asked this same Barère, who was entrusted with the mission of announcing to the Convention the victories won by the the army, "not to make such a song about them any more." In fact there was no longer any excuse for the existence of the Public Safety Committee.

However the Terror had continued and the people only revolted against it all the more. During the first few months, only the great nobles, priests, well-known bourgeois, deputies, financiers, former politicians, former King's officers had been guillotined; but, with the lust for murder becoming unrestrained, the foul passion for denunciation unbridled, and with private vengeance being given free rein, the prisons were soon filled with a crowd of unimportant citizens, servants, artisans, shopkeepers and farmers, all imprisoned as "enemies of the Republic" under the weirdest and most varied pretexts. In the terrible days after Prairial (sixth month of Republican year) the number of minor citizens sacrificed greatly exceeded that of the highest blood. The whole nation believed itself threatened and before such a fearsome menace everyone trembled without any distinction of class, although the parents and friends of those lowly victims were indignant. The government of the Terror only worked because it was well constructed with its committees, members of committees, secret agents, police, denouncers, prisons, judges and executioners. One felt as if caught in a monstrous snare which no one dared to break. As so often has happened in France everyone just waited for a miracle.

Robespierre's fall seemed to be the miracle. He embodied the Terror as has been said—wrongly, according to his champions. But, admitting that on the eve of Thermidor,

Maximilien might really have put an end to the rule by
guillotine—after an enormous blood-letting moreover—how
could the people have believed it? The man had made himself the Terror's great theorist, its dazzling apologist. "The
Terror without which virtue is powerless." And, besides, the
people knew him to have the Committees in the hollow of
his hand. They knew that the Commune, which, at the
Hôtel de Ville, had collaborated in the massacres, and General Henriot, who, as commander of the army in Paris, had
placed the latter at the service of the terrorist régime, were
Robespierre's creatures. They also knew that the public
prosecutor, Fouquier-Tinville, the president of the tribunal,
Dumas, and the very jurors themselves were Robespierre's
friends and tools. Naturally the people could only think
that he was the Terror and when they learned of his fall
and death, after a momentary stupefaction caused by the
announcement they all cried with one voice: "The guillotine must be suppressed, the prisons emptied, the scaffold
destroyed, the Terror abolished!" There was only one sentiment in the immense cry of joy which arose from the Place
de la Revolution when his head had fallen: it was the intoxicating feeling that at last they were to escape from a terrifying nightmare.

The Convention began its first session on the morning of
the 9th Thermidor and remained shut up in the Tuileries
twenty-four hours, only ending the session in the afternoon
of the 10th. They did not know of the interpretation placed
on Robespierre's overthrow and that of his friends by the
people who thought themselves freed and almost resuscitated.
The names of Robespierre's adversaries were all over Paris
and an enormous crowd gathered at the Tuileries to acclaim
them. When the Assembly came out they were dumbfounded

at the welcome and rather worried, not being sure of its reason. But when the crowd recognized Tallien, Fréron and Barras it became delirious. "Market-women presented them with flowers and I saw young men kiss the skirts of their coats," wrote an eyewitness. Spellbound, these executioners of the day before—and strongly disposed to continue the rôle the day after—learned that they had just put an end to the Terror.

But it was obviously inexpedient to undeceive the public since the popularity arising out of this event might be lost.

Collot d'Herbois and Billaud-Varenne were sectarians armed with an immutable faith to which they would remain loyal: but Barras, Fréron and Tallien were politicians, sceptics, sensualists to the marrow, schemers whose intrigues led them into the worst excesses, without any faith or principles, and who did not believe in any system of government. Suddenly, all bespattered with blood as they were, they entered into the spirit of the applauding crowds. They even had the audacity to declare that they wished to free the whole nation from the fear of death, having overthrown the tyrant. Then, realizing clearly that a reaction was inevitable they had dreams of assuming its leadership—if need be, against their old allies of the 9th of Thermidor. They would sacrifice Billaud, Collot, Fouché, Barère and Vadier to popular vengeance if by so doing they could escape it themselves.

Thus forced towards a reaction these politicians were to carry it further, because in making an appeal to the Centre against Robespierre, they found to their astonishment that the Centre, which had appeared inert and almost moribund for a year, had taken on a new lease of life and now claimed the leadership of the movement.

Since the fall of the Girondist Right wing, the Centre had

lived in the midst of the Terror more than any section of the nation. Composed as it was of level-headed bourgeois—only slightly revolutionary and still less republican in tendency—it had discreetly helped the Girondists in the first sessions. But it left itself free to acclaim Danton when he arrived and voted for the "maintenance of private property" from the very first. The Girondist leaders had bewildered these quasi-conservatives by being the first to vote for the King's death. The greater part of the deputies had followed their calamitous gesture, and, from Cambacérès to Sieyès, had voted for death. But they then broke off relations with the Right from whom they could only expect blunders and inconsequential acts. On the 2nd of June they gave up their alliance with the Girondists.

They had then willingly rallied round Danton but again they had abandoned him, being grateful—as they said—to Robespierre for having crushed Hébert's *"levelling"* party. They had accepted everything of his, even the detested Terror. Durand de Maillane depicts rather naïvely their lifeless rôle: "I was one of those honest deputies who *took no active part in the unprincipled debates.*" Burying themselves in the technical Committees—legislation, educational and public works—they sought in these an alibi. They did not often go to the sessions and avoided the tribune. By these methods they hoped to forget that the arrest of seventy-three members supposed to be their friends had wrecked the Right wing. To avoid a like fate they remained in the background. And so, spiritually and physically, shaken with fear, these bourgeois had managed to live through the Terror although Vergniaud, Brissot, Desmoulins, Hérault de Séchelles and Danton had died. They had achieved the miracle: for as Sieyès of their party put it, they had "lived."

The Mountain mistrusted them. The Centre had been

nicknamed "the Plain" but as a result of their lifeless attitude they were renamed the "Marsh" and the Mountain jeered at "these Marsh toads" whenever they gave vent to a "croak." In return for their mistrust the Marsh hated the Mountain; but they were also afraid of them. Indeed Robespierre, anxious to crush "his enemies" of the Left wing, had made advances to the Marsh in later months calling them "these honest gentlemen" and they had seemed attracted by this suggestion. Durand de Maillane had congratulated the dictator on his spiritual qualities while Boissy d'Anglas professed regard for the adversary of the levelling theories, and Cambacérès allowed himself to be flattered by him. All the same, when Robespierre appealed to them on the 9th Thermidor, calling them: "And you, honest, honourable gentlemen!" . . . they betrayed him as they had already betrayed Vergniaud and Danton.

For some hours they had hesitated because they hated and feared Robespierre's attackers more than their victim. But they also had understood the cheers of the crowd on the 10th at the end of the session. The Centre had made a decisive gesture. They were complimented on their "courage" and, not being used to this kind of congratulations, they were rather intoxicated by them. "I am a fearsome fellow now," Cambacérès might have said. Then they became a force to be reckoned with: in the Convention, whose Right was decimated and whose Left was appreciably smaller, they numbered at least three hundred—a majority. If they could have recalled the seventy-three members of the Right they could have voted a good tax-paying constitution—and put an end to the Revolution to the profit of the bourgeois who had started it —instead of the ridiculously impracticable constitution of 1794. Meanwhile, followed by certain Thermidorians, or recanting revolutionaries, they succeeded in purifying the

Mountain, and overthrew Collot, Billaud, Fouché, Vadier and some others thus taking the power into their own hands. One of the Centre wrote proudly that "the Mountain was now the servant after having played the master for so long." And seeing the truth of this, Barras, Fréron and even Tallien himself shamelessly sat in this resuscitated Centre. The month of Thermidor was the starting point of a complete rearrangement of the Conventional benches.

Public opinion had not been led in this case: it had preceded the event. From the 10th a mad joy had raised the hopes of those victims—resigned to death the day before —in the prisons where the fatal roll-call was no longer read. Soon the doors were opened and more than seven thousand people came out into Paris alone. But, before this, more than fifty thousand who had hid in burrows expecting a worse fate, suddenly had arisen from their refuges. All this section of the people was mad with joy and the whole nation rejoiced in sympathy. "It was as if they had arisen from the dead," wrote Thibaudeau.

Perhaps the majority of the people were content with the fact that their lives were safe, but others after a few days cried aloud for vengeance. During the first few days Tallien, Fréron and Barras, who went in fear of reprisals, still hoped that they would evade them content, as was acutely said of them, "to be, at the time of the cleavage which was taking place in the heart of the Convention, on the side of the judges when it was very possible that they might be mistaken for the accused." At first they asked for an amnesty. "A free people, having made a revolution, should never look back," cried Legendre. But now the continually increasing cry of the people was for *"Vengeance!"*

The desire for a reactionary movement and for reprisals

became general. The outlawed came back and the Girondist, Louvet, materialized like a ghost, eager to avenge his friends; he reassumed the editorship of the *"Sentinel"* but this time attacked the Revolution. In the south of France another returned outlaw, Isnard, cried to the anti-revolutionists: "If you haven't any weapons then dig up the bones of your brothers and use them to exterminate the brigands." The liberated press then furiously attacked "Robespierre's tail." It was not considered enough to have sent to the guillotine the members of his Commune, of his tribunal and of his jury. The provinces declared for the punishment of Carrier and Le Bon, who were, as a matter of fact, executed later on; they demanded the denunciation of Collot, Billaud and even Barère because they had signed terrible letters with Robespierre, Saint-Just and Couthon, congratulating these executioners and urging them on to further excesses.

The movement would have lacked the Parisian touch if it had not burst in the theatre. From the day after Thermidor, play after play was produced on the Varieté's stage, all anti-Jacobin in character, beginning with the *Day of Thermidor* which enabled the people to hiss Robespierre, so lately fallen. Then came the *Session of the Revolutionary Committees* in which the hated faces of tyrants, denouncers, minor executioners were recognized and immediately heaped with insults; suddenly the audience turned towards a stall in which a pilloried man, pallid with fear, rose quickly and dashed out. Even the classical pieces were used against the defeated Terrorists. Voltaire's *Mahomet* became popular because the youth of the audience enthusiastically applauded every evening the two lines:

> Him destroy, Great God, from out our ken,
> Who delights to shed the blood of men.

It was indeed a crusade of youth against the former "blood-suckers" but, contrary to general opinion, this youth was not composed of members of the aristocracy at all. These "gilded youths" were Basoche [3] clerks and shop assistants and as a matter of fact were led by men of the lowliest origin. But only the young took an active part in this movement. The youth of France had been under restraint for the three years' reign of Virtue and now, being set free from a detested puritanism, it burst into transports of joy. How intoxicating it was to be free of that Spartan mode of life! to be able to make a noise with everybody's benevolent approval and moreover thus winning smiles from the girls, because, of course, the women joined in with them. Robespierre loathed Woman, and now the female sex took its revenge by urging the young men to thrash the Jacobin and to attack Robespierre's Tail. Armed with cudgels these young men pursued all those who had been marked down as erstwhile secret agents or informers: the red cap, once common in Paris, was now seldom seen. Soon these dandies were the masters of the streets with the enthusiastic support of their inhabitants.

Fréron became the head of the movement. He had deliberately decided to throw in his lot with the reactionary movement—the more reactionary the better. Barras and Tallien shared the same views. They now determined to demand the heads of their former allies of Thermidor: of Collot, Billaud, Barère, Vadier, and some supernumeraries—those whose evidence might inconvenience them. That was the time when even Fouché, the cold-hearted butcher of the Plain des Broteaux, had the audacity to sympathize, from the Conventional tribune, with "those horrible scenes that

[3] An association of clerks in the royal Parliament. Henry III suppressed their practice of choosing a "king."

had taken place in Lyons under the name of Maximilien the First," as he jeered.

Fréron hardly deserves pardon less than Fouché, Barras and Tallien. An examination of the moral character of these three Revolutionaries will prove more useful than any dissertation to show why the Republic descended from a régime of blood to one of infamy.

Stanislas Fréron was the son of Elie Fréron, an aggressive Catholic who, as a bitter opponent of Voltaire and the *Encyclopédie,* had incurred the hatred of the philosophers. Thanks to his father's connections with Royalty he was the godson of a king and a princess of the Blood, Stanislas Leckzinski and Madame Adélaïde, daughter of Louis XV. Idle, sensual, elegant and dissolute, from the year 1789 he had denied all his father's gods and, as is common enough, had gone to the opposite extreme. At Louis-le-Grand he had had Robespierre and Desmoulins as his fellow-students and after 1789 cultivated their friendship assiduously. Desmoulins brought him to Danton's notice; he then invaded the "damned .ground" of the Cordeliers and quickly became a familiar figure in Lucile Desmoulin's salon and at the Dantons' table. Then, because he had a renegade's soul, this godson of princes became involved in the Revolution before any of the others. In his scandalous publication *The People's Orator* he agreed with Marat of *The People's Friend* demanding, before Danton, the King's overthrow. Then he took an active part in the Revolution of the 10th of August and became a member of the notorious Commune of the massacres. Elected a deputy of Paris with all Danton's protégés, he sat in the extremest part of the Mountain, demanding—still before anyone else—the "tyrant's" execution. He voted for the death of the grandson of his royal godfather without an instant's delay, hoping that both old Élie Fréron, who had opposed the philosophical doctrines, and the many princes who had bent over his own cradle thirty-five years before, would be forgotten in these revolutionary gestures.

Moreover, through all this blood-bespattered tragedy, he retained the manners of a rake; he made loose living an art; he was handsome and an all-conquering Don Juan. Even little Lucile, although so attached to her Camille, was sore put to it to resist him for he considered this dandyism of his of some importance. This is obvious from a letter requesting the release of a citizen Wilkers who, he wrote, had—a very unexpected proof of citizenship—"always provided very elegant braces."

However this fine fellow wanted to progress from mere statements to actual deeds; the dandy wished to be an executioner. Reference has been made to his mission in Provence where, in conjunction with Barras, he organized the "Cordelier bludgeonings." "We shall only be really happy when we have baptized Toulon with blood and fire," wrote the young dandy. He had entered that rebellious town with troops, "his face alight with an unholy joy" as a witness described him, and before eight days had passed he had written to the Convention: "Everything is going very well; we have requisitioned twelve hundred bricklayers to demolish and to raze the town to the ground. Every day since our entry two hundred people have been executed." This amiable young pro-consul's letters are terrifying. Still a journalist, he joked, made catch-phrases, told stories, and trumpeted gaily amidst all the bloodshed. Having found a worthy comrade-in-arms in Barras he lived like a provincial governor surrounded with an elegant, corrupt court. Hébert denounced to the Jacobins Fréron's abuse of power at Nice, saying that "he was surrounded by a crowd of nobly-born women and lived dreadfully extravagantly." It is worth mentioning that

Fréron and Barras, in the name of the principles of Reason, looted silver from Churches as Fouché had done in Nivernais, but nothing obtained from this raid ever went into the Treasury. This was the reign of what Maximilien called "Terror without Virtue."

The Master had recalled them both and demanded an account—not so much of the blood spilt but of the dissolute habits they had displayed and of the stolen gold. They had tried to disclaim all responsibility using the meanest excuses, but they had read their death-warrants on his grim face. When Fréron had been expelled by the Jacobins, he and Barras had become involved in the Thermidorian intrigue in order to save—with the gold they had acquired—their threatened existence.

And now the man declared himself in favour of a reaction. Under the pretext of avenging "his friend" Danton, and the Desmoulins, he pursued with an unheard of ferocity Robespierre's comrades, then the former members of the Committee of Public Safety whom he dared—he, the butcher of Toulon—to call "terrorists." He then hunted those Jacobins, who to please Maximilien, had expelled him from their party. Every day there appeared in *"The People's Orator"* an article in which he demanded the executions, "in the name of Justice," of those who, like himself and sometimes of not such a high standard of villainy, had been terrorists. The mob was raised to heights of enthusiasm by these articles from his bitingly active pen. The phrase "Have you read Fréron" opened the conversation at any of the evening gatherings. "This devil Fréron doesn't give his enemies a minute's breathing space." This appeared in a paper. He then launched an attack on Collot, Billaud, Amar and Barère. "Your graves yawn for you," he cried to the unfortunate men, "and you merely struggle in vain." To those who expressed any astonishment at this he confided with a sentimental expression that he meant to avenge his little friend, Lucile Desmoulins, who had been sacrificed by these cowards. From writing in the papers he took to tub-thumping and put himself at the head of the "gilded youth." He led them on expeditions against the "blood-suckers" and the hand that had organized "the Cordelier bludgeonings" now organized, with the help of the black-collared royalist insurrectionists, "the dandy's cudgel." In the Convention he urged the hesitant Centre to take action against the remnant of the Mountain. But, between a session at the Tuileries and an expedition against the Jacobins, the former terrorist was to be seen, elegantly dressed and perfumed, setting the fashions and, in citizeness Tallien's drawing-room, forgetting poor guillotined Lucile easily enough. The "gilded youth" shouted for Fréron, sometimes tearing him away from Madame Tallien and often from his pen. Had they not called him "the capital's strongest club"—the terror of the Jacobins?

Barras also was a renegade because, by birth the viscount Paul de Barras, he was connected with all the noble families of Provence. At least he claimed in his *Memoirs* to be related to the families of Blacas, Castellane, and Vogüé. Formerly an officer under the King he had seen service in the Indies and had developed a taste for adventure. Heavily in debt and having no moral scruples he had welcomed the Revolution and from 1789 had gone almost without any intermediate steps into the ranks of the extremists. Carnot later on spoke of him very feelingly, stating that he had "the savagery of a Caligula under a crust of feigned *insouciance.*" In reality he was not "savage," a word which would imply a more passionate feeling than he was capable of. "A roué of the most debauched type." Thus a foreign agent under the Directory described him. And Mallet called him "a proper filibuster." And thirty witnesses could be produced who agree over this. At forty years of age this handsome fellow with his full face and high complexion had some noble traits in spite of the degradation of his soul and his perverted morals. First impressions of him were deceptive. His mortal enemy, Larivellière said he had "a charming smile" which often masked an expression which easily became sinister.

Some pictured the Revolution as the shining temple of Liberty; to others it appeared as an arena. But Barras, the bad character, with his taste for adventure, only saw in it a scope for his powers of intrigue and a career financially profitable. Like Fréron he led a fast life but he was of a more calculating disposition, so that while Fréron ended up in disgrace, oblivion and almost poverty Barras became a Republican director, lord of the manor of Grosbois and multi-millionaire. His mental powers, which only gave way after four years of power under the strain imposed on them by his mode of life, were very acute and his aptitude for intrigue was "untiring" as Larivellière put it. He sounded all the parties and flattered them; then, as he was capable of playing any rôle, took up the part of an executioner. Then he returned to Paris under the goad of Robespierre's threats and, like Fouché, knotted the threads of the plot against his master. For two days during the month of Thermidor he said nothing though he had made ready his plans to strike. But when an unerring leader was required to go at the head of the troops in order to arrest Robespierre at the Hôtel de Ville it was recalled that he had been an officer. When he was offered the part he accepted. For the occasion he wore a large sabre which afterwards he never relinquished, and, from that day onwards he always styled himself "General Barras."

Like Fréron he considered that they were all lost if they were not at the head of the post-Thermidorian reaction, and so well did he know how to obtain this position that he joined the Committee of Public Safety. Then, in spite of his colossal vanity and his lack of depth, he progressed from the Committee to the Directory and thence, after five years, to power by an extraordinary genius for intrigue. "If he stole without remorse," wrote a foreign ambassador, "he also spent lavishly without regret; it was an absolute necessity to him to throw his money about. He would throw up the Republic to-morrow if it didn't pay for his dogs, horses, mistresses, food and his gambling." In 1794 he was not the worn out Barras whom in Brumaire, Year VIII, Bonaparte was to brush aside with a gesture. He threw himself wholeheartedly into the reactionary movement but he did not intend to allow it to get out of hand and would know the right moment to stop it if it theatened to sweep away its leaders. He negotiated secretly with the Bourbons but was quite resolved only to allow them to return on the day when he received letters from Louis XVIII, pardoning him on the charge of regicide—and as many letters as possible containing money.

Tallien probably followed the same course of action: Louis XVIII may have received letters from him as well. He had more need even than Fréron and Barras to be pardoned.

He was neither the godson of a king nor the descendant of Provençal nobility but the son of a steward of the Marquis de Bercy and had dragged out a ragamuffin childhood on the Paris streets. He had been a dismissed clerk, shop-assistant, foreman of a printing-office and even, it is said, a theatre commissionaire. He certainly belonged to

those disturbing elements that poison and bring dishonour
upon a revolution.

Of course he had joined the extremists. His intellect was
as mediocre as his courage and his whole outlook cowardly
and mean. He had a valet's temperament—a feeling of infe-
riority. Embroiled in the September massacres he had,
thanks to Danton, been elected a member of the Convention,
but he had escaped from the tribune's clutches and during
the King's trial had shown himself to be very extreme even
going as far as to wish to refuse the King the right to appoint an advocate. When sent to Bordeaux he had drenched
the Girondist stronghold with blood, and, being a rake of
the lowest order, he had there enforced "the Terror without Virtue." Money and women alone were able to temper
his harshness and he soon amasssed a respectable fortune
and some pleasant recollections. And then he had met
Therezia Cabarrus and had fallen madly in love with her;
she began to exercise great influence upon him so much so
in fact that to please her he tempered his zeal in his desire
for executions. Robespierre then recalled him and he also
knew some anxious times in the spring and summer of
Year II. He was in despair at Therezia's imprisonment and
the thought of this woman condemned to death perhaps
contributed to make this coward a brave man for a moment.

But suddenly he had become enormously popular, partly
because he had dared more than anyone else, partly because
he had attacked Maximilien so fiercely and because he had
seemed to be the chief factor in his overthrow. To most
people Tallien, more than Barras or Fréron, represents the
Thermidorian type. This failure, with his face marred by a
birthmark, and the soul of a valet, became all in a moment
the most prominent man in France. From the Convention
he had gone into the Committee of Public Safety where he

had done nothing of any use, and finally had reached the tribune—*his* Thermidorian tribune. From this position he had hurled anathemas against the Terror, of which he had been one of the most despicable instruments, and sometimes even against the "infamous Commune" although he had been quite the most "infamous" of the lot, having dipped his arms up to the elbows in blood in September. Now he was cheered and carried about in triumph by the "gilded youths" in the streets and a new and amusing society besieged his house from which issued the day's law.

It was there that Therezia Tallien ruled with him, dominating him, over the worlds of politics, art, pleasure and fashion all at the same time.

She was the daughter of the banker Cabarrus of Madrid and while very young she had married a Marquis de Fontenoy. Then as divorce was introduced in 1791 she freed herself from his authority. Contemporary writers never tired of painting her charms although as a matter of fact her portraits do not disclose them. It is true her attraction lay less in her features than in her charm of manner, in her voluptuous glances and in the seductive quality of her voice. Tallien when in Bordeaux had very easily made this lady first his mistress then his wife.

She was absolutely devoid of any morals, virtue or scruples but she had good qualities as long as they were not taxed too heavily by difficulties. Although not really interested in politics she played at being a Jacobin. Did not the one time Vicomtesse de Beauharnais, Joséphine, future Empress of the French, sign a letter to Vadier: "Joséphine La Pagerie Beauharnais, *Jacobin of the Mountain faction.*" Therezia Cabarrus, former Marquise de Fontenoy and future Princesse de Chimay, might have signed herself very willingly in the same terms at that time. To please Tallien she had taken the part of Liberty in a revolutionary ceremony in a red bonnet—a very pretty little bonnet, it is true, of red velvet trimmed with fur. In the Jacobin Club she had read a paper on principles of national education although no one would think nowadays of bringing up children on them. But by means of these little acts of compliance she had soon obtained some favours of the proconsul as well as a more lenient attitude. When Tallien had been denounced to Robespierre, he had been recalled, and a month after, Therezia was arrested at Bordeaux and sent to the Prison des Carmes in Paris. Thanks to the Thermidorian movement she went from prison to the highest pinnacle of power.

The part she had played in Thermidor was greatly exaggerated and the country treated her like a goddess calling her Our Lady of Thermidor, Our Lady of Great Help and, on account of the reliefs she had obtained for the people, Our Lady of Mercy. She didn't need anyone's help in bolstering up and enlarging this legend. "This is the tiny hand," she declared one day, "that put an end to tyranny." She urged Tallien and his friends to open the prisons and then to finish off the Jacobins. "The Herodias of Mercy" as an inimical historian calls her. And it is true that, by her hatred of the former rules of denunciations, she urged on her friends to similar excesses. The hunted members of the Mountain were not wrong when one of them, a good classicist, wrote: "The scoundrels have promised our heads to their concubines. We shall die because new Fulvias bound to new Antonys have their bodkins all ready to pierce our tongues." Tallien thought he ought to defend Therezia even at the tribune in the Convention which shows how deeply in love he was. "She is called Cabarrus' daughter. . . . Well, I state in the midst of my colleagues and in the midst of the people that this woman is my wife!" And, amidst general and prolonged applause, he spoke in moving terms of his wife's fidelity and awarded her the honours of the session.

She reigned as Queen: "Her Serene Highness, Madame Cabarrus," wrote a journalist, mockingly, "honoured with her presence the fortunate inhabitants of Saint-Cloud. Her august husband, Monsieur Tallien, accompanied her." The fact that she rose to such a high position in the Revolution which Fréron, Barras and Tallien dominated goes to prove that Virtue's reign was closed indeed.

The Republic, however, seemed to have lost its head. Since it had no real head and since the workings of the Committee of Public Safety had been stopped the Revolution became a whirlwind.

After three months' hesitation the Thermidorians had decided to denounce their too inconvenient allies of Thermidor; Collot, Billaud, Vadier were already condemned to death in their friends' minds. But the Jacobins showed their teeth from the first; every evening in the club the reaction was denounced because it curried favour with "rotters." But Thermidor and its consequences had decreased the number of these proud Jacobins. One evening the "gilded youth" assaulted the Club and made them capitulate; the members of this proud club, which had once led France, had to undergo the indignity of low jests and were even spat on. As it had become a nuisance the Convention decided to shut the club. Fréron who had been expelled from the club on the eve of Thermidor would not let anybody else execute the decree. He went with Merlin de Thionville, shut the door and took back the keys to the Convention. Therezia Tallien had gone with them to be present at his triumph. And the fettered tiger had to bear the insulting laughter of that beautiful courtesan.

With the Club closed it was possible to strike at its former friends. The Convention seemed definitely to have decided in favour of the reactionary movement. The Right wing had been reconstructed by the recall of the seventy-three imprisoned members, then sixteen obscure survivors of the Girondist group. The latter had changed their views on the Republic. A witness said the Convention were only thinking of "turning back along the road." Collot, Billaud and their friends were sent to a convict prison.

The remaining few Jacobins attempted to resist by raising the suburbs on two occasions. Twice, on the 12th Germinal and the 1st Prairial, the Convention was invaded by artisans exasperated by hunger and urged on by the remaining revolutionaries; and twice the Convention, with the help of the "gilded youth," was able to repulse the invasion and to suppress the revolt. This was done with great severity because in each battle the Convention had been perturbed and now it became more afraid than ever of the Left and consequently reacted more and more each succeeding day.

The evolution of the party seemed, however, to be more rapid than ever. The royalist element had joined little by little the "gilded youth" and set a course, more or less openly towards new aims. The Marseillaise was no longer sung and if it was started on the stage it was at once drowned by the Thermidorian song, *The Awakening of the People*.

> "The tardy day of vengeance
> Now makes the butchers pale."

Amongst the *black-collars*, as Fréron's young men were called, appeared men from the Vendée or from the south, young royalist insurrectionists or young ruffians who talked of taking Louis XVII from the Temple. Then when he died they spoke of bringing back the Count of Lille, the exiled Louis XVIII.

Even in the Convention a party began to form in the Centre which thought seriously of restoring the Throne. The Bourbons would be asked to accept what was reasonable in the Revolution—some of the 1789 principles and a constitution assuring control by the Houses—and above all to promise an amnesty which would put an end to all fear of reprisals. Another big party with the same views was formed in the provinces which had formerly welcomed the 1789 movement but which had repudiated nearly all of what had happened in Paris during the six years. To tell the truth, the Thermidorians of the Left were distrustful: each one of them was negotiating for his own particular amnesty for further safety. There is little doubt that Fréron, Tallien and Barras were only in communication with royalist agents in order to make terms of surrender and perhaps, if they agreed to a restoration, to feather the nest to which they would have to retreat.

Suddenly all these dreams were rudely shattered. Louis XVIII, hailed as king after the death of his nephew by all the French royalists and by those abroad, was at Verona. Everyone expected an announcement and it came. The old régime was to be restored in its entirety: absolute monarchy re-established, liberty suppressed, property newly acquired by the sale of national possessions abolished, and all those who had fought against the throne during the seven years, punished royalist agents in France, with an eye to rebellion, encouraged the rumor that the Count d'Artois was preparing to land on the West Coast an army composed of armed emigrés to set alight the Vendée which was just becoming quiet.

The regicides were startled in the Centre as well as on the Left. There were still nearly three hundred of them who had voted for the King's death and they formed a solid mass. Émile Faguet, summing up in a word the two large volumes I have just published on Fouché, wrote of the latter that after Jan. 21, 1793, until his death he saw all the events "through the glass of Louis XVI's scaffold." This dismal, but perfectly correct, saying applies to all the regicides. They knew they were unpopular in the country on account of the Terror. So by means of a pardon they might willingly have sought security in a conditional restoration of the Crown. But as a form of bait they were shown the rope. They were frightened but found an inclination to support them in the country. The enormous mass of owners of national possessions were solidly with the revolutionaries. Tallien had already taken his seat anew in the old Mountain being dissatisfied with the disquieting attitude adopted by the Centre.

The Thermidorian leaders recovered their equilibrium when, amidst all this, news arrived in Paris that the expected landing of the emigrés had taken place at Quiberon on seventh Messidor (June 26th, 1795). The expedition had been escorted by an English squadron but after the landing the escort had abandoned the force. The army, badly supported by the inhabitants and surrounded by Hoche's troops, had capitulated. Tallien's joy was unbounded. Threatened with the gallows if Louis XVIII was restored, he now saw in the Quiberon affair a chance to bring back to the Thermidorian Republic the moderates who were terrified by the "King's" declarations. He also hoped to reconquer the suburbs which, since the time of the revolt, had done nothing but talk of the "rotters" who were certainly in the pay of the "despots." The Bordeaux executioner awoke in him: since the "King" would not give him any guarantee of safety he preferred to dig deep the ditch between the France of the Revolution and the France of the Kings. He gave the order to shoot the Quiberon force although these hundreds of unfortunate emigrés were protected by the word of a great soldier. And with one blow the neo-royalist movement was checked. On the 9th of Thermidor, Year III, the anniversary of that memorable day, a banquet took place attended by all those who had taken part in it. It was noticeable that the Centre and the Left were represented at that reunion—and even the Right by Lanjuinais. The toast of the banquet was the common hatred of all tyrants and in the evening the Convention, having sung the *People's Awakening,* struck up the Marseillaise which had been banned for a year.

However the Convention voted a tax-paying Constitution and Boissy d'Anglas using it as a basis stated his proposition that "a country governed by its landowners is democratic." This constitution organized a Republic led by *directors* with two *Councils,* elected by the tax-payers and a *Directory* elected by the Councils. But the country, just deterred from restoring the Crown by the imprudent Verona proclamation, was on the other hand distrustful of the former terrorists and of their accomplice the Convention. Obviously the Nation was prepared to choose its new representatives and governors from others, who had never been besmirched, rather than these men.

So the Thermidorians were greatly perturbed. The regicides formed a kind of governing oligarchy which saw no possibility of avoiding the danger of reprisals unless it continued in office. Besides, those worthy men were just reaping the tangible benefits of power in a society given up to amusement and pleasure. Barras, Tallien, Fréron and many others lived like princes in the houses they had usurped. It was not only the one-time butcher Legendre, Danton's friend, having become a violent reactionary after Thermidor, who amused himself with Mlle. Contat of the Comédie-Française theatre. In order to continue to enjoy themselves they desired to remain in power.

Now their agents warned them—their reports are still in existence—that it was being said everywhere that "these rogues would not be re-elected";—not one; for "the old ones would spoil the new-comers." The members of the Convention were forewarned: except about fifty of them—the moderate members of the Centre and some members left from the old Right wing—the outgoing deputies, from Boissy d'Anglas to Lanjuinais, would all be swept away.

It began to look as if the Thermidorians were to run aground in harbour and they fired up. When a party believed its existence threatened—the procedure was always the same —it declared that the Republic was in danger. Tallien said that if the voters were left free in their choice "the counter-revolution would be made constitutionally in three months." This was indeed a strange confession. So he had two important measures passed which enacted that two-thirds of the deputies elected to the legislative body—five hundred out of seven hundred and fifty—were obliged to be taken from the retiring members of the Convention, and that the Convention would make up the two-thirds from members of its own choice, thus avoiding an appeal to the electorate.

The country rebelled against this astute move to obtain a majority which aimed at binding the country to the regicidal oligarchy, now the Thermidorian party. Already the country prepared to go further and in any case to elect only the non-regicidal members of the Convention. But once more the hard-pressed royalists played into the hands of the threatened Left. The rising of the 13th Vendémiaire, crushed by Barras, allowed the Thermidorians to regain their grasp of the situation. And so it was that the new Councils were composed only of two-thirds of the Conventional clique, and the Directory, dominated by Barras, continued simply as the old Thermidorian committee.

In reality after Robespierre's fall and the end of the Terror, the country, although it had acclaimed the men responsible for these events, saw through these faithless politicians pretty clearly. After some months it realized plainly that these rascals, with their bombastic gestures about generosity, had only favoured the reactionary movement in order to establish an alibi for the time when they would have to render an account of their stewardship. Six months after Thermidor, Tallien, once so popular, was fiercely attacked. Some papers even mentioned his scandalous private life and the extravagant follies of "the Cabarrus" as being an insult to the increasing misery of the people. Comment was also made on the attention showed by Barras to this "prostitute" on whose back, it was said, a placard should be placed with "national property" written on it. The crushed suburbs seethed with suppressed fury. Gracchus Babeuf, apostle of an inarticulate communism, already sowed his doctrine; in the severe famine it was said that under Robespierre at least, the misery of the famished people had not been outraged by extravagance and debauchery. The royalists, who had expected to make capital out of Thermidor and to involve Tallien, branded the bloodshed at Quiberon as another September massacre. And so great was his unpopularity that Tallien had not managed to get into the Directory with Barras, and Fréron, who was also involved, shared his disgrace. But it sufficed that Barras, now captivated by Therezia Tallien, should seem the most influential member of the

Directory in order that this body might be tainted, from the very first, with the unpopularity, which, in later months, had nearly wrecked the Thermidorian party. This unpopularity had overtaken Robespierre in the same way that he had struck down Hébert and Danton. The latter in their turn had overthrown Vergniaud and Brissot, the destroyers in earlier times of the friends of Barnave and La Fayette. Each party, including the Thermidorians, were finally over-whelmed in this same disgrace.

The nation was tired of parties and wanted a national Re-public; but here was this Thermidorian party, formed out of the ruins of all the other parties, forcing itself on France for goodness knows how many more years! It was so unpopular that Sieyès, when elected to the Directory with Barras, had haughtily refused his seat; and this refusal had enhanced his reputation. It was thought that this philosopher might give France at last the Republican government and ideal Constitu-tion which it was said he had been preparing during the last seven years. But if Sieyès failed it would be the end. As they could not consider a return to a King, owing to the ridiculous conditions attached to a restoration, and as they certainly did not want a republic controlled by a party of debauched revolutionaries and self-seeking Jacobins, the people sought everywhere for someone to extricate them from their pre-dicament.

Then, on 17 Vendémiaire—three weeks before the end of the session—the Convention had observed the arrival of a group of officers whose services in materially helping Barras to suppress the royalist rising were highly praised by that "victor of the 13th Vendémiaire." The Convention had con-gratulated them and Fréron, pointing out one of the generals, desired the Convention especially to recognize his ability. So this young Corsican soldier was appointed commander-in-

chief of the Home armies. This appointment put an end to
the dying struggles of the parties for, by one of its last acts,
the Convention had started General Napoleon Bonaparte up
the ladder of fame.

CHAPTER X

L'ABBÉ SIÉYÈS

CHAPTER X

SIEYÈS

On the 2 Messidor, Year III (June 21st, 1795) the National Convention, whose term of office was drawing to its close, discussed the Constitution which it meant to bequeath to the country before its dissolution. The badly constructed Constitution of 1791 had collapsed along with the throne on August 10th, 1792. A proposal for a republican constitution drawn up by Condorcet and the Girondins in the last months of 1792—very nearly voted for—had foundered together with its authors. The ultrapopular Constitution of 1793, which originated in the mind of Hérault de Séchelles— a follower of Danton—was voted for; but although sanctioned by a referendum of the country it had been considered impracticable and after 9th Thermidor it was decided to fashion another out of it. Now for some days numerous proposals were brought to the tribune—some complete, others only partly so—and the Convention grew worn-out over its political problem. They draggled along in the mud and lost all interest in the debate.

Suddenly the President rose up and said that Citizen Sieyès wanted to speak.

This name caused a sensation. The speaker who was at the tribune immediately gave up his place with a great show of deference. The chattering deputies grew silent and the half-empty Assembly rapidly refilled. The name, "Sieyès! Citizen Sieyès!" passed from mouth to mouth, some—falling into the old habit—saying: "Abbé Sieyès!"

He went up to the tribune with solemn step as if ascending Mount Tabor. About forty-six years old, he was of medium height although the erectness of his carriage made him seem quite tall; his black hair and sombre attire—still rather clerical—rendered still more striking the pallor of his complexion; his eyes, also pale, were cold and steady; his close-lipped mouth seemed made for silence. His gestures were studied and his whole manner pontifical. But he was encouraged in this pose by the Assembly's deferential attitude.

This Emmanuel Sieyès was considered to be "the premier political architect" of his time according to the writings of one who was there. If the Constitution of 1791 had foundered so quickly, if that of Condorcet in 1792 and that of Hérault de Séchelles in 1793, had appeared impracticable on examination, it was, as was said, because the Abbé Sieyès had on three occasions refused to co-operate in the great task. Once more elected to the Commission of the 1795 Constitution he had resigned, declaring that his hour had not yet come, and when Daunou, the chief author of the proposal under discussion, had very humbly come to ask him to give his advice, he had replied: "I have indeed studied these matters very deeply but you did not understand me"—which was scarcely kind to his colleagues.

One day in 1790, Mirabeau, in the Constituent Assembly, had proclaimed that the Abbé Sieyès' "silence and inaction were a public calamity," and had, amidst applause, implored him to bestir himself. But the oracle had remained silent; he had stayed silent in 1792 and 1793 and it looked as if he wished to remain mute in 1795. Now suddenly the oracle was going to speak.

He spoke with that dry voice and lifeless delivery which made him, to his secret vexation, such a mediocre orator. As a matter of fact he considered his ideas sufficiently cogent to make up for failings as a speaker; but his theories were more methodical than forceful. "The science of politics," he said, "is not the science of what actually is but of what ought to be." His disdain for history was apparent in this oft proclaimed philosophy ("These alleged historical truths," he said arrogantly) as was his distrust of "contemptible theories always fitting in with events." And these theories stamped him as the most idealistic of all the idealists, who, from 1789 to 1799, had tenanted the Assembly benches, holding that realities ought to be disregarded and that philosophy alone was the mistress of facts.

He developed his system very thoroughly, using strange formulæ. Under the eyes of those men to whom seven years of revolution had restored very materialistic views, he built up a complicated edifice which looked as if it had been produced by a professorial academy legislating for an Utopian realm. It looked like some curiously- though delicately-wrought machinery, garnished with names sometimes invented by himself for in his more youthful days he had shown an inclination to reform the human language.

They did not understand him and their acute distress was visible on their faces: some affected an appearance of approval so as to seem as profound as the oracle itself, while others frankly showed their disappointment. The Benches were full of bored faces.

When at last he descended, it was amidst some polite applause—and his scheme was rejected. He smiled bitterly on them and did not appear again for several weeks. From that day he condemned in his own mind the Constitution which was finally decided upon as well as the régime that was evolved out of it. In the meantime he carefully laid aside the Constitution which he had in mind: one day he was to show it again to the amazed eyes of the greatest realist of modern times—the Consul Bonaparte—only this was to be quite a different matter; for out of that idealistic structure the soldier was to build up a Constitution worthy of a Caesar. On that day the Abbé Sieyès, formerly the oracle of the incipient Revolution, would, without wishing to do so, have laid the foundations of the Empire.

The life of this strange man frames an excellent review in miniature of the drama of ideas, which was played behind the tragedy of events, from the hours which preceded the Revolution to those which saw its close. "What did you do during the Terror?" Sieyès was asked. "I lived," he replied, and indeed, for a person as much in the public eye as Sieyès was from 1789, it was a miracle to have kept alive when everyone else came to grief. When the tragedy was over he was the only one who, having avoided death, imprisonment, exile and even disgrace, survived. And that is why his life makes an excellent opportunity to review the Revolution.

He had revealed himself as the oracle even before the Assemblies were united. He had been the forerunner, because he was the philosopher of the new era, and because he had retained of the priestly profession, to which he belonged, only a form of authoritative sermonizing used to defend dogmas.

For a man who came from the south of France he was singularly cold. His father was recorder at Fréjus. His parents, being pious people, wanted him to take up the Church as a career. Very imaginative and fanciful as he was, he had, as a child, dreamed of a dazzling career in the army; but as he was undersized and delicate, developed late, and was often ill, he could not have endured the hardships of war. Talleyrand was a priest because he was a cripple: Sieyès was a priest on account of his ill-health. At that time strange offerings were made to God.

As befitted a child of his time, he was very apt in philosophical studies but unlike his contemporaries he did not adopt a master. Proud and egotistical, he disdained a Rousseau or a Voltaire as much as a Montesquieu—being Sieyès. Brought up in Draguignan's doctrines, he took to the Saint-Sulpice College a philosophical mind unaffected by the teachings of philosophers. His ecclesiastical tutors considered him physically infirm but mentally dangerous. "I am afraid," wrote one of them, "that his particular choice in reading only gives him a taste for the new philosophical theories,"—which were, after all, "not at all suitable for a priest," and, as another of his tutors added, "He will never be anything but an honest canon." He was then ordained a priest.

Monsignor de Lubersac, a bishop who came from his own province, took him to Tréguier in Brittany as a secretary, then to Chartres where he was, in fact, made a canon. He was very bored there and shirked his duties unceasingly. He wanted to be appointed chaplain to one of Louis XV's daughters, and, as his bishop was opposed to this course, he conceived a violent dislike for him. "My bishop has played me false." From that day, Lubersac being a noble and a prelate, the recorder's son experienced a feeling of rebellion. Moreover he was in some financial difficulty having spent the small allowance given him by his father. In remedying this he grew soured. The spirit of the Tiers État surged within him. Though a priest, he no longer possessed any beliefs if, indeed, he had ever had any, and thought to see Christianity founder in a short while before philosophy, if the latter produced a Revolution. What fault did he have to find with Christianity? Probably the defect of not having been invented by himself.

However he was working at a defence of his theories and the States-General were about to assemble. The Abbé issued his famous lampoon, the most celebrated of the Revolution: *"What is the Tiers État? Everything.—What has it been up to the present? Nothing.—What ought it to become? Something."* This description alone was like a firebrand. Besides, he was twice in error in his first two statements: that the Tiers État was "nothing" in a country which had been governed by hundreds of plebeian ministers—from Sugar, a peasant's son, to Colbert, son of a family of shopkeepers. This error indeed showed a lovely unconcern of "these alleged historical truths" which he held so cheap. The statement that the Tiers État ought to be "Everything," in a country in which the nobility formerly, and the Church, at all times, had rendered so many services to the nation, was merely nonsense. But, in addition the Abbé concocted a theory directed against the nobles and which on that occasion deserved to be styled "alleged history": the nobility were all descended, he said, from the conquering race, which, coming from Germany, had enslaved the enormous mass of Latin Celts who made up the Tiers État. The nobles were to be sent back "into their Franconian forests." The absolutely fantastic theory of the two races lent a nationalistic colour to the claims of the Tiers État which thus became the sole representative of the original inhabitants of France. "The Tiers État alone is the French nation; and it is therefore certain that the non-privileged members only are capable of being electors or representatives in the National Assembly. So the Tiers État is quite sufficient to do all that is hoped of a National Assembly. . . ."

The success that this pamphlet attained can be imagined. In January, 1789, the Tiers État hailed this priest as—even more valuable than a defender—the precious theorist of its rights. The "forests of Franconia" were in themselves, alone, a find; but the title, which was both showy and flattering, would have sufficed. It is very pleasant, having persuaded oneself that one is "nothing," to learn suddenly that one ought to be "everything." In two months thirty thousand copies were sold and Sieyès' name was famous. The Revolution had no sooner begun than it had found its mouthpiece.

Election time arrived; but the clergy of Chartres did not appear eager to elect the canon as their representative and he, on his part moreover, wished to be the chosen of the Tiers État—which was to be "everything." Considering himself to be sufficiently well-known already, he went off to show himself in Paris. Nevertheless his election was not an easy matter: the Tiers État wanted bourgeois representatives only,—and one from amongst themselves at that. Sieyès was the very last to be elected.

As, in addition, the Parisian elections were so long-drawn-out, the deputation from the capital only appeared at the States-General on the 25th of May. For three weeks they had struggled amidst difficulties. The nobility and clergy refused, as you know, to sit with the Tiers État to confirm the powers in common, which would have been the first step towards the fusion of the three Orders. The Tiers État did not dare to break with the two other Orders and the Court which supported them in their resistance. Negotiations were begun but only ended in exasperating all parties. The Parisian deputies arrived, bubbling with enthusiasm and their entry was greeted with rapture: the Abbé Sieyès in particular was an object of interest. Would the author of the famous pamphlet written on their behalf fail to live up to general expectations? Outwardly so calm, would he open the bag containing the tempests? On the 10th of June he only made one remark: would the Tiers État remain fettered? "The cable must be cut!" The phrase was acclaimed with transports of joy; it made Sieyès' fortune. He was remembered by everyone during the whole of the Revolution as the author of this phrase. His "cable" was fastened to him.

On the 12th of June, as Mirabeau announced to the Assembly "that a Parisian deputy" wanted to bring forward a motion, Sieyès appeared solemn and imposing. He read an address to the privileged classes no longer *"beseeching"* but *"summoning"* them for the last time to sit together; and he decided that the Tiers État could confirm the powers of *all* the deputies of the three Orders. And it was Sieyès who, on the 15th proposed briefly that the Tiers État should proclaim itself alone the *National Assembly*. Not being a man of violent gestures, he left it to Mirabeau, on the 23rd of June, to overwhelm with his fury the King's envoy; but, when the latter had retired, the Abbé said drily: "You are to-day, Gentlemen, what you were yesterday: let us deliberate on the matter." And so he laid the foundations of his renown as an oracle: the secret of all oracles has always been the fact that they never chatter.

It was over: the National Assembly, baptized by this peculiar priest, began its first session. A proper constitution was to be given to the realm. Everyone turned expectantly towards him and his real career began. He was enthusiastically elected to the Committee where he drafted the outline of the *"Declaration of the Rights of Man,"* but not all the clauses that he had written were accepted so he was offended. However he framed some ideas upon which a Constitution could be built. They were very much admired but he expressed his thoughts so vaguely that no one understood them. In the Committee of the Constitution his ideas were not adopted and, according to his characteristic custom in these cases, he took no further interest; he smiled coldly and shunned from that time any further invitation.

It was worse in the Assembly. In that enormous mass of orators—or better, speakers—he did not know how to make himself understood. "Is it necessary to gild ideas so much?" he said bitterly after hearing the successful speeches of others. He did not know how to "gild," nor even how to colour his ideas which were dull, and so he was silent listening to the discussions with a haughty, reserved manner. Although his intellect was fallacious yet he possessed a rigid sense of morality and so he was opposed to the suppression of clerical tithes without reparation. This was looked upon as defending his old Order and the Left Wing was scandalized. Was Sieyès looking back? In spite of him the tithes were suppressed without any redemption. He remarked bitterly: "They wish for freedom and they know nothing of justice." In spite of having helped to lay the foundation of the Jacobin Clubs he dropped his old friends, of whom he deeply disapproved. "These people put forward outrages as expedients." The rabble invaded the Club and, as a lofty philosopher, he had a horror of the mob and even of the people. The people, on their side, began to have suspicions of the old defender of the Tiers État, while the Assembly did not pass any of his proposals. Only one exception was made —the case of dividing France into departments, which is his work and obviously bears his stamp so much has history, tradition, good sense and nature itself been violated all at the same time. But when he demanded that the freedom of the press be destroyed, he no longer had any following. Marat, one of those whom he wished to curb, wrote furiously: "Do not let us lose sight of Abbé Sieyès."

All this embittered him. The Assembly remained full of veneration for him and elected him to the presidency which post he first refused then accepted. But, having given a scholarly discourse, cold, solemn and dull, he demanded a successor. He then shut himself up in a frozen silence. Mirabeau, who was looking everywhere for help, wanted to enroll him as a supporter. Knowing how vain he was, he flattered him outrageously, calling him "his master" and, when confronted with the Abbé's reserve, insisted: "Yes, you are my master in spite of yourself." In a speech he gave Sieyès this title and deplored "this culpable silence . . . of a man *who has revealed to the world the real principles of representative government.*" "I implore you to seek his advice which he ought not to keep to himself, to rouse up now from his discouragement a man whose silence and inaction I consider to be a public calamity." There was applause; but Sieyès, glued to his seat, seemed not to understand. His silence, which held a world of disdain, satisfied his pride.

People, who were bewildered by this attitude, sought its explanation, sure that he was working behind the scenes. "He played the most important part at the beginning *and he will again play the same rôle at the end,*" as one of the deputies wrote of the 1st of February, 1790.

It looked for a moment as if he would justify this expectation. With Mirabeau dead it appeared as if he would lead the battle against the Extreme Left, whom he hated. Barnave's friends made him break with the Jacobins, after having sent against him Danton who withered with his fiery tongue the gloomy intrigues of "that priest." Robespierre, of whom he had shown his disdain, took an immediate dislike to him. He succeeded in exasperating all those Jacobins by combatting every republican fancy, after the flight of the King. To account for his preference for the monarchical system he gave some reasons which, as usual, were shrouded in strange phrases. He preferred government by a monarch "because it ended in a head" while republicanism "ended in a platform." Although the Assembly admitted him to be right, that did not prevent his progress from being hampered by the bitter animosity which he had aroused. He was no longer seen on the tribune. Nevertheless he watched the Assembly finish its work with that cold smile which expressed his bitter rancour.

However he voted for the civil Constitution of the Clergy —not that he approved it. He had dreamed of the suppression of all clergy, of the coming of a natural religion, of Philosophy taking the place of the Church; so, quite naturally, he refused the bishopric of Paris when it was offered to him. When, on the contrary, he had accepted a place on the Council of the Paris Department, he quickly resigned and with extreme rancour shut himself up in a villa at Auteuil— a place then considered remote.

For a year he brooded over his sorrows, mistakes, deceptions and cynicisms, watching from afar the Girondins agitating in the Legislative Assembly, Danton roaring in the Clubs, the imminence of invasion, its occurrence and the fall of the Throne. All these catastrophies were the result, in his opinion, of not accepting *his* Constitution—and these great misfortunes were a sort of consolation to him.

Perhaps others thought the same as well; for, in September, 1792, he was elected to the Convention by three departments.

He went there without much enthusiasm and took his seat in the Centre without saying a word.

During the session of the Constituent Assembly he did not definitely join any particular party, nor did he mean to act otherwise in the Convention, deeming himself above them all. But, as he had once been insulted by Danton, threatened by Marat and attacked by Robespierre, the Girondins reckoned on the assistance of this visionary seer. He, himself, would willingly have stood in with them, but he had not only retained the hauteur and pride of an ex-Abbé, he was also timid. "The most cowardly of mortals," as Mallet du Pan was to say and Talleyrand eventually wrote less brutally: "Fear is the only feeling that exercises any real influence on Sieyès." He certainly disliked taking sides between abusively violent parties and in mortal combat. Besides, as he deemed himself a theorist, he put forward this pretext as an excuse for not exposing the man of ideas to the risk of capture in the quarrel of men without ideas— and saved his skin. He loved to forbear from action, to disappear and to act in the dark. Charles de Constant wishing to have Sieyès pointed out to him by his neighbour, the latter, not seeing him, said of him: "If there was a curtain in the hall, I would be quite certain to find him behind it."

He had a redoubtable enemy in the Convention: Robespierre. The latter had not forgotten Sieyès' disdain and their acrimonious disputes in the Jacobin Club. The ex-Abbé knew now that he was dangerous and discreetly advised the Girondins to make use of Danton to fight their battles against him. When the latter recovered from the attack made upon him, it boded ill for the Girondin attempt and he did not mean to give grounds to the Incorruptible for action against him.

On the other hand, though these Girondins used Sieyès, yet they did not make sufficient use of him. They ought to have entrusted him with the Constitution which they were preparing. Unfortunately they already had a high priest, an oracle, a Constructor of constitutions: Condorcet.

In the Legislative Assembly, which Sieyès did not attend, Condorcet took up his rôle and moreover suffered more or less the same fate. "This professor of special morality," as he was called, was the permanent secretary of the Academy of Science, member of the French Academy and with the "Encyclopédie" as his heritage. He, also, had arrived with a reputation and it was generally admitted that he would be the Left's spiritual advisor; but unfortunately he also was very boring as he used complicated and obscure phrases in his speeches. Madame Roland wrote of him that "His intellect was like an exquisite liqueur drunk through cotton-wool." As Rivarol more brutally expressed it, "He used a drugged pen to write on leaden pages." So he was wearisome; but that did not cause even a tremor to his pedestal of fame. There are, and always will be, in any Assembly these rather tiresome high priests who are respected.

But he had been re-elected to the Convention in which Sieyès found him already in undisputed possession, an ally of the Girondins and consulted and admired by them. His well-known phrase was recalled: "Their highest sentiments were joined in one"; it scarcely looked as if the highest thoughts of Sieyès and Condorcet would so mingle since the two oracles did not love each other. Naturally Sieyès was nominated for the Committee of the Constitution, but, when he found that Condorcet prevailed there, he beat his usual retreat and shut himself up. He left the other philosopher to build his monument; but he did not experience any great grief when the Convention adjourned the discussion after the trial of Louis XVI. He did not love other people's work.

It is not very surprising that he voted for the King's death. "A cold heart, a pusillanimous spirit, *but an inflexible will*," as Talleyrand wrote later. That ferocious saying, "Death without any talking about it," has long been ascribed to him. But he was not savage—only prudent. He simply said *"Death"* and if he could have voted in fewer words he would have done so. The more the Mountain (the Extremists) gained in power the more he kept in the background. The Girondins were declared outlaws and he allowed them to be proscribed: seventy-three deputies of the Right Wing courageously protested but he did not associate himself with them. He became accustomed to being silent. Some private notes of his on these times were found: they all end with these words, *"Be silent."*

A new Constitution—that of the Year I—was drafted, but it was distressingly demagogic. A member of the Committee, who came to get his opinion, boasted about the proposal to him. He listened to it, then shrugged his shoulders and went off without saying a word.

On the other hand, when he produced a really magnificent scheme for public education and though, moreover, he had taken the precaution to get his colleague Lakanal to sign it, Robespierre maliciously tore it to shreds. In the Jacobin Club, Maximilien had previously ordered the chemist, Hassenfratz, one of his men, to attack him. "It needed all Sieyès *rascality* to conceive a scheme so *fatal to the cause of liberty*," cried that wild fanatic. Robespierre attacked the "fatal" plan from the tribune, and tried to prevent the' re-election of its author to the Committee of Public Instruction which up till then had been his great place of refuge and almost an alibi. Sieyès did not recriminate but once more became silent. This silence of his, amidst all the broiling and fighting, is very amazing. Then he wrote in his notes, *"What would the offering of my glass matter in such a deluge of spirits."* The whole of his dislike of this wild régime can be felt in that saying: it is possible to sense also, amongst other traits, his fear of being seized by Robespierre who was keeping an eye on him. When, at the Fête of Reason, he declared that he had for a long time renounced his title of priest, "his profession of faith to the old recognized religion," Robespierre only saw in it another reason to hate the one-time priest. This pale, speechless man, who sat in the Centre, worried and exasperated him. "The Abbé Sieyès no longer shows himself in the forefront," he said, "but he does not cease to work behind the scenes of the Assembly. *He is the Revolutionary mole."*

But he was not working any more than he was talking. He was simply trying not to die, to "live" and to have the last word. When, on the 9th Thermidor, Robespierre, turning to the deputies of the Centre with outstretched arms, left them to fight it out with the Extremists, he may have met the Abbé's cold regard. From what is known of the latter, it is safe to say that he was not the first to rise to vote for the dictator's overthrow nor certainly was he the last.

With his enemy defeated Sieyès recovered his freedom of action. Making a splendid case out of the general hatred for this fallen Catiline,[1] he forced himself on the Thermidorians.

He mistrusted them—naturally—and perhaps even more than he had mistrusted anyone. Since he was austere in his habits, led a pure private life and possessed a kind of disinterestedness in money matters, he considered himself the incarnation of virtue, especially as he disdained women although he associated with those who pandered to his vanity.

---

[1] A Roman demagogue and conspirator of the 1st century. His plot against the Senate was denounced by Cicero. His name typifies the plotter.

He could only hate those terrorists such as Barras, Tallien, Fréron and their like who, having dabbled in blood, amassed large fortunes from it to satisfy their taste for the vilest debauches. That these men could govern the Revolution was a disgrace to the country and a condemnation of the régime. Now that Robespierre was dead he tried to assert himself.

He published a "Notice" about himself extolling his "virtue"—that virtue to which he was indebted for the hate of "scoundrels" who fell in Thermidor. But he overwhelmed with that virtue the band who had taken a part in it. He threw in his lot with certain members of the Right—back again on the benches of the Convention—against the Girondins; and Julie Talma arranged for their meetings to take place at her house. Under the moral presidency of the ex-Abbé Sieyès the destiny of the State was, wrote Malet, decided at the home of that pedantic artiste. He wrote again, "Many sincerely believe that, if the Revolution has only led to wild extravagances and crime, it is because its essentials have not been grasped, and because it has been badly organized and abandoned to the leadership of scoundrels. But if it had been based on abstract philosophical principles and led by such honest men as the philosophers, it would have ensured the millennium." He mentioned Sieyès and Condorcet: they had "proposed a scheme of Republican philosophy which was stifled at its inception."

Condorcet having disappeared tragically, Sieyès survived and again took up the idea. The Republic would be one based on philosophy or else it would not exist at all.

When it was decided to make a fourth Constitution he was once more appealed to for help as he was still on the Commission. But he might have wished that they should all come to him and accept in advance the whole of his scheme. He resigned after some days and when he was requested to give his opinion on the adopted Constitution, he replied haughtily, "They probably would not listen to me." He went to the tribune with the idea of crushing the proposal with his own, but the terrible disillusionment he experienced has already been mentioned.

In addition, he still retained his acerbity. Although he was elected president of the Convention he refused it again, smiling coldly, but he accepted a place on the Committee of Public Safety towards its end. There he undertook foreign affairs. Since he had not been able to alter France to his own satisfaction, it pleased him to make alterations in Europe.

Europe, conquered by the Revolutionary armies, began to capitulate. Holland became a vassal state of France; Spain gave up the struggle; Prussia seceded from the coalition; Austria alone, not having experienced her share of defeat, prepared for another campaign, urged on and supported by England. Sieyès shared the pride of the post-Thermidorian Committee before this first collapse of the coalition. This Committee had declared the Rhine frontier to be thenceforth immutable and even went so far as to include in the Constitution itself the principle of natural boundaries—called "constitutional" boundaries. Prussia had recognized France's possession of the left bank of the Rhine and Austria had to be brought to the same way of thinking. To do this, England had to be brought to her knees. Sieyès had his plans. Prussia was to be promised the control of a Germany of the North— the condition being war with Austria. England was to be reduced by a blockade. As a beginning Sieyès obtained leave to absent himself from the Committee to impose the treaty on Holland which would be the starting point of the great new system.

When he came back the Constitution was voted and the Convention was on the point of dissolution to make way for the Directory.

It is well known what Sieyès thought of the Constitution: "It is not yet good," he confided to one of his satellites. "He had a new code of laws in his portfolio," wrote Malet, "and he did not wish to waste it."

Although it was said that his "metaphysical dictums had lost their prestige" his· reputation as a great thinker still existed supported by his work on the Committee. They said of him that he was no longer thinking of France alone but of Europe as well. He had an amazing triumph at the elections being elected by *nineteen departments*—a quarter of France. This was not calculated to increase his modesty and from then on it was considered that he alone was sure of being elected to the Directory and—as was written on the 7th Brumaire, Year IV,—that "he would be in complete control."

He was, as a matter of fact, elected to the Directory but, to the general surprise, he refused to take his seat. He was greatly annoyed at the election of Rewbell, a brutal politician with whom he had quarrelled on the Committee, and with the successful candidature of Larevellière-Lépeaux who, during the debate on the Constitution, had dared to chaff him; that Barras, whom he distrusted on account of his dissolute habits, should also be returned, greatly angered him. He did not wish to have anything to do with such men. Besides he did not believe in the durability of the new government and was already meditating changes in the construction of the State. He took up a very high-handed attitude in which were collected the accumulated hatreds of seven years: "I cannot believe," he wrote with obvious acerbity to the two Councils, *"that a man who has since the Revolution kept aloof from all parties can form a rallying* centre for every form of faith. My real place is in the Council of the Five Hundred. My mind is made up. I stay there." And persisting in his resignation he buried himself in the Financial Commission where he was better able than anywhere else to confirm his view that France was ruined.

He was not, however, in favour of a royalist restoration and the fact that he had voted for the King's execution left a definite mark on his political career as on those of many others. So he approved of the coup d'État at Fructidor (September 4th, 1797), declaring that it proved the noxiousness of the Constitution and the necessity of altering it. He was already dreaming of another kind of restoration in which a foreign prince or a popular soldier would perhaps accept his Constitution. Under the protection of a strong authority an hierarchical state on the principles of rationalist philosophy would be organized: a pyramidical State, he described it, and one that would not end in a directorial platform, but in a "point"—the famous "point" which he used as an argument, in 1791, in favour of monarchism.

He kept out of public life, pondering over his ideas and trying to perfect his theory of government. For a whole year nobody heard of him. Only one peculiar incident brought his name before the public; he was made—very strangely—the object of attempted assassination. The Abbé Poulle, a mentally unbalanced priest, obtained an interview with him and shot him in the arm. He remained quite calm merely saying to his doorkeeper: "When he comes again to see me say that I am not in." He divided his time between two houses in which he was regarded as a god—that of Madame de Staël, another visionary, and at Madame Helvétius' in Auteuil, for a long time the *rendezvous* of philosophers. He used to go to the Institute, of which, of course, he had been made a member, and was a great influence on his colleagues who were also all philosophers. There his ideas on the restoration of the State met with a favourable reception. The Institute of France as is well known was to produce the keenest supporters of the overthrow of the Directory by Napoleon,— the "coup de Brumaire" as it was called (November 9th, 1799).

But he was already opening up new avenues for a coup d'état for he found fault with everything that was done at the Palais du Luxembourg. He smiled bitterly if Larevellière's eccentricities or Barras' debauches were mentioned; he denounced the government's weakness in proscribing a number of good citizens along with the royalists; he decried their action in letting the Jacobins recover and in allowing the rabble to have any influence on the elections. "The Directory," according to Barras in Germinal, Year VI (March and April, 1798), "is worried by this continual buzzing."

Finally to get rid of this buzzing he was sent on a mission to Berlin to bring to a triumphal conclusion his scheme of a Prussian alliance. "Disillusioned by modern republicans," someone wrote, "and even more so on the subject of republics, he wanted to get away from his country which no longer held any attraction for him." He appeared in Berlin where he was a public figure from the day after his arrival to the crowning of the new King Frederic-William III who later suffered defeat at Jena. The effect produced by the appearance of Sieyès has been well described by Albert Sorel: "Amidst the be-ribboned diplomats, generals and ministers all dressed in the customary uniforms walked a stranger of medium height with a decisive profile and a pallid complexion; he was dressed very severely in black, his black hair being unpowdered, while he wore a large tricolour scarf across his breast. It was Sieyès. Everyone pointed to him.

This haughty regicide's appearance caused a shudder to disturb the dignity of this royal procession."

Perhaps he was too "haughty": in any case he was the very antithesis of a diplomat on account of his natural reserve and overweening pride. He failed in his mission but very soon broke away from it. The Directory, which had crushed the Councils when they became Jacobin in sentiment, was in danger in its turn of being crushed by them. Paris was in confusion, chaos and anarchy. One party hailed with loud cries the coming of the philosopher who would put the City in order again. Rewbell no longer being in the Directory, Sieyès was elected by the Councils, and this time he accepted, considering that it was the right moment. He foresaw that at last there was great work for him to do, so he left Berlin precipitately.

His coming was awaited at Paris with anxious curiosity. "The entry of Sieyès into the Directory," wrote a foreign diplomat, "has caused a greater sensation than the accession of most sovereigns under difficult circumstances. At this moment he is the cynosure of all eyes." It was as if the Republic was playing its last card. If philosophy failed only the army remained to be tried.

The Directors, very much worried, awaited their distinguished, but dangerous, colleague. He did not come to the Luxembourg, but he lodged at a friend's house from which veiled threats issued and he allowed those gentlemen to revel in their anxiety for several days. Meanwhile he plotted with his friends to get rid of Larevellière-Lépeaux and Merlin, whom he hated, from the Directory. Barras' support was necessary to him because he was popular with everyone. The latter had said with a sneer: "I will always agree with him and he will believe me as spiritual as himself; so we shall

get on famously together." The hoped-for scheme materialized and Sieyès, who had taken his seat, helped with an expressionless face in the overthrow of his two enemies. They
were replaced by two incompetent men who certainly did
not hinder him since they overwhelmed him with flattery,
but he distrusted them all the more. He wrote in his private
memoirs: *"They pursue me and I hate their society because they do not believe in moral goodness. They offend me,*
and my first act, if I was carried away, would be to say to
them: 'You ought to be ashamed; just because you are
scoundrels and villains you lightly suppose that everyone
must be like you.' I shall end by hating them."

He did hate them all but he was their master for they
bowed down before him. He forced them to fight in a body
against the Jacobin rabble which had elected these newcomers to the Directory. As President of the Directory, he declared war on the Jacobin Club, which had been weakly allowed to reopen, and caused it to be closed. Thus purifying
the Directory, he had, as he described it to a minister,
"cleansed the Temple, after Our Lord's example, of those who
sold, bartered and dishonoured the Republic." It became
necessary to destroy the scoundrels who wanted to bring back
the Reign of Terror: but the latter seemed to be too numerous
and they headed the poll. Discouraged and disillusioned, exasperated and alarmed, the philosopher declared he would not
act alone and, in his turn, was forced to consider an appeal to
the army.

The only event that could save the Revolution now
would be the arrival of a Caesar to take complete control of
it. This moment had been foreseen by clear-headed thinkers
five years before. The only question was who would be the
Caesar?

Sieyès did not possess the Caesarian spirit, but, nevertheless, some of his conceptions inclined him to try to force a strong authority on a society deeply hierarchical. Perhaps he had dreamed of being this supreme authority; but he realized the difficulties and his cowardice proved too great an obstacle to his pride. The Jacobins heaped insults upon him and hurled threats at him. Besides he knew that the Government, of which he was President, was weak, as he thought it was shakily based on a bad Constitution; he also considered it to be discredited by its viciousness and contemptible absurdities. He confided to a friend that "his was an infernal profession." So certain of his superiority, he felt outdone and he became very sceptical about the Assembly's regime. After the revolutionary movement of Floréal (the eighth month of the Republican year) Barras asked him which of the deputies it would be well to dismiss, and he said: *"Deputies are either very good or very bad according to the way they are used."* But the best thing was to get rid of them all. The man whom Mirabeau had proclaimed as the founder of representative government now desired to paralyze the Houses. "It is impossible to build anything with the help of blunderers and babblers," as he said to Fouché whom he made Minister of Police, *"two things are necessary: a head and a sword."* In his opinion he was the head and he was looking about for the sword.

Bonaparte, then on his triumphant visit in Paris after Campo-Formio, had covered the then inimical philosopher with flattery. Citizen Sieyès was, according to him, the only statesman of the Republic; he it was who ought to give the Revolution its definite form. The flattered Sieyès said of Italy's conqueror: "He is the politest general in the army." But Bonaparte seemed to him to be a man to be feared, besides in the summer of 1799, the General was a captive in his own conquered Egypt. Hoche had just died rather mysteriously at the age of twenty-seven. Sieyès put aside Bernadotte who, he said, "was only a gosling though he had an eagle's profile"; he even had him turned out of the War Ministry where he was considered to be the representative of his enemies, the Jacobins. Then he thought of the young and fascinating General Joubert with whom he had a good understanding. But Joubert was killed in Italy in rather dubious circumstances like those in which Hoche had succumbed. All this rather pointed to the fact that it was not healthy for a general to be suspected of holding hopes of a dictatorship. Then Sieyès adopted Moreau as a candidate but the latter was too procrastinating temperamentally: he hesitated. One day in Vendémiaire (the second month of the Republican year) Sieyès was in the Luxembourg reproving him when a breathless messenger arrived with the news that Bonaparte had landed at Fréjus. "There's your man," said Moreau and vanished. "The die is cast," declared Sieyès a few minutes later to Lucien Bonaparte. "It is round your brother that we must rally."

The General visited him as soon as he got to Paris. His materialistic mind convinced him that the Abbé's ideas were really all wrong, but he said, "I have seen Sieyès. . . . One must throw in one's lot with those whom one loves and esteems least." The soldier flattered the philosopher. "We have no government because we have no Constitution—at any rate of the kind that we need. *Your genius must supply us with one.*" Sieyès could now see the Promised Land from the top of Sinai where he was at last to write the Law.

He lent his aid to every plan for a revolutionary movement and in the evening of the 19th Brumaire, after many vicissitudes, Bonaparte was made consul—and Sieyès with him.

The latter set about the Constitution, or rather allowed the principles to be torn from him, bit by bit, by Boulay de la Meurthe, who was entrusted with the job of attending its birth. Albert Vandal has related in a masterly way the manner in which the poor legislator was tricked when the scheme was finished. Bonaparte took over his system so scientifically complex and well balanced and, without demolishing it entirely, extracted everything on which he could build up his despotic rule.

Sieyès did what he had always done. He did not defend his Constitution, but, sulky and disdainful he retired into his shell, and allowed the Caesarian structure to be cut out of his work. And when all was done the General turned to him in an important conference and begged him, after a due amount of flattery, to nominate the Consuls—which was a delightful way of telling him that he would not be one.

As a consolation he was appointed President of the Senate —to square the account after having eliminated him so quickly.

He had now come to the state when, disabused for good, the politician only sought to extract the bits worth saving from a badly broken situation. Bonaparte caused a decree to be passed offering him a castle in the name of the Nation in recognition "of great services rendered by Citizen Sieyès." Indifferent as he had been, up to that time, to the lure of worldly rewards, he was weak enough to accept this sop for his abdication. It was the Château de Crosne and there was a poem about it which ran as follows:—

Sieyès had made to Bonaparte a present of a throne,
And thought 'neath the ruins of majesty to fix his burial-place;
Now Bonaparte, his gift to Sieyès was the great Château de Crosne,
This was how he paid his man and brought him to disgrace.

He was given a good endowment and later was made a *Count of the Empire*. On May 20th, 1808, the Chancellor Cambacérès—his old neighbour on the Marsh in the Convention—signed the letters patent which gave him the right henceforth to a coat of arms "with the title of the Count Sieyès": "Argent on a mound vert a pine tree of the second; a canton sinister azure charged in the sinister chief with a head of Boreas cantoned in gold, blowing a blast of wind argent. Liveries, blue and white braided with green."

When Monsieur le Comte Sieyès placed this parchment in the drawer of his desk perhaps he found at the same time an old yellow pamphlet. *"What is the Tiers État? Nothing. What ought it to be? Everything. What does it want to become? Something."* The Tiers État became ennobled and the nobility became endowed.

He lived to be an old man dying at the age of eighty-eight. Louis-Philippe had forgotten, with so many other surviving members of the National Convention, to make him a peer of the tricolour Monarchy. And he could say that right up to the end no one had known how to do him justice. Such was the extraordinary career of the Abbé Sieyès who, though a priest and a canon, had refused a constitutional mitre, but came near to wearing a revolutionary crown.

When Bonaparte arrived in Paris he found that the only notable personality to have survived the Revolution was Sieyès; and he was brushed aside by the soldier because that "great man" was in reality only a wind-bag. "Head of Boreas cantoned in gold, blowing a blast of wind argent"—was the description in his new coat of arms. Around this greatly overrated high priest the general found a crowd of unimportant revolutionaries, ex-tribunes of Assemblies, former proconsuls of the Terror, erstwhile members of Committees, all very passionate gentlemen in days gone by. But ten years of revolution had opened their eyes to a political and a personal materialism. Fouché, Minister of Police, was a typical example of those worn-out revolutionaries. It is now time to judge the fruits of the Revolution since it is ended; it is now time to realize its effects on institutions and laws; also it is time to calculate the profits accruing to those who had carried it through and who had the hardihood to survive.

With La Fayette thrown aside—and what was worse—practically disgraced; with Mirabeau's painful end, Talleyrand exiled, then resigned to the playing of minor rôles; Bailly and Barnave guillotined, Brissot, Vergniaud, Barbarroux guillotined; Buzot, Pétion, Condorcet dead by their own hands; Hérault de Séchelles, Fabre d'Eglantine, Camille Desmoulins, Jacques Danton, in Germinal Year II, Saint-Just, Couthon and Maximilien Robespierre thrown to the executioner in Thermidor, Year II; out of all these great men of the Revolution the only one to survive, after Thermidor, was the over-rated wind-bag, Sieyès, who, with his own hands, had prepared the way for Bonaparte as if acting on the behalf of others.

What would they have done if confronted by Bonaparte? —an idle question, because as they were all dead when this happened we may well suppose that had they been alive he might not have handled the reins of power in spite of his genius.

Perhaps it was fated that they should all die to enable him to appear, because few human events give, as the Revolution does, the impression of a long and certain misfortune.

The Revolution was part of a great misunderstanding. The people, who were deeply monarchical in feeling, desired a new method of government, but one that supported by the King's authority, would be based on the equality of rights. That was all. Attracted by Philosophy, the bourgeois had added to the programme, liberty, which the 1789 electorate had, at least, placed in the background and which, moreover, they only understood subject to the King's consent and agreement.

The Nation realized its chief desire when the feudal system was abolished on the 4th of August, 1789. This was the opinion of Mirabeau who, although a strong adherent to the theory of a final authority, cherished the newly acquired equality. He was almost a genius and neither the King nor the Assembly understood him. That Assembly meant to turn the whole state upside down and to legislate for humanity. The *Declaration of Rights*, which was a superb manifesto of sincere philosophy given to the whole world by the representatives of French democracy, threw the Revolution out of its proper course. It was too exhilarating a theme and clouded men's reason. It resulted in a wholesale destruction without any plan of rational practical reconstruction being prepared. It was impossible to alter the Constitution to fit this magnificent Declaration without provoking anarchy, and so the former belied the latter. Although it weakened the royal power it failed to make democracy a fact; but in weakening authority, whilst the Declaration authorized the rebellion, it unloosed chronic disorder on the Nation. Nearly all the men who had voted for it were sincere and honest, men carried away by a noble faith and often inspired by a cultured mind but blended by despotic ideas and sometimes bemused by emotion. That admirable French gentleman, La Fayette, saw too many visions: he was to give way under the load of mistakes with which one scarcely dares to reproach him on account of the nobility of his character. And he was a finished example of the greater part of those members of the Constituent Assembly who might have cried: "Let everything else perish rather than cede one principle." On the other hand there was Talleyrand, a politician who had a genius for treason: he was a representative of the other kind of man who did not believe in the movement but exploited it, betraying his party and leading the nation astray. Then the determined, resolute Mirabeau, with his practical mind, might have saved the State, but, time after time, both the King and the Assembly refused to trust him on account of his bad reputation. In vain did he try to prevent his friends in the Assembly from taking the bit of idealism between their teeth. In vain did he warn them particularly against that pacifism which, by a celebrated display of public feeling, encouraged Europe to rise up against the new France.

This foreign invasion resulted in the Revolution being a total loss, because, although it was in reality directed against the ordinary everyday France, it seemed to be aimed at the Revolution. The latter became wildly excited by a savage patriotism and it seemed a good thing that a new revolutionary wave should brush aside the men of the first group, La Fayette, Talleyrand and even Barnave, who having driven his colleagues to acts of violence for which he did not hold them responsible, had, too late in the day, thrown in his lot with the policy of resistance to anarchy after Mirabeau's death. Then this *second revolution*, ridding itself of the old lot, created new men with no experience in public affairs— men even more blinded than their predecessors by their narrow outlook and, in addition, made dangerous by their eloquent ability to excite public feeling. These were the Girondins who by their *romantic* conception of politics and their oratorical attitude, paved the way to fresh excesses. Not only did they plunge rashly into war, but they took as their guide a woman, Madame Roland, who was an extremist. Out of the national crisis—the country's frontiers being threatened—came the downfall of the throne.

The second revolutionary group had not wanted to gain anything from the disorder they had caused, and, what was worse, blind, inconsequent and irresolute as they were, they were swept away by a third band who were determined to stop at nothing. Although beaten and dying they refused to disown any of the ideals they had defended; at the same time —quite illogically—they deplored their fatal consequences.

Third group, or the extreme Jacobins, seemed at first to be entirely controlled by the absorbing personality of Jacques Danton. In common with Mirabeau he possessed a materialistic mind but a fiery spirit and he made lavish use of ideals when invasion was threatening. Faced by the peril from without, he tried to unite the nation which had just been terribly rent by the massacres he had permitted. And it was this wish for unity which he had himself rendered impossible from the very beginning, that inclined him also to adopt—as always, too late—a more restrained and reactionary policy. La Fayette, the nation's idol, had been denounced and given over to the people's fury by Danton himself on account of his reactionary views and he had given way; for his reactionary principles, Barnave, the man who admitted that blood would be shed if he was not judged to be "pure," after an unwholesome popularity had experienced lifelong disgrace. In the same case Vergniaud, who had nailed his Sovereigns to the pillory, had been treated as "a second Barnave." And now Danton, having overthrown La Fayette, Barnave and Vergniaud, tried, in his turn "to hitch on to the Revolutionary hearse." So he also became suspected.

All the revolutionaries whom he had inconvenienced—
from Robespierre to Hébert—attacked him, having under-
mined his position. The Titan was able to crush Hébert before his own fall; but Robespierre, being free of Hébert, in
turn overthrew Danton and had him killed, making himself
master of the situation. Then this prophet, driven by Saint-
Just who was his master's superior in intelligence and will-
power, tried to build up on the Terror a new revolutionary
State, dedicated to Virtue; he proscribed all the enemies of
the Revolution and all those who opposed the three dogmas
of Public Safety, God and Morality. In Europe it was
thought that he was going to construct a new system and he
dreamed of doing so but he only had one life.

He was overthrown by the very ones he aimed at, who,
fearing that the executioner of to-day might be the victim of
to-morrow, attacked him in a paroxysm of delirious fear.
Their only idea was to get rid of a dangerous enemy in Robespierre. But he was the only man who appeared able to hold
the Reign of Terror within bounds and his death, to the dis-
may of his enemies, was the signal for a still further anarchical reaction.

The Thermidorian leaders, from Barras to Tallien were
men of very moderate intelligence and vile morals, and they
became engulfed in the mire of the Revolution, already
splashed with so much blood. For a long time France had
stood aside from the Revolution, now doubly defiled, retain-
ing her desire to build up a strong government based on the
principle of equality. But the result was a weak government
under the control of a few leaders, who had forced themselves on a disgusted nation. Indeed it looked as if "this
breathless tyranny" was to be perpetuated under the Directory. Meanwhile Barras, Merlin de Douai and Larevellière-

Lépeaux, minor revolutionaries, who had reached the highest rung by reason of the successive downfalls of the really great leaders, fought like jackals for five years over the remains of these stricken kings of the forest. The disgusted country looked for a man who, by materializing the dreams of 1789, would strengthen the results of the Revolution. It wanted a man who would end the Revolution at once by restoring authority and establishing equality on a definite basis.

Caesar's coming was facilitated by the Revolution's last leader. Sieyès, who had seemed to have opened its floodgates by advancing the claims of the Tiers État in the autumn of 1789, was, curiously enough, called on to hand it over to its last master. This former priest, who became the Revolution's oracle, high priest, spiritual leader, threw in his lot with the soldier and placed him in command. His work did not please him so as usual he yielded and disappeared.

Bonaparte found the stage empty; all the great leaders had come to grief. Then he turned to that great secondary mass of Revolutionaries and invited them to help in the Caesarian rule, since he did not intend to stifle, but to establish, the régime created by the Revolution. Some of these were members of the Constituent Assembly quite recovered from their idealistic theories; others were members of the National Convention prepared from their own experience to support a rule by authority. Four years afterwards these men, who had escaped death in the Revolution, had become hard-working, faithful servants of the Imperial régime.

END